Challenge and Change in Social Work Education: Toward a World View

Selected Papers by Herman D. Stein

Collected by Nina L. Aronoff

Foreword by Darlyne Bailey

Preface by Katherine A. Kendall

D1363864

Council on Social Work Education
Alexandria, Virginia

The Council on Social Work Education acknowledges the support of the Mandel School of Applied Social Sciences, Case Western Reserve University, for publication of this work.

Council on Social Work Education
1725 Duke Street, Suite 500
Alexandria, VA 22314-3457
www.cswe.org

Printed in the United States of America

Challenge and Change in Social Work Education: Toward a World View
ISBN: 0-87293-100-5

To the memory of Charmion

Contents

Foreword

During the last half of the 20th century Professor Herman D. Stein was one of the most respected and influential figures in social work education and practice, internationally as well as in the United States. His professional stature was recognized in part by his presidency of the Council on Social Work Education (CSWE) and the International Association of Schools of Social Work (IASSW), as well as other leadership positions. It is also reflected in the broad array of honors he has received for his teaching, international work, writing, advocacy, and academic innovations.

Stein's international activity began in 1947 when he left his faculty post at the Columbia University School of Social Work (CUSSW) to join the American Jewish Joint Distribution Committee (JDC) in its Paris headquarters, as director of the Welfare Department. The JDC, whose mission was rescue, relief, and reconstruction, was then operating the largest private social agency in history. It had mobilized huge resources to help meet the needs of survivors of the Holocaust, refugees, displaced persons, and broken communities.

He subsequently was advisor to the United Nations Division of Social Development (to begin with, on social work training around the world), and was senior advisor in 1968 to the secretariat of the United Nations Conference of Ministers Responsible for Social Welfare.

Stein's most varied and extended international activity was with the United Nations Children's Fund (UNICEF), with which he was involved both on a full-time and part-time basis for over 20 years. His relationship to UNICEF began in 1962 with a year in Tanganyika (now Tanzania) to work with its new government in community development, and it continued in UNICEF headquarters where he became senior advisor to the executive director. In this capacity he had repeated missions to over 25 developing countries and also directed the agency's inter-regional staff seminars for 10 years in different parts of the world, drawing on indigenous expertise.

Stein had a significant role in organizing the 1964 UNICEF Bellagio Conference on planning for children in developing countries, and he wrote its final report. This conference is credited with expanding the mission of UNICEF and putting the well-being of children on the agenda of development planning. Professor Stein's interest in social development was long standing. His teaching included lectures given over 14 years at the Harvard University School of Public Health in planning for the social sectors in developing countries. He devoted his first year as a fellow at the Stanford University Center for Advanced Study in the Behavioral Sciences in study of this area.

During his presidency of IASSW, working with Dr. Katherine A. Kendall as secretary general, he led the association in reaching out to training centers in third-world countries. IASSW became a more wide-reaching and inclusive organization than it had been, and was involved in issues such as population and urbanization. His teaching on the subject of international social welfare was pioneering.

At CUSSW Stein introduced courses to prepare students to apply creatively, in their practice, concepts and theory from the social and behavioral sciences. The 1950s was a time when human behavior was still generally interpreted in schools of social work principally, and often solely, in intra-psychic terms. Professor Stein developed seminars for field instructors and faculty to reinforce what students were learning in becoming sensitive to applying such concepts as class, race, ethnicity, and power in their practice. He was teaching, writing, and lecturing in universities across the country, and he had a decided impact in this area of social work education. There were repercussions also in Europe where he was invited by the United Nations Educational, Scientific and Cultural Organization in 1960 to lead a conference on social work and social science.

Stein served in a leadership capacity in a number of national and local bodies. He was a member of training and research panels at the National Institute of Mental Health and the Social Security Administration, among others. In Cleveland one of his daunting challenges was to serve as chairman of Mayor Carl Stokes's Commission on the Crisis of Welfare in Cleveland.

Early in his career Professor Stein developed a strong interest in organizational theory and management in the human services. He consulted for organizations in the public, private, and nonprofit areas. For one of his two years at the Stanford Center he organized a cross-disciplinary conference on organizational theory and concepts as they are reflected in for-profit and nonprofit organizations.

After serving on the faculty of CUSSW a total of 16 years Dr. Stein assumed the deanship of Western Reserve University School of Applied Social Sciences (now Mandel School of Applied Social Sciences). His leadership propelled the school to even higher standards than it had and influenced the school's direction to this day. When Western Reserve University merged with Case Institute of Technology he became provost of behavioral social sciences and then the first provost of the university. In this capacity his educational vision and crisis management during the turbulence of the late 1960s were widely recognized. As university professor a few years later he took leave with UNICEF and returned to the university to organize and direct a public lecture series called Global Currents. He resumed his earlier capacity as provost during a two-year transition period in the presidency of the university. During this period he helped to encourage an international outlook in professional schools and academic departments. With a colleague he presented the first course in global issues and perspectives in the undergraduate curriculum.

This volume not only illustrates the career of one social work leader, but also ideas and activity that have helped shape social work education for decades. It is a privilege for the Mandel School of Applied Social Sciences to have joined with CSWE in making possible its publication.

Darlyne Bailey, PhD
Dean and Professor, 1994–2002
Mandel School of Applied Social Sciences
Case Western Reserve University
Cleveland, Ohio

Vice-President for Academic Affairs
Teachers College
Columbia University

Preface

It is a happy coincidence that the publication of selected papers by Herman D. Stein should coincide with the 50th anniversary of the creation of the Council on Social Work Education (CSWE). There is scarcely any phase of the Council's history or facet of its work in this half century that has not benefited from his varied contributions. Many of the challenges and the resulting advances that took place in social work education in this period bear the mark of Herman Stein's leadership. In fact, his own career, with its many mutations, could almost serve as a mirror of the way professional education progressed from a major investment in psychoanalytically oriented casework to the multifaceted preparation for professional practice that it enjoys today. This collection of selected papers provides an illuminating guide to the source of many of the changes that have taken place. Historical material of this nature is of immense value in producing a better understanding and appreciation of how challenges met in the past shape the present and constitute essential building blocks for future development of the profession.

When Stein embarked on his career in the mid-1940s, most, although by no means all, of the schools of that period had one central mission—the preparation of social workers skilled in providing direct services to individuals and families through immersion in psychoanalytically oriented casework. A recurrent theme in many of the papers recognizes both the value of this absorption and its limitations. As a young faculty member, he admires the way in which gifted teachers helped students absorb the skills and attributes of what was called a "professional self," but he soon senses the need for a broader preparation. It is no wonder then that he was at the forefront of a movement to push education and practice beyond its preoccupation with psychoanalytic theory and practice and a primary concern with the individual as the major focus of change

His leadership in this area was undoubtedly bolstered by his own professional experience working with displaced persons and survivors of the

Holocaust following World War II. In 1947 he left a promising teaching career at the Columbia University School of Social Work to join the American Joint Distribution Committee in Europe and North Africa. Encountering in Europe the unspeakable tragedy of lives tortured and destroyed and experiencing at first hand in Africa the sights and smells of mass poverty made him aware of the limitations and potentials of existing professional education for social work. In comments at a Columbia alumni conference, he noted that a great deal of what he had learned at the school was indispensable to his work overseas, but the international experience taught him much that was completely foreign to American social work, although essential to it.[1]

In this collection of papers, we see the beginnings of his successful campaign to strengthen professional education through a more fruitful and reciprocal relationship between social work and the social sciences. Upon rejoining the faculty at Columbia in the early 1950s, he found a more welcome climate than earlier for broadening the theoretical base for social work practice. Although the Freudian emphasis continued into the 1950s, the experience of the Depression and initiation of broad social legislation demanded a broader role for social work in dealing with problems associated with poverty. The influx of G.I. Bill veterans, older and more tough-minded than previous recruits to the profession, also contributed to the growing concern about how to do a better job in dealing with problems caused by social forces beyond the control of the individual.

He makes it quite clear that while he regards concepts drawn from the social and behavioral sciences as indispensable in education for social work, he does not consider social work an applied social science. What he stresses as a pivotal concern is the relevance of social science content to practice. Again and again he underlines the importance of testing relevance within the context of acknowledged social work functions. What may seem routine today emerged then as a breath of fresh air in thinking about the social work curriculum. The social science concepts he outlined and taught as central, the connections he built with related disciplines, and the research he stimulated all contributed to the enrichment and clarification of the knowledge base of social work practice.

It is significant to note, also, that his various educational initiatives

---

[1] Herman Stein, "Which Way is Up?" *Alumni Newsletter*, Winter, 1975 (New York: Alumni Association of Columbia University), p. 3.

are firmly linked to competent practice in the traditional functions of service to individuals, groups, and communities. In Chapter 3, for example, "Social Work's Developmental and Change Functions," he contends that the influence and credibility of the profession as a partner in social development and system change rests on its first-hand knowledge of the problems to be addressed and the people to be served. He is equally clear that real progress on a broad social front cannot be achieved by any one profession acting alone and urges social work to engage with other disciplines and diverse interest groups to bring about systemic change.

His interest in moving the profession forward from a defined but restricted practice base took on special significance for the Council on Social Work Education in the late 1950s when he assumed responsibility as chair of its first Curriculum Committee. It was my privilege, as the Council staff member in charge of educational services, to work with him on the production of the official Curriculum Policy Statement adopted in 1962. This was no ordinary assignment. Each of the 13 volumes of the controversial curriculum study published in 1959[2] had to be analyzed for policy implications and for use in curriculum building. The previous change in 1952 to a generic curriculum with the intent to eliminate all specialized sequences had led to the production of statements of practice by nine specialized groups. Their recommendations of necessary content from their fields of practice required special attention. The results of a graduate and undergraduate survey of curriculum trends, issues, and concerns along with suggestions from the National Association of Social Workers Commission on Social Work Practice also produced a mountain of material . All of this had to be gleaned for relevance to the purposes and content of a new official statement of curriculum policy.

Herman Stein was the perfect fit for this Herculean task. He had earned respect and admiration as a chairman who not only listened to differing points of view, but created opportunities for their exploration. He encouraged discussion to achieve consensus, a necessary outcome of any work on official policy documents. Best of all, he brought to the assignment a comprehensive knowledge of social work history, changes and trends in curriculum development, the characteristics of professions, and the place of social work in the academic world. The breadth and depth of this knowl-

---

[2] Council on Social Work Education, *Social work curriculum study.* New York: Council on Social Work Education, 1959.

edge and his many references to the primacy of competent practice in gaining influence and credibility emerges clearly from a number of the papers in this collection.

One notable example can be found in Chapter 5, "Observations on Determinants of Social Work Education in the United States," which presents a comprehensive view of social work education in the 1960s—its roots in the values of the American society, its historical development, and its structure and content as seen in the official statement of curriculum policy he did so much to produce. Unquestionably, his masterful and successful handling of the promoters of change, the defenders of tradition, the many special interests, and the plenitude of issues had much to do with the final favorable acceptance by the entire constituency of the Council of the Curriculum Policy Statement of 1962.

Herman Stein again appeared, almost a decade later, as an interpreter of new challenges and revolutionary change facing the profession in the troublous and restless times of the late 1960s. In his valedictory address as president of the Council in 1969—published here in Chapter 2 as "Reflections on Competence and Ideology in Social Work Education"—he reflects, in inimitable fashion, on the ferment in the field. This was a period of passionate concern about how to combat racism, poverty, and all forms of injustice. He applauds the deep commitment among faculty and students to wide-ranging social causes, but warns that high-sounding proclamations about social justice achieve little unless harnessed to competence and the capacity for action. Again, as in many of the collected papers, he stresses the dual responsibility of social work for providing direct services of a remedial and ameliorative nature, while taking strong action within its professional expertise to prevent social injustice and solve social problems. He notes a difference in roles in carrying out this responsibility and calls for their reinforcement, not competition, within the profession.

While serving as Council president and also as provost and vice-president of Case Western Reserve University, his Solomon-like wisdom in dealing with student and faculty unrest was a source of admiration and amazement. He listened, he learned, and he encouraged open expression and debate on the full range of viewpoints on current issues. Educators were urged to capture the zeal of demonstrating students and channel their idealism into constructive channels for change. This listening and learning had much to do with a major restructuring of the Council's board of directors, the opening up of opportunities for minorities, and a greater flexibility in curriculum policy.

This account of his contributions to social work education, as described thus far, has been limited to the United States, but that only begins to tell the story behind the papers in this collection. Almost from the outset of his social work career, he has been a key figure in international social work, serving for many years as a senior advisor to the heads of the United Nations Children's Fund, performing significant assignments for the United Nations, participating in social science projects with the United Nations Educational, Scientific and Cultural Organization, and giving leadership to social work education around the world as president and long-time board of directors member of the International Association of Schools of Social Work. The wide reach of his international experience reflects both the breadth of his interests and his professional versatility.

His assessment of international social work in the United States in the early 1960s is described in a keynote presentation for a conference sponsored by the Council, the U.S. Department of State, and the U.S. Department of Health, Education, and Welfare—and presented here as Chapter 15, "International Responsibilities of U.S. Social Work Education." Along with high ranking officials from federal agencies and American educators from social work and related disciplines, the participants included representatives from the United Nations, the Organization of American States, and delegates from a number of developing countries. The establishment of social welfare ministries and expansion of social welfare programs in new nations following World War II created a vast demand for trained social welfare personnel. The conference focused on how to work with other countries in meeting this need.

In the address Stein comments on the considerable contribution already made by U.S. educators overseas as advisers, consultants, and trainers. The relatively formless and haphazard nature of the preparation of faculty members for such assignments leads him to propose a long-range plan of action for better preparation of faculty for international service. That plan includes more effective programs for foreign students, introduction of an international dimension to American social work education for all students, interdisciplinary involvement within and among universities, and encouragement of research on the social welfare component of social and economic development. Stein concludes that we neglect our responsibilities as educators when our students do not develop a world view and as a profession when we fail to contribute to and learn from international service. Social work education in the United States today could greatly benefit from the revival of many of the hopes and agreements on international responsibility as expressed at this landmark conference.

A major expression of his own sense of international responsibility can be found in numerous papers, published and unpublished, that record his reports as a rapporteur or summarizer of seminars and conferences. An excellent example in this collection is Chapter 6, "Cross-National Themes in Social Work Education," his brilliant review of the central concepts emerging from an international congress of schools of social work that teemed with ideas and ideologies, concerns and commitments. Well worth noting is his assertion that a major function of an international congress is its ability to shake up and change our know-it-all assumptions as well as to reinforce our feelings of shared values and knowledge. Capturing the essence of a conference at the end of days of presentations and discussions is a rare talent, of which Herman Stein is a master. His performance has been well described by a high-ranking UNICEF official as "like listening to a world-class virtuoso musician."[3]

Fortunately, Herman Stein's many achievements and outstanding qualities have been flavored by a quick wit and robust sense of humor. His great talent as a performer, carried over from his first career as an actor, has lightened many an occasion. No collection of his papers would be complete without the inclusion of one of his side-splitting monologues. For an excellent example, see Goldilocks in this book's Epilogue. His wit has also been enshrined in the skits gently satirizing curriculum concerns or other issues of the day that were a feature of CSWE Annual Program Meetings in the 1950s and 1960s.

In sponsoring this publication of Herman Stein's selected papers, the Mandel School of Applied Social Sciences has made available the wisdom and experience of a colleague, internationally renowned as a teacher, scholar, innovator, dean, and university administrator. Through the mirror of the past as reflected in this collection, we become aware of continuities as well as significant changes in the structure and content of programs

---

[3] Comment in an article about Dr. Stein, *CWRU*, an in-house magazine of Case Western Reserve University.

of professional education. The greater maturity and sophistication of those programs evolved to a large extent out of beginnings recorded here. There are also visions that have been lost, particularly in the international arena. What readers will find and cherish in this volume is a world view of social work education rooted in humanistic values and committed to the goals of providing for all humankind the highest attainable measure of economic and social development, social justice, and personal well-being.

Katherine A. Kendall, PhD, ACSW
Former Executive Director, CSWE
Retired Secretary-General, IASSW

Part One
SOCIAL WORK: THE PROFESSION

1. Professions and Universities

INTRODUCTION—OVERVIEW AND DEFINITION

I approach the theme of "professions and universities" by sketching a framework within which certain issues governing the relationship of professions to universities may be discerned, and of presenting a point of view regarding these issues.

There are some preliminary essentials to be emphasized concerning the nature of professions before I proceed with the main theme. Any discussion of professions initially requires paying respects to the pioneering work of Carr-Saunders and Wilson, on the history of the professions in England particularly, and on the European continent and the developing countries generally. For the moment, it will suffice to remind ourselves that professions originated in the universities of medieval Europe, which were, in fact, "training schools for work of a kind that we now class as professional."[1]

Professionalism was at first coextensive with the church. As religion lost its central dominance, the professions became secularized and then separately organized. Before the nineteenth century the recognition of new professions—other than theology, law, and medicine—was an extremely slow process, but since the mid-nineteenth century various other intellectual specialists were gradually added, especially in engineering and the sciences, to handle the increasingly complex functions of society. However, the twentieth century was well begun before formal education became an accepted avenue to professional status in most fields.[2] Apprenticeship and short training courses were still the major routes.

Reprinted with permission from *Journal of Education for Social Work*, Vol. 4, No. 2 (Fall, 1968), and originally delivered to the Colloquium of the Paul Baerwald School of Social Work, Hebrew University, Jerusalem, Israel, April 16–19,1967.

[1] Alexander Carr-Saunders and P. A. Wilson, "Professionalism," *Encyclopedia of the Social Sciences,* Vol. VI (New York: Macmillan, 1937), p. 476.

[2] Earl J. McGrath, *Liberal Education in the Professions* (New York: Bureau of Publications, Teachers College, Columbia University, 1959), p. 28.

In the United States the professionals per 100,000 of the population increased from 859 in 1870 to 3,310 in 1950.[3] Of first degrees granted in 1901, a total of only 4.1 percent were in the four fields of agriculture, business, education, and engineering. In 1951-53, the percentage had risen to 46.4.[4] The new professions have surpassed the old, and medicine, for example, accounts for only about two percent of professional degrees.[5]

One hundred years ago 75 percent of all professional men and women in the United States were in four fields: medicine, law, theology, and teaching. Now there are 2,200 occupations requiring highly-trained manpower and 10 to 20 are added annually.[6] Only a small proportion of these occupations may properly be termed professions in any rigorous sense, but the small proportion adds up to a goodly number.

What can one mean by a profession "in a rigorous sense"? The definitions abound, but there are some ingredients one can feel secure in selecting. "To profess" originally meant to take the vows of a religious order, but by the seventeenth century was secularized to mean "that professes to be duly qualified: professional."[7] Everett Hughes notes that professions "profess to know better than others the nature of certain matters and to know better than their clients what ails them or their affairs. This is the essence of the professional idea and the professional claim."

Carr-Saunders and Wilson similarly point out that it is the possession of an intellectual technique acquired by special training which can be applied to some sphere of everyday life that forms the distinguishing mark of a profession. Indeed, one dictionary defines a profession as "a vocation in which a professed knowledge of some department of learning or science is used in its application to the affairs of others or in the practice of an art founded upon it."

Carr-Saunders and Wilson go on to define a profession more fully: "We recognize a profession as a vocation founded upon prolonged and specialized intellectual training which enables a particular service to be rendered." They then go on to assert the necessity for practitioners to form

---

[3] William J. Goode, "Community Within a Community: the Professions," *American Sociological Review,* Vol. XXII (1957), pp. 194-200.

[4] William J. McGlothlin, *The Professional Schools* (New York: The Center for Applied Research in Education, Inc., 1964), p. 29.

[5] *Ibid.,* p. 17.

[6] *Ibid.,* p. 2.

[7] Everett C. Hughes, "Professions," *Daedalus,* Vol. XCII, No. 4 of the proceedings of the American Academy of Arts and Sciences (Fall, 1963), pp. 665-68.

associations before they can "become a profession in the full sense of the word." In another passage they refer to regulation. "Where professions are not regulated, the professional associations set up their own tests of competence. They go further; they recognize that because their work consists in the application of specialized knowledge which members of the public do not possess, their clients are entitled to expect from them a higher standard of integrity and fair dealing than is required in the ordinary transactions of life, and they desire that the practitioners whom they hallmark shall be not only competent but also honorable. Therefore, they elaborate ethical codes and exclude from membership those who offend."[8]

In these passages, three elements in the concept of a profession are highlighted: (1) that there is a defined area of practice expertness which the professional "professes"; (2) that the professionals are organized into a professional association; (3) that there are ethical standards, usually self-regulated, and if not, regulated by the state.

To these commonly agreed-upon criteria of a profession may be added at least three. One, and therefore a fourth criterion in our listing, is an essential theoretical and knowledge base. Without such fundamentals in principles, there is no basis for research, for judgment in practice, or for innovations, and what is left is purely technical preparation. Adam Flexner speaks specifically to this point:

> How are, we to distinguish professions that belong to universities from vocations that do not belong to them? The criteria are not difficult to discern. Professions are, as a matter of history—and very rightly "learned professions"; there are no unlearned professions. Unlearned professions—a contradiction in terms—would be vocations, callings or occupations.[9]

Whitehead similarly stresses that a profession is "An avocation whose activities are subject to theoretical analysis, and are modified by theoretical conclusions derived from that analysis."[10]

A fifth element which we may add is a defined and accepted mode of

---

[8] Carr-Saunders and Wilson, *op. cit.*, p. 479.

[9] Abraham Flexner, *Universities: American, English, German* (New York: Oxford University Press, 1930), p. 29.

[10] Alfred North Whitehead, *Adventure of Ideas* (New York: Macmillan, 1933), p. 73-74.

educational preparation and entry to the profession. Whether it is via state licensing or by a self-imposed, internal method within the organized, profession, there is a *droit de passage*—organized, systematic, visible, and usually with symbols attached, which makes it possible for someone to say that today he is a full fledged member of the professions, whereas yesterday he was not.

Finally, and sixth there is an aspect of the profession that should be made explicit, although it is usually implicit: that the function of the profession is clearly recognized by society as a function to be performed by the professionals. In other words the expertise which they profess has to be accepted by the society within which they profess it.

There has been scores of definitions of professions, and the process of definitions of professions, and the process of definitions is seemingly endless,[11] but it would probably be generally agreed that the six specific elements are the most central. To change the order, and paraphrase, they are:

1. A defined area of competence which is professed.

2. Acceptance by society of the professional function and competence.

3. A base of theory and knowledge undergirding the professional expertise.

4. Commonly accepted standards of education for preparation and entry into the profession.

5. A recognized and organized professional association.

---

[11] Among the more recent, see, for example, Morris L. Cogan, "Toward A Definition of Profession," *Harvard Educational Review*, Vol. XXIII (Winter, 1953), p. 48-49. "A profession is a vocation whose practice is founded upon an understanding of the theoretical structure of some department of learning or science, and upon the abilities accompanying such understanding. This understanding and these abilities are applied to the vital practical affairs of man. The practices of the profession are modified by knowledge of a generalized nature and by the accumulated wisdom and experience of mankind which service to correct the errors of specialism. The profession serving the vital needs of man, considers its first ethical imperative to be altruistic service to the client. . . ."

The profession has also been represented as "a socially divisive, institutionalized elite [whose] members are clearly superior beings addicted to ritual, who preserve an aura of mystery about their craft." (Thomas Raison, "In Defense of the Professions," *New Society*, August 18, 1966, p. 262—quoted by Henry David in his paper on "Education for the Professions," presented at the Council on Social Work Education Annual Meeting, January, 1957.)

6. Ethical standards based on altruistic societal obligations, and regulated either by the organized profession, itself, by the state, or both.

EMERGING PROFESSIONS

Not all occupations which can substantially meet these criteria in any country at a particular time can necessarily meet them in other countries. There are occupations—such as engineering, librarianship, architecture, journalism, social work—that have either achieved or have been in the process of achieving or have been in the process of achieving professional status in some countries that simply have no such claim in others. The single most important influence now affecting its capacity to meet these criteria of a profession is the extent to which the preparatory education is rooted in a university base.

This is not to say that the teaching of a technical skill in a university is sufficient to make a profession out of it. A university base is increasingly necessary, but hardly sufficient. If plumbing or basket-weaving or salesmanship were taught in a university, these vocations would remain honorable and perhaps well-taught, but they would hardly meet the requisites of professions.

There are, however, existing professions which can be categorized as marginal, in the sense that they are in the process of obtaining professional recognition by society. To a greater or lesser degree they meet the preconditions of a learned profession with sanctioned professional expertise, and are on the way to meeting these and other criteria more fully. In such marginal professions, as Bernard Barber has noted, "Its members are not homogeneous with respect to the amount of knowledge and community orientation they possess. . . but the elite of these occupations, such as the director of a university library, or the dean of a major university school of social work, are clearly professional. It is the elite of an emerging profession that takes the lead in pushing for the advancement of professionalism in its occupational group and in claiming public recognition of its new status."[12]

Note that in this passage Barber makes reference to elite figures in universities. Professions which may be considered marginal at any one

---

[12] Bernard Barber, "Some Problems in the Sociology of the Professions," *Daedalus,* Vol. XCII, 4 of the proceedings of the American Academy of Arts and Sciences (Fall, 1963), pp. 676-77.

time are not necessarily marginal in the future nor are they necessarily marginal with respect to all their constituency at any one time, or in all important attributes of a profession. It therefore becomes the responsibility of such an occupational group, with a professional leadership group meriting that designation, to strive to have their calling live up to the hardest criteria of a profession in all respects. It is also the responsibility of the society at large, and particularly the universities within it, to make it possible for those emerging professions to which they wish to give stability, recognition, and development, to move towards the fulfillment and achievement of these criteria. It is essential to bear in mind that through the university the leading figures of the newer professions receive not only their own claim to professional leadership, but their capacity to help advance their entire field to professional status.

When a profession's growth is fostered, the objective should, of course, be not the well-being and self-interest of its members, but the economic and social development the profession affords a particular society, and the resources within that society for the profession's growth. We have a useful illustration in the development of librarianship, whose status in different countries was recently surveyed. Librarianship had, until a few decades ago, nowhere achieved professional status, but the demands made upon it, with the scientific revolution, became increasingly formidable. Several countries began to recognize the increasing importance of the professional librarian's activity for the country's scientific and cultural development. They recognized as well the learning that had to go into leadership competence in this field, and therefore strengthened the development of library science. Where both the will and the resources existed in the countries—resources in the form of a reservoir of educated manpower as well as the necessary capital to nurture professional leadership—postgraduate education for those discharging the most senior library responsibilities has become increasingly essential.

The illustration of librarianship is particularly appropriate to our subject because in this field there are diverse levels of skills requiring different kinds of training, and only the elite, organized as such, qualify as professionals as distinct from technicians. It is a field where apprenticeship had in recent years been considered sufficient, and where now a strong base in liberal arts and sciences prior to post-graduate training is essential, where theoretical underpinnings have been developed and practice innovations have followed. A country's involvement in such a profession's development requires both resources and conviction as to its necessity for the country's future

How rapidly the development can take place may be illustrated by the fact, as an English authority writes, that, "as recently as September, 1959, it was possible for the Education Officer of the Library Association to attempt to describe the British system of library education. . . without making a single reference to the actual or potential role of the universities." Yet by 1963 this was unthinkable, and the writer notes: "The higher professional positions to be occupied by the future leaders of the profession will inevitably and increasingly be reserved for the university graduate who has acquired his professional qualification at a post-graduate library school."[13]

And so we note that, over 10 years ago, the Hebrew University accepted the proposal for a post-graduate library school. We see countries such as Egypt moving towards professional education, Poland and Yugoslavia establishing education for librarians at the baccalaureate level. We observe that the countries of Latin America have moved from short courses, to more formal training, to a three-year undergraduate program, and to contemplation of a four-year program; and we recognize that in Latin America an imminent prospect for graduate education is prevented by lack of economic resources.[14]

What we see in the development of librarianship is a prototype of many of the newer and emerging professions. First comes apprenticeship, then short courses, followed by systematic technical training. As the knowledge base becomes more substantial, the necessity for drawing imaginatively on fundamental principles becomes more demanding, the responsibility for independent judgment greater, the expertise required more complex, the interdependence with other institutions of society, other sciences and professions closer and more varied, professionalism begins to emerge. This phase leads toward systematic education on an undergraduate level. Finally comes postgraduate professional education at the master's level, and then at the doctoral level, for the leadership of a full-fledged profession which, by this time, has several layers of personnel, ranging, in the case of librarianship, from those with clerical and mechani-

---

[13] V. Clement Harrison, *Library Trends*, Vol. XII, No. 2 (October, 1963), an issue devoted to "Education for Librarianship Abroad in Different Countries."

[14] *Ibid., passim.*

cal duties to the most erudite experts in the management of information systems, computer technology for data retrieval, and scientific collections. How very close to the history of an old profession, medicine, which moved in many countries from apprenticeship to proprietary schools, to university schools of medicine, to pre-professional requirements, and now, increasingly, to a general education preceding the professional one.

In contrast is journalism, which is much less widely recognized by the hard criteria of a profession. In the United States, as elsewhere, journalism schools suffered the disdain of universities for years, establishing their base in the state universities, which were most receptive to new fields of study and least affected by centuries-old university tradition. Thus, aside from Columbia University—where a journalism school was established because of a specific bequest, and reluctantly accepted only after great internal conflict—the strongest schools of journalism are in state universities."[15] There are none at Harvard, Yale, or Princeton. While it would be hard to say that journalism has acquired throughout the United States the status of a profession, the attitude within the field has virtually disappeared that journalism can be learned solely on the job, by the apprenticeship method. Yet this attitude remains the rule in western Europe. In England the need for some systematic training has been recognized and there is now a national scheme of pre-apprenticeship training. In the west European countries where there are journalism institutes, the training, except in France, tends to be primarily in technical skills for specific jobs, rather than the inclusion of a broad base of knowledge.

In Italy, interestingly enough, a law has recently been passed making it compulsory for anyone who wants to work as a "professional" journalist to pass a proficiency test, "and it is believed this is going to lead to some curriculum changes."[16]

Thus, only in the United States has the academic world partially and haltingly begun to recognize journalism as a potential profession, rather than a skilled craft. One wonders, however, whether this lagging recognition does not deprive many countries of the contribution of more journalists who can understand their world and not only their assignment, who have acquired not only technical competence but a social ethic. How much are we losing today, when the need of people everywhere to acquire un-

---

[15] John Tebell, "What Happens to Journalism-School Graduates," *Saturday Review,* March 11, 1967, pp. 126-127.

[16] *Ibid.*

derstanding of what is going on in the world is so desperate, by the sparseness among journalists of professional conscience born of a university-bred sense of freedom of intellectual inquiry, a commitment to which the journalist should be held accountable by society and by his colleagues if he would retain his professional cachet? How we admire and value the objective, searching, thorough, informed journalist who appreciates his societal responsibility as well as his craft! How we suffer from the conscienceless hack who turns out copy without regard to truth or consequence, even in countries where freedom of the press exists!

It is quite possible to foresee the day when universities will begin to look more receptively at this mass communication specialist and begin to move the field, or at least its potential leaders, toward a profession based on knowledge and values, a profession for which the university will take its share of responsibility. In most of the technologically developed countries of the world the resources are not lacking; the conviction of a social need for professional development is lacking.

In the history of teacher education, the evidence points to the fact that where preparation of the teacher has been separated from the universities, through separate teacher training institutes or colleges, both society and teacher have suffered. The teachers not only had or have inferior status, but they also tend to be less competent under such training. Their sense of dignity and commitment, as well as the objects of their tutelage, suffer.

In architecture the tradition of apprenticeship has been very strong, but increasingly the preparation of the architect is being viewed—in those countries where there exist both the conviction and the resources—as requiring a basic university education. Today the urban architect, for example, in addition to his design capacity, must have a good understanding of the city and its people and its myriad needs and problems, and such learning does not take place over a drawing board.

I will not dwell on my own profession, social work—which I dare to call a profession—but it is fair to say that where it has become professionalized, as in the United States, the principal index and influence towards professional development has been the gradual incorporation of social work education into universities, and the growth of graduate degree programs based on undergraduate liberal arts education. Even if every one of the hallmarks of a profession has not been fully realized, they are all sufficiently developed to have merited professional recognition within universities from other academic disciplines and professions, so that the fulfillment of the professional criteria themselves is constantly being enhanced. (The relationship to graduate professional education of undergraduate, two-year college, and other training programs in social work, is a subject of considerable importance in the United States, but is outside the scope of the present discussion.)

PROFESSIONS AND ECONOMIC DEVELOPMENT

I have referred to the problem, of resources, related to professional development. Permit me to expand. There is, of course, a direct relationship between a country's investment in education and its level of economic development. The pioneering study by Harbison and Myers, *Education, Manpower and Economic Growth,* has helped to establish this relationship, but it also points out the possibility for a country to invest inefficiently in human resource development and to emphasize the wrong kinds of education. The author suggests that: "The social and political pressures for education are powered by economic motivations, and for this reason an educational system which fails to prepare persons for available jobs is clearly out of balance and is by any definition inefficient."[17] Goode notes that "an industrializing society is a professionalizing society,"[18] but one may add that just where one professionalizes may help determine whether and how fast one industrializes.

Harbison and Myers note that the university system introduced by the British produced an important part of the high-level manpower subsequently required by independent India. After independence there was a phenomenal expansion in Indian universities. However, India continues to be plagued with excessive university enrollments in fields which are not related to India's present stage of economic growth. In 1958 nearly 58% of those enrolled were in humanities, fine arts, and law. One notes as well the necessity for a balanced relationship between the high-level professionals and technicians ancillary to the professional service. In Iran, for example, it was recently estimated that there are seven times as many doctors as nurses, and more professional engineers than technicians.

---

[17] Frederick Harbison and Charles A. Myers, *Education, Manpower and Economic Growth,* Strategies of Human Resource Development (New York: McGraw Hill, 1964), p. 186.

[18] William J. Goode, "Encroachment, Charlatanism, and the Emerging Profession: Psychology, Sociology, and Medicine," *American Sociological Review,* Vol. XXV (1960), pp. 194-200. (Quoted by Bernard Barber, *op. cit.)*

As I have emphasized, the general direction is to move professional education to higher levels, upon a base of broad liberal education. This, however, remains so where the country can afford it. The economic development of the country will determine how much of a general liberal arts and science foundation can precede graduate professional education. In the United States the tendency—not yet the fact in all professions, but definitely the trend—is for professional education to be on a graduate level, with undergraduate education of a more generalized, less specialized, nature increasingly common and available. There is similar pressure for greater depth in professional education on the European continent and an increasing connection of such education with universities, particularly in western Europe.

Let me make it clear that I do not hold my own country responsible for providing the universal international model for university organization, or even specifically in the relationship of professions to the universities. We have had too many illustrations in the United States of the incorporation of rather odd vocations in universities with seemingly professional programs. We have recognized some failings, and undoubtedly failed to recognize others. As one of our students of the professions notes, we have ignored the difference "in intellectual rigor between professional and vocational training; we tacitly assume that if only funds and facilities were made available the nation could call into being as many professionals as it needed."[19] He criticizes as well the prejudice against women in the professions, pointing out that in the Soviet Union 379,000 women are engineers and 332,400 doctors and surgeons, whereas there are only 14,000 women doctors in the United States and but a handful of women engineers. He also criticizes our professions for clinging to too-formal standards of training the insistence of educationists that with out education courses a person cannot qualify as a school teacher and the refusal of doctors delegate significant authority to social workers.

Professor Titmus has commented on the enormous advantages accruing to the United States by its utilization of high-level personnel for whom other countries had provided the training investment. The higher financial rewards that attract those professionals who migrate to the United States, noted by Professor Titmus, is, however, only one side of the pic-

---

[19] Kenneth S. Lynn, "Introduction to the Issue 'The Professions,'" *Daedalus,* Vol. XCIT, No. 4 (Fall, 1963), p. 651.

ture. There is a good deal to be said for the net impact of the relatively easy movement of professions into the universities in the United States-a result primarily of the Jeffersonian policy in the establishment of state colleges and universities-and its effect on economic and technological development.

In a recent edition of *The New York Times* there was a report on the technology gap between Europe and the United States, committed to the latter mission and to great concern having been registered on both sides of the Atlantic about the rate at which the United States was surpassing western Europe technologically.[20] Differences in education were cited as key factors in the advance enjoyed by the United States. The report marked the relative weakness particularly of European higher education.

> In European education there is a tradition of rigid professorial kingdoms. There is little flexibility to permit the kind of interdisciplinary work that produces so many of today's discoveries. . .[21]

These observations are borne out by reports in the *International Yearbook of Education,* which note, for example, that in Sweden "the risk of the idiocy of specialism is often discussed and deplored"[22] and which consider that the high degree of specialization and separation among professional groups severely limits university education for the professions. In Switzerland concern is expressed that its universities should be centers of culture rather than faculties and institutes unconnected with each other, with the consequent risk of becoming mere higher vocational schools.[23] Universities in the United States have their own problems in this regard, but the opportunities to interconnect among disciplines and professions tend to be greater because of greater organizational flexibility and not only greater affluence.

Incorporating professional education along priorities of need and convictions and as resources permit it is a way universities have of being responsive to societal needs. Yet universities also have to be centers of learning, with their own mission of freedom in teaching and in the search

---

[20] "Technology Gap Upsets Europe," *New York Times*, Vol. CXVI, No. 39859, March 12, 1967, p. 1, p. 72.

[21] *Op. cit.* Quoted from an informed interviewee.

[22] George Z. F. Bereday and Joseph A. Lauwerys, editors, International Yearbook of Education (London: Evans Brothers Ltd., 1959), p. 194,

[23] *Ibid.*, p. 401

for knowledge. For a professional school to be committed to the latter mission and to function well in a university requires an intimate interaction between it and the relevant disciplines upon which it builds, and a similar interaction upon which relevant professions. The one leads to a richer mutual feedback of knowledge, the other to the prospect of solving problems either beyond the capacity of any one professions or requiring the participation of more than one. Thus, we have combinations such as psychiatry–law; medicine–engineering; public administration–city planning–architecture; social work–law; management–education. These combinations can best be brought together in a university, which can provide the opportunities for collaborative research and teaching and can stimulate creativity.

I should like now to return to the first point and develop briefly theme of societal obligation, or "involvement," today's word that represent the antithesis of the "ivory tower."

THE PROFESSIONS, THE UNIVERSITY, AND THE "IVORY TOWER"

The first use of the term "ivory tower" is credited to Sainte-Beuve in a poem where he refers to the poet de Vigny:

. . . et Vigny, plus secret,

Comme en sa tour d'ivoire, avant midi, rentrait.

Sainte-Beuve was using the expression to characterize de Vigny—as he had made clear in his essay on the poet—as one less concerned with the real world than with philosophical matters, which he treated with great delicacy and refinement, abstracted from the natural environment or the course of human events. The phrase "ivory tower" has persisted with remarkable tenacity in its original meaning, and has frequently been applied to the university and its scholars, as well as to the reluctance of universities to become engaged with professions other than medicine, law, or theology.

There is, of course, a case to be made for exclusion or restriction of the newer professions from the university establishment, but not because of the fear of contamination by greater involvement with the society around the university. Whatever the situation has been in the past in universities in various countries, non-involvement is no longer possible. The primary basis for restricting entrance to the university circle, even for those fields of activity which have lived up to the essential criteria of professions, is a matter of resources, not of principle. Does one have or can one afford to develop the faculty necessary to teach at a professional level? Can one draw from an adequate source of students to seek this professional education? Is the development of this profession of sufficient priority in the country? Is there a reservoir of technicians or sub-professionals to aid in delivery of professional service? Negative answers to these kinds of questions might dictate slowing the pace of incorporation of particular professions into the university. It cannot be the "ivory tower" concept.

All over the world there is an increasing back-and-forth flow of faculty between the university and the worlds of government, industry, private professional practice, and politics. Where the very existence of the profession is determined by society's needs, especially if the state has made an investment in higher education in the particular professions as part of its plan for economic and social development, one cannot escape the societal obligation and mutual relationship with the state.[24] "Moreover, students more and more bring the world into the universities with them, even where there might be some desire to keep the world out.

The university maintains its distinctiveness not in separating itself from mundane affairs, but in exercising its primary function as a center for free and unfettered search for knowledge and its transmission.

There are those who feel that even this freedom can be overdone. Thus, John D. Millett, Chairman of the Board of Higher Education in my own state of Ohio, has recently written reminding the academic world of Aristotle's concern for the excess of virtues as well as defects, and he suggests as possible excesses the free use of knowledge and the self-direction of academic activity. "One extreme of self-direction results in the academic communities withdrawing or escaping from contemporary society. The other is the extreme of self-immersion and self-identification with contemporary society that blocks intellectual progress."[25]

He observes that Oxford and Cambridge withdrew from British society in the 19th century. The universities found the growth of business, industry, and democracy distasteful. "Only in this century, in large part

---

[24] France, through the Napoleonic reorganization, was one of the first countries to meet the need for professionally trained personnel through national planning for institutions of higher learning.

[25] John D. Millett, "The Ethics of Higher Education," *Educational Record,* Vol. XLVIII, No. 1 (Winter, 1967), p. 17.

because of increased financial support from the government, have the British universities been dragged into the 20th century." So much for the excess of separation from society. As for the other, he stresses the danger of universities' being too free in their search for knowledge and neglecting the benefit of man. He states, "As a social utility, higher education has no choice but to accept social direction."[26]

While I agree in part with Dr. Millett's observations, I find myself less concerned than he with the dangers of the excess of virtue in the free search for knowledge. It is part of the university's glory, where it has been unfettered in its intellectual climate, that it has served as a bulwark in the defense of freedoms generally and as a source of social criticism. Not all universities have been able to preserve their domain as a sanctuary, immune to political pressure. The course of recent history has made this all too evident throughout the world. In my own country, the universities were on the defensive during the heyday of the late Senator Joseph McCarthy in the 1950's, and only a few great universities, such as Harvard, were able to maintain in this period a climate of intellectual integrity and freedom.

In recent years it has been of interest to observe the different perspectives upon social issues of the professional schools within universities as contrasted to professional societies. Thus, when Medicare-the incorporation of health service into social security, particularly for the aged-was under debate in the United States, the faculties of medical schools tended to take a more accepting attitude than did the medical societies, and their moral influence helped to take a bit of the sting out of the negative attitude manifested generally, if not universally, by the professional societies. It is another illustration of the thesis that the principle of a free search for knowledge and an essential social commitment in universities provides a salutary underpinning for the ethics of all professions. Moreover, universities, in providing the context for interprofessional and interdisciplinary collaboration, generate not only a broader academic and practice base for effectiveness and creativity in research and practice, but help mitigate the tendency towards professional insularity and self-interest.

In this connection, a word might be said about the relationship of professional schools to their surrounding professional communities. This relationship naturally increases the university's "involvement," but it is not

---

[26] *Ibid.*, p. 19.

always an unmixed blessing, for it contains constraints as well as advantages for the university. The advantages include the prospect of financial and other support by professional groups eager to recruit the products of professional schools, or engage in research with the schools, or simply support them as loyal alumni. The professional community provides opportunities for research as well as practice experience as part of professional education, and is a source for stimulation of new research and practice developments. The constraints, on the other hand, reflect the special interests of any professional community. They can include pressures for particular curricular emphasis or the demand for participation in academic policy because of the contribution they make to professional education, financial or otherwise. Quite often there is also pressure for more technically-oriented rather than broader professional preparation on the part of professionals and professional groups who have arrived and are eager to recruit, not those presumed to be over-theoretical, but graduates who can "do a day's work." My general feeling here is that the advantages for a close relationship to the professional community far outweigh the potential strains, and are, in any event, essential, but professional schools often do have a problem in defining their orientation as between the university base and the professional community.

THE NEED FOR A LIBERAL EDUCATION

One hardly need develop the point that the prodigious growth of knowledge in all fields demands more systematic preparation for all professions and a broad theoretical base for later innovation on the part of the fledgling professional and for his continuing education. Without this fundamental preparation in principles as well as techniques, the growth of professional invention is impaired, as is the rapidity with which the profession can take advantage of advances in the sciences on which it depends. But beyond this it is also important, as I have perhaps too often noted, for the professional to have a liberal education—by which we generally mean the possession of a broad knowledge of the natural sciences, the social sciences, the arts, and the humanities—and to see the meaning of his calling within the society in which he practices it. A professional can be well-trained but poorly-educated, and he is much less able to meet his professional obligations without a background of liberal education which can best take place within the university.

One of our keen students of the professions states:

Unless professional education inspires the desire to learn, to extend the scope of one's knowledge, to increase one's insights into the nature of things, it has condemned its recipients to eventual ignorance and mental stagnation, for the exponential increase of knowledge is the most arresting fact in today's world and swiftly accelerating change the most characteristic feature of modern life. Hence, even if higher education were able to supply each student with all the knowledge needed to understand the world in which he currently lives, and even if it could sharpen the intellectual skills to a fine point, it would have failed if it had not added to these achievements the inculcation of the irresistible desire to learn and to know. . . unless education initiates a chain reaction in which each advance and understanding sets off a desire for greater growth and wisdom, those who leave our campuses will soon reach a state of permanent intellectual rest.[27]

We have been witnessing recently a slow but inexorable revolution in the preparation of professionals. In medicine and law, as well as in engineering, in public administration, and in management, in architecture, and even in journalism, not only has apprenticeship ceased to be the model for professional learning, but even special institutes or special schools unrelated to universities have now come full circle to the realization that without a broad base in liberal education they will still be turning out advanced technicians or technologists. They are very useful and important, but they are not truly well-rounded professionals, who are even more valuable in the modern world.

One of our great tasks is to prevent the mass production of the crass "professional," thoroughly ignorant of all but his vocation, and yet on whom we are dependent for his special competence. This is the kind of man whom Ortega y Gasset assails in these terms: "This new barbarian is above all the professional man, more learned than ever but at the same time more uncultured—the engineer, the physician, the lawyer, the scientist."[28]

It is an unhappy prospect, and it can be prevented. The main hope is liberal education, the kind that provides the capacity to develop one's full

---

[27] McGrath, *op cit.*, p. 25.

[28] Ortega y Gasset, *Mission in the University*, translated by H. L. Nostrand (New Jersey: Princeton University Press, 1944), p. 58.

intellectual resources, to bring objectivity and wisdom to bear on problems, to know what one does not know, to be able to utilize the resources of other academic disciplines or professions, to cultivate an esthetic sense and to deepen one's sense of values.

Moreover, the ethical commitment, which is one of the principal hallmarks of a profession, cannot easily be discharged without the opportunity of the professional practitioner to have experienced, partly within the university, a broad sense of ethics in the large, rather than in connection only with his technical specialty, for only so can his education help him develop deep commitments to fundamental social values.

If there is one keystone to the culture of the university, it is the commitment to the unremitting pursuit of knowledge, where ever it leads. It is that search and that sense of unfettered intellectual independence which is most soundly generated by the best of liberal education. All professions need this ethic and need it constantly reinforced.

For these reasons, I believe the case can be made for the increasing provision of a broad liberal education as a requirement or as a component of professional education.

CONCLUSIONS

The professional school, new and old, can be highly compatible with the academic tradition of the university. Indeed, it can reinforce it and make it more fruitful. The problems that exist in the relationship do not lie in the myth that the academic disciplines are purer in scholarship, higher in standards of research or teaching, than are the professional schools of medicine or law, or library science, or social work, or management. Academic standards can and should be kept at least as high in the professional schools as in the academic departments, and often they are indeed higher. The real problem lies in the willingness of the university to lend a helping hand to the emerging professions which it wishes to incorporate, to aid its absorption into the academic community in all respects. Without such encouragement-which does not, of course, suggest any compromise in academic quality-and a perspective of equality in all essential conditions of belonging to the university family, the school and its faculty are handicapped in advancing the profession itself. With such encouragement and support, the professional school cannot only fully live up to the best of university ideals, but help make the university itself a more effective force for research, teaching, and service to its society.

2.   Reflections on Competence and Ideology in Social Work Education

INTRODUCTION

The presidency of this organization is not honorific; its responsibilities are heavy and continuous. I must admit that it also sometimes—has been fun, and that well-known "learning experience" always. I will not recite the litany of achievements in restructuring, broadened participation, or responsiveness to changing needs and conditions of the Council on Social Work Education (CSWE) during these years. It has been a time of growth, change and incessant self-questioning, calling not for self-congratulation at achievements—neither Board nor staff, commissions and committees had any time for that—but rather for hard self-scrutiny and action to keep pace with, anticipate, and try to effect significant changes in social work education and its environment.

It has, of course, also been a period where there has been the characteristic ferment within social work education itself in a number of widely different areas. Interdisciplinary education with much more utilization of university resources has grown markedly, particularly with new relationships with public administration, political science, public health and operations research, as well as with the social and behavioral science fields. There has been progress in promoting preparation for administrative responsibilities, new course developments in areas of poverty and race, innovations for training and practice for community mental health, and experiments with the period of time required as well as the content of social work education, both on graduate and undergraduate levels. The utilization of new technology in the form of video tape, closed circuit T.V. and program instruction have also begun to take hold.

This text was originally presented as the Presidential Address at the Annual Program Meeting of the Council on Social Work Education, January 23, 1969, Cleveland, Ohio. It has been slightly revised for this volume.

There have been two areas of highest activity. One has been experimentation with different curricular models, including efforts towards merging methods, organizing curriculum around problem areas, revising and refining the traditional organization of curriculum by practice methods, and trying other variations on the specialized generic theme.

The second area which has taken life more vigorously has been the involvement of students in various modes of participation in policy and planning for the schools—as part, of rapid developments within all of higher education—and in the affairs of the CSWE itself.

My emphasis in this paper, however, is not to dwell on what has been happening these past few years in social work education or the CSWE, so much as to comment on certain issues that are before us currently, with a view to the prospects that lie ahead. My main theme is competence and ideology, but I will approach it discursively.

CERTAIN DISTINCTIONS AMONG PROFESSIONS

Professions may roughly be divided into Group A, those that rank high on one or more of the criteria of power, drama, adventure, financial risks at stake, or sophisticated material technology—such professions would include medicine, law, engineering—and Group B, those that are characterized more by humanitarianism, compassion, artistic expression, constructive and ameliorative services that make life more livable, and aid in the growth and development of people. Such professions have traditionally included teaching, nursing, dentistry, clinical psychology, library science and social work.

This is not really a breakdown into two groupings, but is more in the nature of two clusters at each end of a spectrum. Architecture, for example, is sort of in-between. Yet, we can, at least loosely, refer to two classifications, depending on how they fall on either end of this spectrum.

I had thought of calling the first group the more masculine professions—in terms of masculine attributes, not in sex distribution of personnel—and the latter group the more feminine professions, but decided against it. It not only would offend a lot of people straight off, but everything with potential sexual connotations leads to complications and a temptation to make jokes, which won't do for such a serious paper. So let's just call those groups "M" and "F"—no, we will stay with A and B.

Of course, none of these professions is wholly one thing or the other. In medicine, for example, surgery is perceived to have much more life-and-death drama and power than pediatrics.

When a profession is in the throes of moving from one identity to the other, however, or of including significant components of the other, strains in professional identities and confusions of image of image arise. Library science, for example, has moved far away from checking books in and out, and cataloging, to include computer technology with its information retrieval systems. What is meant by a "trained librarian" these days is therefore no longer as clear as it was a decade ago. Nursing, with its Ph.D. programs, has taken on or is struggling to take on large administrative, research and scientific responsibilities previously associated solely with medicine.

In social work we are also going through a metamorphosis, from having interpreted ourselves traditionally and being perceived as essentially in the B grouping, concentrating on the service-humanist attributes, to our attempt to incorporate some of the A elements. Thus, our increasing effort to interpret our role with respect to the billions of dollars expended through public and voluntary welfare, our efforts to influence political decisions, to enter significantly into the fray of the urban crisis, and to engage in large-scale research with computer technology. The planning and social action functions we now ascribe to ourselves lie in the first category. These A elements in our self-definition are emerging, while the public still identifies us as among the most B of fields, and while the actual distribution of social work activities lies in the B framework. There are many who smart at both this public perception and this reality, and would hasten the movement to more engagement, for example, with power—in the sense of the opportunity to define and influence the resolution of significant social issues.

The cry for greater impact increasingly reflects the wish that the profession represent movers and shakers, that social workers be A people, and not B people. The frustration at our not having all that muscle leads, however, not to scaling down our aspirations., but to intensifying our commitment to social change and social reform—in other words, to enhancing the accent on ideology. Yet, ideology without the means to achieve ends—without competence and institutionalized means to translate that competence into action—is futile for a profession.

COMPETENCE AND IDEOLOGY

The restlessness being experienced within social work education, as in social vote, itself, reflects in part a fundamental dilemma in the relationship between competence and ideology.

By competence I am referring essentially to knowledge and skill. There is no profession that can call itself such without a defined sphere of competence. To demand of society that we have professional recognition is to make the claim that we know how to do certain things which society needs, and that by virtue of our special educational preparation and experience we know how to do certain things which society needs better than anyone else. This is not to say that each professional can possibly leave competence in the entire range of sectors which a profession has staked out. In social work, however, we do not yet have a clear map of what it is we *have* staked out. We may be able to speak fairly clearly about certain treatment and administrative fields, but when we move into such areas as social planning, of stimulation and participation in social change, or even of social research expertise, we are not yet on very firm ground, either as to the nature of the capacities we claim or the uniqueness of such competence.

The pressure to build into undergraduate and graduate curriculum background knowledge and skill in course and field experience, to make these aspirations for competence genuinely realized, is becoming intense. The struggle within schools and within social work education broadly for maximum room, within sharply delimited curricular space, for competing methods of practice, or problem areas, or new terrain for professional service, shows no signs of diminishing. And this is as it should be.

By ideology I am referring not simply to underlying humanistic values, but to clear social objectives and the commitment to struggle for them. We have properly become preoccupied in recent years with emphasizing the need for ideology, in this sense, in order to prevent over-professionalism and a narrow technical orientation in our curriculum, and more important, to prevent such provincialism being transmitted to our students. But it is quite clear that our students themselves will prevent such an orientation, hopefully with rather than against faculty.

It is not easy to define what a consistent and coherent ideology is. The most pressing and deeply held commitments within social work today are to combat racism and poverty, to end the deprivations to which blacks and other minority groups are subject, and to advocacy both on behalf of clientele and of the interests of the poor and disinherited. The demand is keen and persistent in social work education at all levels, for engagement with the burning social issues of the day.

These are vital and essential. convictions, but they do not constitute ideology sufficient for purposeful direction. Specific programs and specific capacities are required to turn ideology into reality. We need more passion and more commitment, but if they are not harnessed to competence and to the organizational instruments and power for action, we spin our wheels while we spin our slogans. Moreover,, the ideology of professions, particularly those addressing human needs, tends to differ from that of society at large, and that is true of social work.

SHIFTS IN SOCIAL OBJECTIVES

We are a culture that goes in heavily for changes of fashions, not only in hem-lines and hair-styles, but in art and child-rearing, and yes, even in causes, which change not only because of changing events, but because of rapidly shifting ideologies and shifting groups of adherents to given ideologies.

For these aspects of ideology which are reflected in social reform, this particular cultural trait often results in frustration and weakness. Causes which run high in passion, can also lose stem just as fast, and we tire from some prematurely. There have been social reforms which been, essentially won—child labor and workman's compensation, for example—and their success ensured by law and organizations devoted to their protection. There are other causes, however, which have zoomed on the horizon, deposited an army of agencies and practitioners and receded from the list of causes receiving priority dedication, even ,when no fundamental changes have occurred. In prison reform, for example, for much of America, we are still in the dark ages. Prevention of distress for the aged—progress, yes—success, hardly. Mental health continues to be a heavy preoccupation, but the block-buster attack on the shame of the state hospitals, which Albert Deutsch and others were decrying thirty years ago, has lost ground as an object for fervent commitment without our having solved the problem, and even the community mental health movement has lost some of its luster as a shining priority. It is as if, since we have organizations presumably devoted to doing something about these problems, we are rid of them. It isn't so. If our society is to progress, our causes must not be permitted to drop out of sight until they are won.

A philosopher was recently quoted as stating that the philosophical function is to say, after everyone has agreed on a position—"However." One social work function is to react, when everyone has agreed on how much progress we have made in any social field, to prevent any complacency, and with questions of "Are you quite sure? And what else has to be done to improve the lot of people?" To be preoccupied with causes cannot be regarded as a sometime thing with social work. It is apart of our natural habitat, just as fires are part of the natural habitat of firemen.

Social work's contribution to the resolution of social problem cannot derive from proclamations that we believe in justice, freedom and the good of life. Nor can they derive even from the sensitization of our students to social problems and the attempt at inculcation of attitudes of commitment, for those not already committed. Our students eventually become practitioners who, with the rest of us, will enrage in ritual dances on annual or biennial occasions, depending on the professional tribal group, where we exorcise the evil spirits of our society and dust off our deities. These ceremonies have, to be sure, valuable functions. They reinforce our collective moral dedication, and occasionally they lead to the establishment or influence of programs and events that have some significance. These occasions can also give us the illusion of having done something when we have only said something. They permit us to feel that we are among the righteous, so that we can return spiritually refreshed to our daily chores, which may or may not have anything to contribute to the social objectives formulated with such care for clear prose, constructive content and democratic process.

An outpouring of energy for the analysis and formulation of policy without comparable investment in necessarily related competence and action, may be intellectually and spiritually satisfying, but will not necessarily produce change.

The optimal relationship between ideology and competence is to have the first ahead of the second, but attainable. We should keep our social objectives beyond what we may be able currently to deliver, develop our capacity to meet them, and go on to new objectives.

If we say that comprehensive urban planning is a goal we should help achieve, and we know what we mean, then we have to develop people prepared to contribute to this goal. If we want to engage in designing and implementing basic new income maintenance programs, then we have to help provide the underpinnings for careers in social welfare economics. If we feel that delivery of health services needs drastic redesigning and that we ought to make a signal contribution to it, then we have to stake our claim and deliver the people to work at it. If we have goals that imply our participating in the solution of problems of housing or education or employment or community mental health or any of our urban problem areas then we have to train people for them. If a school states that its black social work students should be prepared for leadership in black communities it must organize itself to deliver such preparation.[1] If it cannot so organize itself and develop the necessary resources, then this expectation is empty of meaning.

PORTER R. LEE'S "CAUSE AND FUNCTION"

Those who recall social work history and are sensitive to social work tradition will recognize that this discussion is a re-examination in contemporary terms of competence and ideology, of a classic statement on the relationship of cause and function. It was presented forty years ago in the Presidential Address of 1929 at the National Conference of Social Work,[2] by Porter R. Lee, director of the New York School of Social Work of Columbia University and one of our all-time great social work educators.

Porter R. Lee referred to the history of social work as including both cause and function. He interpreted "a cause as usually a movement directed toward the elimination of an entrenched evil" and "function" as the translation of a cause into one or more administrative operations. He stressed that "Once the objective of a cause is reached, it can be made permanent only by a combination of organization and education."

Contrary to many subsequent allusions to this historic paper, which I trust is known by all social work students, Mr. Lee was not declaring the superiority of cause over function, but was instead warning against the exaggerated expectations in certain kinds of promotion of causes which could only lead to frustration. He warned against the fervid support of causes which the field cannot do anything about, in the way of providing trained manpower. "But our very success may imperil both our functional efficiency and our leadership if we try to develop opportunities for service beyond our resources in qualified personnel."

He cautioned against the tendency "to claim more than we can perform," and stressed the tenuous nature of causes presumed to be won. He quotes Jane Addams, "The good we secure for ourselves is precarious and

---

[1] Gary, Lawrence E., "Social Work Education and The Black Community: A Proposal for Curriculum Revisions," in *Social Work Education Reporter*, Vol. XVI, No. 4, December 1968, p. 47.

[2] Lee, Porter R., *Social Work as Cause and Function and Other Papers*, New York: Columbia University Press, 1937, pp. 3-24.

uncertain, is floating in mid-air, until it is secured for all of us and incorporated into our common life."

When we do not somewhere in our educational establishment prepare the people who can discharge the functions we say are needed to reach the social goals we espouse, we should simply and clearly say that we are for these goals and will support them in various meaningful ways as socially responsible citizens, but not on the claim of our professional expertise or on the promise of delivery of expertise. We cannot depend on the occasional "sport" in social work who through brilliance, talent or accident becomes an expert or leader in new fields without any formal preparation. We point to these individuals with pride when we recognize them as social workers, but we ought to concede that it was not primarily the education we provided which made their contributions possible.

Our educational institutions will individually have to select the kinds of expertise on which they will concentrate, aside from basic underpinnings. Schools will therefore differ considerably, depending on their interests, resources, and their priority commitments to social goals, because there will undoubtedly be great variation in ideological emphasis, as well, although hopefully a shared commitment to social goals along with all others in the social work profession. Schools of social work, and undergraduate programs which prepare people for practice in social work, will have a clear obligation not simply to declare their educational goals, but the specific spheres of competence for which they are providing the fundamentals, and these spheres will increasingly differ in character.

It will be less and less desirable to require, or even seek, consistent—let along uniform—curricula with respect to areas of competence. Common cores of competence and much overlap will continue to exist, but with much greater variation than we are now accustomed to. It is no longer experimentation with curricular innovation that I am referring to, but large-scale changes through painstaking development by schools, which can justify society's confidence in the capacity of the profession to produce expertise for existing and for emerging new areas of practice.

DIRECT SERVICE AND SOCIAL CHANCE

Social workers have a certain measure of credibility now for expertise in many areas of service and administration, for the most part in remedial and ameliorative fields. This is nothing to be depreciated, as is one of our current tendencies. No matter what massive social, economic or political solutions are found, there will be distressed children and anxious mothers and distraught fathers and forlorn old people and other lonely people who need careful, painstaking, sensitive help, one at a time or in pairs and small groups. And they deserve the best we have to offer when they *need* the help, without waiting for the millenium when all human problems will be prevented by social and economic reconstruction. This is not to say that individual problems are not related to broad social conditions, but people still suffer one by one.

Preventive public health does a great deal of prevention of illness, but if I have a heart attack, I want a doctor just for me, and I don't want at that moment to write my congressman to do something about easing the tensions of modern living.

Let's not keep on knocking remedial and therapeutic work. We have too little of that, not too much, and its availability is now maldistributed— as are so many of the better things in life—with the poor and the minority groups being short changed all the way.

We are witnessing in our schools of social work evidence of great dissatisfaction and strain with the way our society is meeting its social problems, and the question of our profession's potential impact on these problems is being persistently raised. The basis of this strain tends to be more articulated in schools than in the world of practice simply because it is one of the functions of the school to have these issues raised. And one of the great contributions of students is to voice the questions, which thankfully they do not fail to do, and sometimes to answer them in ways different from their elders.

The concern can, however, also take a shape that gets us nowhere but can instead provide the illusion of engaging in a meaningful engagement of issues. Thus, this is a period when it is tempting for some who are primarily concerned with policy development, planning or with an activist, organizing and social change orientation to patronize those performing direct treatment services, just as the reverse was at one time true. The student who wants to work with people who have family problems or who are in hospitals suddenly has to defend his relevance to today's world.

It is not a useless exchange, of course, because out of it, especially if conducted in a spirit of informed inquiry, can come a lasting appreciation of the complexity of the social work system itself on the basis of shared values and an appreciation of the diverse contributions that have to make it up, while social work is itself undergoing change.

It is important to bear in mind that the individual practitioner is not necessarily less concerned with social problems, as an individual, than is the administrator, the social welfare policy teacher, or the planner. The individual practitioner should have a basic and hopefully a continuing education which throws his area of practice against a screen of a larger societal framework. He must also have a way of providing knowledge and action for the resolution of those social problems to which he can contribute expertise, and to have access to the points of view and the avenues of action of those concerned, in their daily professional activity, with the development and execution of policies and plans. It is a differentiation of roles, a division of labor within our field that is essential, within a context where these roles can be mutually reinforcing, through organizational arrangements that make this possible, rather than engaging in wasteful competition about who is more important or who is more relevant.

We need more vigorous social action, and accelerated progress towards all goals of social justice, but the record of history gives little basis for confidence in those who ignore people as individuals, while they presume to serve only what they define as the interests of the masses of humanity. A profession need not choose between the two. We must have individual caring and compassionate services in that Group B humanist tradition, while we also try to grapple with the larger massive issues from which so many individual needs stem.

Having said this, it must also be recognized that the remedial function, and its practitioners, have contributed an overly dominant emphasis in our field and our education. Let me digress for a moment to refer to the historic United Nations Conference of Ministers Responsible for Social Welfare held at the United Nations in August, 1968. Eighty-eight countries sent delegations, sixty-one headed by a government leader of ministerial rank. The final document of this conference[3], approved word-by-word in the plenary sessions, contains these statements:

> The Conference gave emphasis to the principle that the objectives
> of national development everywhere are designed to enhance the

---

[3] Draft Final Document of the Conference. E/Conf. 55/L.7, 7 Sept. 1968 United Nations Economic and Social Council.

well-being of people by raising their level of living, by ensuring social justice and the more equitable distribution of the national wealth, and by enhancing the opportunity of the people to develop their highest capacities as healthy, educated, participating and contributing citizens. Social welfare, whatever the precise meaning given to its function and programs in different states, is an essential component force to such development objectives. Its contributions are manifold. They may be characterized as developmental, preventive, and remedial.

It goes on to define the development function in social welfare as "fundamentally engaged in the development of human resources, including the strengthening of family life and the preparation of people to improve their own lives as they contribute to national development. Social welfare contributes its particular expertise to planning and to the formulation of social policy, including the design of needed legislation. . ." And further on, "Strong emphasis was given to the preparation of personnel for combined social and economic planning and in social policy analysis. . ."

Those of us who were involved in the preparations and the procedures for the conference know how seriously all this was taken and how meaningful, particularly for the representatives from the developing countries. But one could not help having certain misgivings as an American as to whether the service we were giving to the developmental, in our society, was not mostly lip service. The document clearly calls for a connection between ideology and competence. It speaks of goals of social justice and economic and social advance, to which social welfare would make a significant contribution through trained capacities. How far have we moved in the United States and Canada in this connection? We have moved some—but not very far.

SOCIAL PROBLEMS

I have emphasized—not too originally—that the remedial function and the goal of attacking social problems, must both be retained in our field. Let me make clear that I use the term *social problem* as a problem which, in addition to other criteria. has its origins in significant measure within the social structure itself. The extent to which it is so derived is a key index of the extent to which it is a *social* problem. It is not a social problem alone because many people have whatever it is, or suffer from it, or even because the public is concerned about it, but it is a social problem if, in addition to these, it is recognized that its causes lie to a significant extent within the social environment. If juvenile delinquency were defined as the totality of behavior of individual juveniles, each with a distinct psychological problem, it could not, from this premise, simultaneously be defined as a social problem. It becomes one to the extent that part of its etiology is social, and the direction to prevention, therefore, at least partly related to effecting changes in relevant segments of the social structure.

The clearest analogy can be made with public health, Appendicitis is not a public health problem even though it is very common. Its etiology lies within the individual human organism. There are no public health measures that can prevent it, and the only treatment is to remove or otherwise treat each separate appendix. Lung cancer became a public health or social problem when it was discovered through research that what is inhaled, such as cigarette smoke and other pollutants, can cause or aggravate the condition. The measures to combat lung cancer, therefore, require changes in the social system to reduce cigarette smoking.

No problem arising in any appreciable measure from the social or physical environment can be attacked without reference to modification in the appropriate systems within these environments. Any change in any part of the social system—and not necessarily a revolutionary change—means actual or potential resistance may be anticipated from those whose true or perceived interest it is for the status quo to persist, whether this interest is of a material or ideological nature.

Frustration with the ills and shortcomings of any society gives rise, and must, to demands for change, and within professions for demand that they contribute to such change, and thus be prepared to deal with conflict and resistance. But no profession can be relevant to everything. Each has its constraints, both on its presumed competence and on its formulation of ideology. An individual professional may be a revolutionary, for example, but a profession cannot, if revolution is defined as the forcible redistribution of power. Every profession, as a profession, is related to its society. It may work for large-scale social reforms that will eventually modify the larger system, but to the extent that it is a profession legitimated by society it has to work within the social system and its rules.

Social work has a long tradition of liberal humanism. This is not a soft tradition. It has had its fighters and strong advocates of the poor and the oppressed, and continues to have. It has also had its periods of decline into provincialism and over-concern with technique. We have, I believe, turned the corner. Commitment to fundamental reform is inherent in the profession, as part of a shared ideology in social work. This commitment gives increasing promise of impact as it is backed up by competence as well as zeal.

STUDENTS

In the shaping and re-shaping of our ideology and social commitments, we must be sensitive to the definitions of issues and the major concerns that are expressed by our students, in the full range and variety of such expression.

The term "students" today is loaded with judgmental connotations. For some, it is part of a demonology—those devil students are at it again! For others it is part of a hagiography—the idealizing of saintly characters—so that students by definition can do no wrong, especially if they do whatever they do in large numbers.

It is, I think, not altogether fatuous to note that students come in an extraordinary diversity of personal maturity, intelligence, political ideologies and social commitments. Generalizations about students are, therefore, subject to enormous error. This is particularly true if we are inclined to exercise the "squeaking hinge" principle—well-known as a disease of administration, whereby those who demand the most attention get the most rewards. The result is compounded in the case of students, by our generalizing about all students on the basis of the voices of any one segment, who deserve a hearing, but may be far from representative of the range of student opinion. It is not, therefore, that all of our young students —comparatively young anyway—are of one mind, or that each viewpoint need be given equal attention with every other. Indeed, all viewpoints should have their forum in which to be articulated and debated, and in our colleges and universities the expression of the full range of student opinion should be encouraged.

We should catch the sentiments and thoughts of our students relatively quickly, on the wing, and as early as possible in their careers as students. They become socialized into the views and lexicon of their mentors all too rapidly as they blend into the professional landscape. Of course, they can remain exciting individuals, with new and invigorating ideas, even after they leave our schools, but that first blush of enthusiasm, possibly naive, but sharp, clear, and even impudent in its expression, should be encouraged before it becomes subdued and channeled. We have to listen to our students—even those who will not speak up unless encouraged to do so—when they are keenest and least fettered. Their eye may be more on the ball than ours.

CONCLUDING COMMENTS

Social work education cannot turn back the clock to a period of narrow over-professionalism. We must be as a profession more fully engaged with the significant issues of our time—move more closely to the power-oriented *A* type, while retaining the traditions of the humanistic *B* type—and try to develop a coherent ideology about social purpose, while we know both that there will be ideological differences among us and that as a profession our emphases will differ from those of most of society. When we select specific social objectives, within a consensus of broad ideology of change and reform to which social work should make a definite contribution, we should also plan to develop the competence that goes with making such contribution.

Since social problems rarely have single causes, nor arise through one single system or subsystem in our society, the approach to dealing with social problems of any significance has to be ramified. No profession alone can deal with any one of our mass of social problems. In social work as in other professions, however, we have the responsibility to define those issues with respect to social problems on which we should take leadership because of our special claim to competence and social responsibility. We should also support the leadership of other professional and interest groups where our objectives and theirs coincide, and, as a profession legitimated by society, we have to work within the basic rules of the society.

Schools of social work will redefine their particular and separate spheres of competence for which they are prepared to educate professionals, as some schools have already done. There will continue to be core competence, in the areas that have been traditional, but the common core among schools, I predict, will be smaller and the variations larger. Schools should be expected to declare what kinds of competence they prepare for, and be evaluated on the extent to which they deliver on what they declare. Moreover, the nature of this competence will change as it combines with and draws from other professions and disciplines. Community psychology, as well as clinical psychology, for example, has great overlap with social work competence, and certain spheres of joint expertise may merge.

In social problem areas there will have to be combined resources from fields of health, education, economics, and political science. It should not be identical targets for training in competence which unites schools of social work, but commonly accepted premises of social purpose, values and commitment, which I have loosely gathered under the term ideology; such commitments should include those which protect the essential and unique values of freedom and rational discourse in universities. The zeal of the best of our students, who wish to help our country live up to its ideals, must not be lost under the weight of narrow technology. They must be in a position to contribute their idealism to the sharpening and development of ideology for all of us, but our education must also couple this dedication with solid knowledge and skill to make it effective. It takes dough as well as yeast to make bread. And on this hungry and not financial note, I take my presidential leave.

3.   Social Work's Developmental and Change Functions: Their Roots in Practice

Social work can progress to the functions of social development and system change by fulfilling its system-maintenance function. System maintenance sustains social stability and cohesion through meeting needs of people in accordance with prevailing social values and institutions. Developmental functions aid in the orderly growth and change of established political, economic, or social institutions. System change challenges significant values and elements in the social structure, including distribution of wealth and power. These functions are overlapping in reality but are sequential in their full development. Under a residual welfare policy, using the models developed by Richard Titmuss, social work will not rise beyond the system maintenance level, while the institutional redistributive model allows more scope for social work in all of its functions.

A maturing profession eventually assumes a wide range of social functions. In nations where social work has a long history one would hope that its range of endeavors would be broad and its professional authority, such as it is, respected. The thesis explored in this paper is that, paradoxical as it may seem, social work in a given nation can progress to essential functions of social development and system change only on the basis of fulfilling its system-maintenance function. I shall forthwith explain these expressions in the sense in which I use them.

Reprinted with permission from *Social Service Review*, Vol. 50, No. 1 (March, 1976), this article was adapted in part from the author's Eileen Younghusband Lecture on the "Societal Functions of Social Work," delivered at the National Institute for Social Work, London, England, November 12, 1973, and prepared while the author was a Fellow at the Center for Advanced Study in the Behavioral Sciences.

System maintenance is hardly a slogan to put on a banner and go marching down the streets with, but it does include supporting and caring activities without which most of us would suffer more than we do. More precisely, the term is being used to refer to all those social provisions and services that have the effect of maintaining social stability and cohesion through meeting needs of people in accordance with prevailing social values and institutions. Such services and provisions include resources for livelihood such as income maintenance and remedial, rehabilitative, and protective services. While system maintenance has the ring of supporting the status quo—and thus is automatically a term of disparagement to those who oppose the "system" being maintained or who feel that social workers should at all times be change agents—this is not necessarily its import, except in the sense of not challenging the fundamental institutions of the society. A system-maintenance function is not to be denied in any society, for it includes not only measures to ensure the coherence, continuity, and stability of the social structure but also measures to plan for and cope with change and the provision of institutionalized ways of helping people in distress. Every socially sanctioned profession in human services fulfills at its core a system-maintenance function in this latter sense—the health professions through care of the sick, the legal profession through preservation of individual and collective rights under the law. Moreover, it can be argued that a system-maintenance function is consistent with activist practitioners in any of the human service professions, protesting to authorities or doing other battle on behalf of the rights and needs of people whose interests they are serving. Such advocacy (as in Ralph Nader's activity) is essential "to keep the system honest" but is not the same as changing the system itself, as, for example, in attempting to change the political structure or in attacking other major institutions. A system-maintenance function does not necessarily mean adjusting the individual to the system. A U.S. public welfare worker, protesting the rigidity of rules on behalf of a welfare recipient, is hardly adjusting the individual to the system, nor is the social worker in India who is struggling to protect the interests of an Untouchable who is deprived of basic rights presumably guaranteed under the law.

System maintenance does, however, involve social control. This is patently manifest in such fields as corrections and evident with less visibility in fields such as social work in schools or in recreational settings. Whether one considers this kind of control function valid or pernicious depends on whether one's values are congruent with those of the institutions through which social workers in these fields practice. Where there are oppressive elements in the system which social work is helping to maintain, social work's values prescribe a struggle against such elements, at least to test the limits of the official constraints. Where the total system of which social work is a part is essentially oppressive, social work either has no place, if it retains pretensions to ethical foundations, or, if its function can be justified at all, it is heavily compromised morally.

The diversity within in political and social institutions, and in cultural values leads inevitably to marked differences in social welfare systems and, therefore, in the ways in which social work exercises system-maintenance functions. Thus, in countries with scarce resources, where social security provisions are unavailable or in a nascent stage, mass income-maintenance programs of any kind are not present, and social workers will therefore not be engaged in such programs. In both the private and public sectors, they would more likely be working in institutional settings or with designated groups such as abandoned, neglected, or delinquent children but unfortunately most often as part of fragmentary, urban-oriented welfare programs.

By developmental functions of social work, I refer to those that have an impact on the analysis, planning, and implementation of broad social policy affecting large segments of the population, again within the framework of prevailing social values and political structure. In this sense developmental functions, while related to social change, are designed more to aid in the orderly growth and change of established political, economic, or social institutions within the framework of national plans and aspirations rather than to attack these institutions.

Developmental directions are derived not only from systematic planning and analysis, however, but also from political considerations unrelated to the planner's criteria. These considerations may have overriding merit for the national welfare, or they may reflect narrow vested interests of power and status. Many decisions in the field of health services, for example, are not solely or even primarily based on national health planning criteria, else we would not be seeing huge hospitals continuing to go up in urban centers of poor countries to the neglect of preventive and service programs in the rural countryside where most of the population resides. Decisions on allocations of resources have in the last analysis to be made by political authorities, whether these decisions are made on rational or on nonrational grounds.

When social workers collaborate, in developing countries, in the formulation of a section of a national development plan for consumer cooperatives, for the promotion of family planning, or for an increase in literacy through nonformal education—or, in industrialized countries, when social work is involved in the recasting of social welfare delivery systems—they are in this sense performing a developmental function which is strengthened when social work is also involved in the administration and implementation of the plan or program. The kind of research that is helpful in strengthening social work in these developmental directions is the study of social problems and social programs.

The major difference between the developmental function and the system-maintenance function is that the latter focuses on remedial and rehabilitative operations usually involving the most vulnerable sectors of the population, whereas the developmental function aims at broader social coverage and at broader social policy and at the strengthening of social institutions to make them more capable of meeting the aspirations of the population. The developmental function of social work is to participate in this process, which is not smooth and is heavily engaged in political considerations but is consistent with at least stated national objectives.

System change, by contrast with system maintenance and developmental functions, aims at directly changing significant elements in the social structure and challenges existing values, organizational investments in the status quo, and distribution of wealth and power. To the extent that it is a professional function, it does not partake of political revolution, aiming at the forcible overthrow of political institutions and the forcible redistribution of power. No profession, by definition legitimated by society, can have revolution as a formal function.[1] But well short of revolution a systemic-change function, which inevitably entails conflict between interest groups, can be sanctioned within a profession. Organizations geared

---

[1] ". . . Social workers in their professional roles cannot be expected to employ militant tactics in bringing about change, however necessary or desirable this change may seem to be. But if one is to work essentially with, rather than in open opposition to the establishment, one can hardly function as an agent of major structural change. My own feeling is that there is more slack within the system than social workers have utilized, that the range of permissible variations in their professional role within society might have permitted more decisive action than they have taken" (Roland L. Warren, "Overview of the Intercultural Seminar," in *An Intercultural Exploration: Universals and Differences in Social Work Values, Functions and Practice* [New York: Council on Social Work Education, 1967] p. 67).

to "advocacy" constitute one manifestation of this function, where such advocacy challenges and seeks to change, through pressure but within the bounds of existing law, inequities practiced by existing institutions.[2]

A program that is system maintenance in one country may be developmental in another and system-change oriented in a third. As the deliberations of the International Congress of Schools of Social Work at The Hague in 1972 indicated,[3] there has been a marked upswing in Latin America, most dramatic in Chile during the Allende regime, in the movement of *concientizacion*—that is, consciousness raising among the poor in urban areas and peasants in the countryside to be aware that they are oppressed and of the sources of their oppression—and in stimulating social workers to be part of this process and to implement action programs. Such effort might take the form of helping peasants organize against landowners or other groups defined as exploiters. From the point of view of the Chilean national perspective during the Allende regime, *concientizacion* was developmental more than it was systemic change, since these efforts were in accordance with official government policy, moving toward national objectives. Today in Chile, as in some other Latin American countries, *concientizacion* would be identified not only as system change but as illegal and subversive. Those who would expound and practice *concientizacion* today could probably do so in such countries only under cover and at risk to their lives and liberty.

I am avoiding the terms "social reform" and "social action" because they have been subject to such broad interpretation that given illustrations can fit into any of the three classifications of societal function, with reform being often more developmental than involved in the more aggressive system change.

Although these functions of social work are overlapping in reality they are sequential in their full development, in the sense that it is necessary for the system-maintenance function of social work to be established, recognized, and respected before the developmental function can be truly exercised and that both functions be institutionalized before a system-change function can be effectively discharged. Otherwise, whatever legitimacy

---

[2] In the United States such advocacy groups have dwindled with the collapse of the Office of Economic Opportunity. In the legal framework Nader's Raiders is an illustration.

[3] Katherine A. Kendall, "Dream or Nightmare? The Future of Social Work Education," *Journal of Education for Social Work*, Vol. 9 (Spring 1973).

social work has as a profession would be threatened. Since most social work practice is of necessity of a systems-maintenance character, this is another way of saying that social work's claim to competent practice in needed direct services has to be recognized before a developmental function can be truly exercised for social work, let alone incorporation of a system change function.

It is not only appropriate but necessary that there be social workers whose main activity is in the development of policy and in planning. However, why should a social worker be engaged to work on a planning commission if all he or she knows that is relevant to planning comes from social science? Unless there is a practice base in the society for them to draw on, there is no more reason for the policy analyst or planner to be a social worker than to be an economist, a sociologist, or a member of any other discipline or profession who has a humanistic orientation and an ability to handle data rationally.

Social work practice involving direct contact with others does not necessarily mean remedial services, clinical or otherwise. When a community development worker in an African country is involved in enhancing community participation in self-help programs, he is engaged in service and is in direct contact with the people he is working with. Whether the welfare service in which he is engaged is of a developmental or a system-maintenance character depends (by the concepts I am using) largely on whether there is current amelioration of people's life conditions or whether it is preparation for the future, and often it is both. If social workers' efforts help a community to accelerate the process of digging wells and getting potable water, they are serving both a system-maintenance and a developmental function.

In almost every country where social work is a principal profession or occupation for carrying out social welfare functions, social workers in direct service tend more often than those in any other helping profession to bear the self-imposed burden of having continuously to answer the question, Is your work making any fundamental difference? It seems that social workers were born into the world of the helping professions tainted not with original sin but with original guilt at being "microoriented" in a "macro" world.

What is more important than drawing the lines too fine in assigning maintenance and developmental labels to specific tasks is that there be a network whereby social workers in direct practice can participate with

people at the policy level who have a social work background in the definition and execution of local, regional, or national social welfare policies
and programs. Planners and researchers need to be linked to the direct
experience of people in the field. Planning and policy personnel with social work background can be more effective in the development of programs in family planning, for example, if they engage the participation of
social workers directly involved in the delivery of family planning services.

The settlement houses in England and the United States which pressed
for reform, whether of developmental or system-change character, drew
their influence and credibility from the fact that they were giving service,
that they knew the problems that they were addressing and knew the
people in whose interest they acted. It is not a public relations image of
credibility that is involved in order for social workers to be in a position to
influence policy, let alone to move into the forefront of systemic-change
efforts, but credibility derived from the reality and the effectiveness of
their own or their colleagues' efforts in direct practice.

IMPLICATIONS FOR SOCIAL WELFARE POLICY

Richard Titmuss, in his last public address, referred to three general
welfare models. One he termed the residual welfare model of social policy,
where welfare institutions come into play only when the private market
and the family resources break down in meeting the needs of individuals.
The second he described as the industrial achievement-performance model,
which holds that social needs should be met on the basis of merit, achieved
status differentials, work performance, and productivity. He characterized
this as a functionalist view of social welfare. The third, which he preferred,
is the institutional redistributive model, in which social welfare is seen as
a basic integrative institution in society, providing outside the market both
universal and selective services on the principle of need.[4]

When the residual welfare policy holds, it may be assumed that social
work will not rise beyond the system-maintenance level. The second model
would permit developmental activity if the national social welfare policy
is indeed governed by pressures toward "work and savings incentives,
capital accumulation, effort and reward, and the formation of class and

---

[4] Richard M. Titmuss, "Developing Social Policy in Conditions of Rapid Change:
The World of Social Welfare," in *Proceedings of the XVIth International Conference on
Social Welfare* (New York: International Council on Social Welfare, 1973), pp. 33-43.

group loyalties."[5] The institutional redistributive model allows freer play for social work in its systemmaintenance, developmental, and system-change functions.

There is irony, however, in that social work is not in a position significantly to influence the development of any kind of social welfare model until social work is perceived as performing its system-maintenance function to the point where it has gained the necessary legitimacy to move into policy and change areas. Yet, the more system maintenance is caught in a residual model of social welfare, as it is in many developing and some European countries, the more difficult and more necessary it is to affect overall welfare policy. Social work cannot as a profession make its views count in social policy, or even develop its own cadre of personnel capable of participating technically in policy development and social planning, until there is some defined field of practice that is accepted, validated, and respected by society; and, further, when such practice exists, those who move into policy positions should be able to draw on the field experience and study of practitioners. Linkages with practice should be formalized.

System-change activities, where confrontation is to be anticipated and conflict engendered with established institutions and vested interests, require a solid base of public support for the profession before this function can be accepted as legitimate and have significant financial or moral support within the social welfare field of operations.

This does not mean that system-change efforts must wait until social work is thus established. System change should be initiated when it is essential and could be effective to achieve ends on behalf of those suffering from inequities. Unless social work is accepted through its practice base, however, such efforts may have to be undertaken outside the boundaries of the social work profession—in social workers' capacities as individual citizens.

There is thus a chronic frustration built into social work, as there is to virtually any profession that draws its sanction from society. One can never achieve via the profession alone all that one wishes to achieve in social goals. Real progress on a broad social front is difficult, painful, and from a single professional base alone, practically impossible. It is a frustration this profession has to live with, but it is also a frustration that provides a constant dynamic to move beyond direct service activities alone, to enhance the well-being of society at large, and particularly to attack inequi-

---

[5] *Ibid.*, p. 40.

ties in economic and social provisions. In so doing, social work must engage itself increasingly in joint efforts with many other disciplines and with diverse interest groups in the society at large.

IMPLICATIONS FOR SOCIAL WORK EDUCATION IN POLICY AND PLANNING

Schools of social work are linked to the functions which social work has in their particular societies. To the extent that a school prepares people for existing jobs in social welfare services, it is helping social work fulfill a system-maintenance function; to the extent that it prepares for competence in policy, planning, and administration, it is serving an existing or potential developmental function; and to the extent that it is concerned with analysis and with strategies for revising elements of the social structure, it contributes to the dynamics for system change.

Training institutions that only prepare people to fill job slots for service occupations do meet a need—that of qualifying personnel for employing agencies—but such training cannot be expected to contain ingredients designed to challenge existing structures or modes of practice. There are many such schools in the world. They are constrained—by political risks, limitations of financial resources, shortage of capable faculty, or by lacks in knowledge or imagination—to an exclusively system-maintenance function and often, indeed, to a stolid, implacable orientation to the status quo.

Most schools have a mix of functions, particularly where the country's political institutions are relatively open and democratic. Where there are many schools in a given country, they may differ considerably among themselves in the nature of their mix. Given maintenance, developmental, and change perspectives in the curriculum, even where the system-maintenance orientations are dominant, the likelihood is that the school will be more future oriented than the welfare system to which it is connected. Indeed, one of the latent functions of any professional school is to keep the professional service establishment on its toes, if not to shake it up. This is one of the main reasons that there is a built-in tension between professional schools on the one hand (in any profession) and employing organizations or professional associations of practitioners on the other, a tension that is constructive even though it can lead to irritations and misunderstandings.

One of the lessons that can be derived from an examination of the societal functions of social work is that training in social policy analysis, social planning, and, indeed, for fulfilling "change-agent" roles, should deal realistically with the constraints in utilizing such training when the students function as social workers. There are many countries where access for social workers, qua social workers, to policy and planning positions ranges from the very difficult to the virtually impossible. This fact hardly suggests that in their training social work students in such countries should not be informed and concerned about the larger social problems and about the part, whether peripheral or central, that social work should and does play in trying to cope with these problems—on the contrary! The point, rather, is to focus on the next steps that social work must take in order to strengthen its capacity to influence policy and program.

It is a frustrating exercise to try to prepare social workers for planning roles from a position of weakness in society's acceptance of their practice competence and utility. That is why it is not only desirable but mandatory to project clearly the stage at which social work exists in a particular country and then what must be done in order to achieve the posture necessary for more leverage on policy and to engender the capacity for change efforts. Where the position of social work is relatively strong, in the sense that its practice base is established and social work research competence has been both demonstrated and relevant to the country's problems and where there are at least a few social work administrators and other social workers who have involvement in or access to policy and planning positions, then training for policy, planning, and, in fact, for effective systemic change is essential and should be rigorous and hardheaded.

R. A. Parker, in his lecture entitled "Social Ills and Public Remedies,"[6] interprets the development of social administration in Britain, distinct from and yet closely connected with social work education. I have not had the firsthand experience with this relationship to be able to comment on it with any serious judgment. Parker's own point, however, should be highlighted-how unusual (from an international point of view) this development has been and in many ways how extraordinarily productive, particularly in pushing forward the frontiers of social analysis and policy development, in close contact with government. The separate but linked growth of service-oriented social work education and policy-and-planning oriented social administration may be peculiarly derived from, and appli-

---

[6] R. A. Parker, "Social Ills and Public Remedies," in *Man and the Social Sciences,* ed. William A. Robson (London: George Allen & Unwin, 1972), pp. 113-129.

cable to, the British context, as Parker suggests, but it may also be a model adaptable for export, as a way of accelerating the developmental and change functions of social work where conditions permit.

In planning and genuine social change situations, social workers will encounter and have to work with representatives of other disciplines, professions, and interest groups in and out of government, and the social work voice is likely to be dissident; it should not be laid open to being faulted on grounds of insufficient expertise. Humanitarian values and semantics alone will not do. In addition to the technical capacity for policy analysis and for planning operations that have to be provided, it is also essential for the social work planner, policymaker, and change-oriented shaker and mover to learn how to be in touch with both the practice world and the political world. The linkage with both constitutes the starting point for the social worker's policy, planning, and change contribution.

4. A Framework for Analyzing Social Work's Contribution to the Identification and Resolution of Social Problems

Herman D. Stein and Irving Sarnoff

Although the term "model" has been applied to the approach being presented here, we prefer to think of it more simply as a framework for analysis. However, since "model" is what it has been called, we will occasionally employ the term, with the reservation understood. The origins of this model lie in a meeting held some three years ago, under the auspices of the National Association of Social Workers (NASW), on social work's potential contribution to the identification and resolution of social problems. During the course of this meeting of consultants, Chairman Nathan E. Cohen, who had somehow sensed that we were thinking along similar lines, asked us to construct this kind of framework. We then developed our ideas to provide a context for the examination of social problems by the various specialists. Eventually, our efforts culminated in a conceptual outline for the written reports on social problems which the NASW has now published.[1] During the course of subsequent give-and-take, the framework was modified and elaborated, but it remains essentially as it was initially proposed.

Clearly, the orientation we have followed is only one of a number that are possible, and there are difficulties with it. We wished, however, to build in provisions that would:

1. Compel us to take nothing for granted that is significant, to make sure that we turn over each rock of hidden bias or assumption, and take a good look

---

Reprinted with permission from National Conference on Social Welfare, *The Social Welfare Forum, 1964*, (New York: Columbia University Press, 1964).

[1] Nathan E. Cohen, ed., *Social Work and Social Problems* (New York: National Association of Social Workers, 1964).

2.   Question the premise that social work is naturally doing good, and is hindered in solving social problems only by absence of more social workers, more agencies, and more of other resources

3.   Identify the additional knowledge that social work must have in order to make more rational decisions regarding the scope and strategy of its interventions.

To these ends we were concerned with searching systematically for conflicts of values, not only between social work and the values of the larger society, but within social work itself; with compelling an evaluation, through the structure of the model, of programs now being sponsored to see whether they serve, to any extent, to perpetuate the very problems they were designed to prevent or resolve. Moreover, we wished to adopt as nonparochial a view as possible, recognizing that social work is one among many social institutions, and that, with respect to broad social problems, the field's potential influence may range from very low to very high impact, but would rarely, if ever, be totally decisive.

The approach does not give detailed consideration to specific techniques of intervention, or to social work processes. Instead, it focuses attention on definable objectives for the profession. To achieve these objectives new modes of intervention may have to be developed, or certain old ones perfected. Our task, in short, was to help develop an approach by which social work could assess its potential contribution to the identification and resolution of social problems.

The model is not intended as a sequence of consecutive steps in an analysis of social problems, but rather as a disciplined way of thinking about them so that the most significant issues will be addressed. It was assumed that theories from the behavioral and social sciences would be drawn upon throughout the application of this, framework, particularly in considering the etiological sources of the diverse problems, the consequences of changes in values, of selecting priorities for change, and of other elements to be specified. While the model may appear abstract indeed as presented, illustrations of all points abound, particularly in the papers prepared for *Social Work and Social Problems*.[2] The social problems dealt with there, with this framework as working basis for analysis, include: racial discrimination, poverty, martial incompatibility, child neglect, unmarried mothers, the broken family, and deterioration of the inner city.

---

[2] *Ibid.*

In considering the application of framework to particular social problems, three important factors should be kept in mind:

1. The sources and intensity of values inside and outside social work that
    impinge on the problem

2. The forces inside and outside social work that have the effect of main-
    taining the problem

3. The forces which currently exist in and out of social work that are di-
    rected toward reducing or resolving the problem.

The steps of the framework, not to be rigidly viewed as consecutive in a
time sequence, follow:

I. The Nature of the Problem Itself

    A. Definition of the Problem

        1. What, for example, does "poverty mean, or "mental illness," or
            "deterioration of the inner city," in conceptual and operational
            terms?

        2. Who "suffers" from the problem? In what ways?

        3. Who defines it as a problem? Why? One cannot assume that
            every social problem is recognized as such throughout the so-
            cial structure. Who says it is a problem? Why do they think so?

        4. Who does *not* define it as a problem? Why not? Is it is due to
            ignorance of the situation, or to knowledge of the situation,
            with, however, the point of view that it does not constitute a
            social problem?

    B. Etiology of the Problem

        1. Are its sources inherent in the social structure?

        2. Are its sources inherent in the individual personalities of those
            who share the problem?

        3. Are its sources located in existing organization designed to
            cope with the problem?

        4. Found in transitory social phenomena, such as an international
            crisis, for example?

        5. Found elsewhere?

There is now no consensus on what constitutes a social problem. Is a social problem one that concerns large numbers of people, each of whom happens to suffer from the same individual difficulty—like appendicitis or dandruff? Or does it uniquely pertain to problems which, to some appreciable extent, are rooted in the social structure and can therefore be prevented or controlled, in part, by modifications in that structure rather than by the provision of more of the existing services to those who are suffering from the problem? Or does it include both? We took the societal or social structural view, recognizing that it is far from universally acceptable.

Since we are interested in social work's contribution to the identification and resolution of social problems, we must confront the relationship of social work's values with those of the broader society. We cannot assume either congruence or incongruence between the two, nor can we assume that the values and norms of either are entirely homogeneous or always even known.

II. Norms and Values

    A. Societal Norms and Values

        1. Are there any norms and values that support the existence of the problem (for example, in crime and delinquency)?

        2. What norms and values oppose existence of the problem?

        3. What norms and values are relatively neutral?

    B. Social Work Norms and Values

        1. Which of these norms and values support the existence of the problem?

        2. Which of these norms and values oppose it?

        3. Which of these norms and values are neutral to it and uninvolved?

This scrutiny and testing of assumptions lead to a quest for incentives of change that are rooted in value positions opposed to the perpetuation of the problem, in the terms defined. Where social work's values are engaged, but are not those of society at large (for example, with respect to unmarried motherhood), one set of considerations would obtain. However, quite a different set would be involved where social work values and modal norms of society are similar (as is true for dealing with physical illness, and may be becoming more true in meeting social problems of mental illness).

We next look within social work at activity related to the problem.

III. Current Operations—"the Actual"

   A. Social Work Operations related to the Problem

      1. If one looks only at what is actually being done rather than what may be said, how does the social work field really seem to be defining the problem.

      2. What are the implicit value positions that seem to understand the actual ongoing operations?

      3. To what extent do these implicit definitions and values, as exemplified by what is actually going on in social work programs, compared with the norms of society?

      4. To what extent are these implicit norms and values within social work congruent with the declared and explicit values of social work?

We then raise the same series of questions about:

   B. Non–Social Work Operations[3] Directed to the Problem

      1. Implicit definition of the problem

      2. Congruence of values with modal societal norms

      3. Congruence with social work norms

In other words, what is being done about the problem, either with or without social work participation? Is the total consonant with social work values? The answer, in effect, maps the existing situation.

Finally, in looking at "the actual," we encounter the consequences of the continuation of the present complex of social work and non-social work operations. Suppose they all went on for long periods to come, what are the results likely to be?

   C. Consequences

      1. For the extension or diminution of the social problem?

      2. For the social work programs related to it?

      3. For the non-social work programs related to it?

Moving from the actual state of affairs, we posit the notion of the ideal state of affairs.

---

[3] These may be more extensive than modal work operations.

IV. Objectives—"the Ideal"

    A. Goal

        1. What is the most desired goal of social work in respect to the problem?

        2. What is its social change objective?

        3. What do we really want to happen?

    B. Implications of This Ideal Position

        1. For the relationship of the most desired goal to existing societal norms and values?

        2. For the change in societal norms?

            a) How much can be done if societal norms are opposed?

            b) Is there a need to try to change these norms before the problem can be effectively tackled?

        3. For the relationship of the valued ideal to the existing norms of the social work profession and to our organizational framework?

            a) What may have to be changed within the field's own institutional patterns to move the actual nearer to the ideal?

We then seek to visualize an entire program that is consistent with the analysis of the etiology of the problem and with social work's value position. This, in turn, is broken down into:

    C. The Sector Appropriate to Social Work

        1. In view of our existing definition of social work scope and function

        2. In view of a possibly revised definition of that scope and function

    D. The Sector Appropriate to Non-Social Work

        1. Identification of non-social work interest groups involved with the objectives of the program

        2. The relationship of social work to each of these interest groups.

We thus try to conceive an optimum program, based on the ideals of social work and related both to social work and non-social work activity.

Finally, we examine the relationship between the actual and the ideal, to discover a viable program for moving forward, beyond the field's present effectiveness in dealing with the problem.

V. Relationship between the Actual and the Ideal

    A. Gaps between the Actual and the Ideal

        1. What is the nature of the gaps?

        2. What programs are needed?

    B. Resistance to Closing the Gap

        1. Does the source lie within social work? (Let us not assume that there is no resistance. We may have our own *status quo* investments in either economic or ideological terms or both.)

        2. Does the source lie outside social work?

    C. Support for Closing the Gap

        1. In social work

        2. Outside social work (We cannot afford the assumption that social work is the only or, necessarily, the most important force for positive change.)

    D. Action Priorities for Social Work

        1. In operations directed toward society at large—direct services, educational, or social action programs—

           What can social theory contribute to our understanding of the strategies useful in modifying general values? In introducing or encouraging countervailing forces, how can social theory aid social work to come closer to ideal solutions to the problem?

           What kinds of knowledge do we need to obtain in order to resolve the impasse between the actual and ideal, in knowing more precisely what it is we should want?

           What changes in social policy are needed, if existing social policy is incompatible with social work's values?

        2. In changing existing norms and organizational framework within social work itself

Does the existing structure of social services require modification?

3.   In relation to non-social work groups and forces, what are the relationships among service systems, organization of the profession, and the power structure of society?

These three steps are designed to map the indicated changes in policy for which social work can take initiative and responsibility, which lead, in turn, to:

4.   Action sequences (alternatives within a total set of priorities) offering the greatest potential for reducing or preventing the problem. (Here, too, social theory comes into play in helping us to evaluate probable consequences and, therefore, in enabling us to make more rational decisions regarding the relative effectiveness of different means for achieving positive results.)

5.   The needs in theory and research (other than the accumulation of available facts but not in our possession)

Can we specify the theoretical exploration needed to help us understand the etiology of a particular problem better? Or would it be necessary to test, through systematic empirical research, any program designed to move us ahead in relation to this kind of analysis?

Important preliminary work has been done by those who have tried to use our framework in examining existing social problems. It is the questions and answers arising from their work, and from similar studies in the future, that are most valuable, and that merit continued exploration. Our framework is only one means of assisting such explorations, of helping them to be more consistent guides to knowledge and action. Undoubtedly, the guide lines we have suggested will be revised and alternative modes of analysis will be forthcoming, as experience accumulates.

Part Two
SOCIAL WORK EDUCATION

5. Observations on Determinants of Social Work Education in the United States

INTRODUCTION

This paper considers certain themes bearing on the development of social work education in the United States as part of an examination to which this Seminar is addressed, of what may be valid across national boundaries in social work education and what is more uniquely tied to a particular society's own history and culture. No pretense is made that these themes are comprehensive or fully developed. They are, rather, notes on some (but not all) relevant strands in the growth of professional social work education, concerned essentially with the values in our society, the historical development of social work in the United States, and the changing nature of social work practice.

My underlying premise remains:[1]

> While the profession of social work is international, and common elements are increasingly in evidence, it is not a technology or a science requiring only minor adaptations to be universally applicable wherever taught. Rather, it is still shaped in its methods, its structure, and to a considerable extent in its idealogy, by the underlying social, economic and cultural elements in each particular society in which it develops. In these respects, education in social work poses at least in degree a different situation from that faced by

---

Prepared for Intercultural Seminar, East-West Center, University of Hawaii, February 21–March 4, 1966.

[1] Herman D. Stein. "Issues in the Professional Education of International Students in Social Work in North American Schools," in Irwin T. Sanders, ed., *The Professional Education of Students from Other Lands*. New York: Council on Social Work Education, 1963, pp. 151-184.

the overseas student in other professions such as engineering or medicine.

SALIENT VALUES IN AMERICAN SOCIETY AFFECTING SOCIAL WORK EDUCATION

Students of national character, or national culture, are aware of the many pitfalls of easy generalization and are not entirely in agreement about how best to identify the essential ingredients of a nation's culture. The point of greatest consensus is that there is such a thing as national culture, or national character, notwithstanding the enormous complexity to be found in many societies with wide variations in religion, regional differences, economic levels, and ethnic backgrounds. Dominant pulls persist in each society which shape the image of "the good life," determine what represents success and failure, good and evil. These pulls vary in intensity in different strata of the population; they are mediated by the family system in which the individual is reared and are affected by the individual's immediate social environment outside the family. Yet, these central tendencies exist for societies as a whole. The problem is to identify those central tendencies that are deeply rooted in time and that most effectively cut across the varied sub-systems and sub-cultures in the society, rather than those that may dramatically appear at any one time but are essentially superficial and soon disappear, or those that are characteristic only of certain segments of the society.

The United States is, of course, a highly diversified and complicated society. Yet, as Gunnar Myrdal has stated about that part of the American creed that deals with belief in man's fulfillment as a human being based on his own natural potential: "It is remarkable that a vast democracy with so many cultural disparities has been able to reach this vast unanimity of ideals and to elevate them supremely over the threshold of popular perception."[2]

PROGRESS

Belief in progress, the capacity to rid oneself of the restraining fetters of the past and to seek to control the future, is one component of these ideals in American Society. In the more recent vocabulary of social science, this may be termed a "future-oriented time dimension," but the roots of this value lie partly in the early history of the United States, settled by people who

---

[2] Gunnar Myrdal. *An American Dilemma*. New York: Harper and Brothers, 1944, p. 6.

faced an uncertain future in a new land and did not by and large revere the past.

> He (American) had little sense of the past or concern for it, was not historically minded, and relegated interest in genealogy to spinsters who could have no legitimate interest in the future. Even the recent past became speedily legendary; children whose parents had heard the war whoop of the Indians and seen vast herds of buffalo cover the plains played at Indians much as English children played at King Arthur. The American saw the present with the eye of the future; saw not the straggling dusty town but a shining city, not the shabby shop but the throbbing factory, not the rutted roads but gleaming rails. In every barefoot boy he saw a future president or millionaire, and as the future belonged to his children, he lived in them, worked for them and pampered them.[3]

Land was plentiful for the American pioneers in the age of an expanding "western frontier" and all the resources were there for economic development, sparked in turn by the belief in man's capacity for self-betterment, in his capacity to harness the future, in short—in progress. The future had to be better than the present, and the past was no necessary guide to what could be done in the future for one's children and the generations to come. In the 18th and early 19th centuries no significant historic tradition indigenous to American life had yet developed. There was only the future, a future that had to be better than the past and in the grasp of those who reached for the new and unexplored.

This orientation to the future, and the tendency to avoid past European associations, had a profound effect on all aspects of American life, including social work. It was an important influence in preventing mutual benefit societies and other formal cooperative associations known in England and France from gaining substantial footholds. At the same time, this zest for the new encouraged the adventurous experimental spirit which contributed not only to the growth of the physical sciences and technology but to the relative ease with which new ideas in philosophy and in the social and behavioral sciences could be introduced, tested and spread.[4]

---

[3] Henry S. Commager. *The American Mind.* New Haven: Yale University, 1950, pp. 5-6.

[4] Herman D. Stein. *Sources of Social Work Development in the United States.* U.S. Committee Report for the Seventh International Conference of Social Work, Toronto, Canada, 1954.

The very introduction and rapid dissemination of Freudian psychology in the United States, accepted so much more readily than in Europe, is a reflection of this temperament. The author of *A History of Psychoanalysis in America* writes:

American psychiatrists, teachers, professors, and sociologists, reared in democracy and less awed by tradition, although not uncritical, were far more ready than their European colleagues to examine and test Freud's ideas in an experimental spirit.[5]

In social work's early incorporation of knowledge and methods from psychoanalysis, it partook of this same spirit. However ingrained psychoanalytic theory became in social work, it was not so much of an orthodoxy to be universally adopted on faith that other schools of thought could not emerge and have their influence—Rankian psychology, neo-Freudian approaches, Rogerian psychology, and "ego psychology." Indeed, one can discern currently a restiveness in American schools of social work about drawing on any one school of psychological thought exclusively without at least acquainting students with others, in a spirit of free inquiry.

The readiness to break new ground, and to be exposed to new ideas, has been manifested most particularly in United States social work's reform tradition, at the turn of the century, during the depression of the 1930s, and in its recent resurgence. This spirit of inquiry is also evident in the research efforts of social work in the United States, in the growing emphasis on research teaching in its professional schools, and in increasing alertness to relevant developments in allied fields of knowledge.

WORK

Combined with the emphasis on the future and man's capacity to control the forces of nature in his own behalf were the underlying Puritan teachings inculcated in America's early settlers, which have remained a

---

[5] Clarence P. Oberndorf. *A History of Psychoanalysis in America.* New York: Grune and Stratton, 1954. Quoted by Franz Alexander in *Saturday Review* (January 9, 1954), p. 12. Dr. Alexander notes: "Americans presented with an innovation, are not much bothered about who proposed it or sanctioned it, or whether it is in line with previous ideas and convictions; Americans are concerned with whether or not it works."

basic theme. In Tawney's words: " . . . emphasis on the moral duty of untiring activity, on work as an end in itself. . . ."[6]

> Work was required for group survival among the moving frontier from the first settlements until the continent had been won. The rule "he who does not work, shall not eat" expressed the deadly struggles of the early settlement period. To this compulsion was added the dawning sense of rich rewards to be had in a land of relatively unappropriated resources. Furthermore, the population was mainly recruited from the working classes of Britain and Europe; except in a few areas of the South and New England, there was no aristocratic class to give prestige to leisure and to stigmatize manual labor and trade.[7]

Work is regarded in American society not only as a means to earn one's living but almost as an end in itself. To be productive, to be useful is a value in its own right, and even leisure is often seen as utilitarian, justified as needed so one can do better in one's work. For an able-bodied man not to be employed is a disgrace, even if his non-employment is due to conditions he cannot control.

To restore an individual to some measure of productivity becomes a matter not only of economic significance but a matter of pride and self-respect, the restoration of a feeling of being worthwhile. Rehabilitation efforts in the United States have, therefore, become a high priority in American social work, in concert with medicine and other professions; and a central theme in social work education is the enhancement of individual capacity through rehabilitative efforts, when functioning has been impaired; or the provision of "habilitation" when optimal social and economic functioning have not had a chance to develop. While the concept of rehabilitation goes far beyond work itself, to restoration of as much physical, psychological, and social growth as is possible for an individual, the capacity to be productive, in some sense, remains the latent objective.

---

[6] Richard R. Tawney. *Religion and the Rise of Capitalism*. New York: Harcourt, Brace and Company, 1926.

[7] Robin Williams. "Value Orientations in American Society," *Social Perspectives on Behavior*, Herman D. Stein and Richard A. Cloward, eds. Glencoe, Illinois: The Free Press, 1958.

Robin Williams,[8] in his analysis of American value patterns, under-scores one aspect of the value of work in American society that has both a positive and questionable side, namely, technical efficiency:

> Efficient is a word of high praise in a society that has long empha-sized adaptability, technological innovation, economic expansion, up-to-dateness, practicality, expediency, "getting things done" ... this crucially important canalization of interest at once sets this society apart from societies placing greater emphasis upon esthetic, contemplative, ritualistic, mystical or other wordly concerns ... A culture that in the first place tends toward an unhistorical and utilitarian orientation will be especially likely to encourage just those behavior patterns in which technical efficiency can become valued for its own sake.

A contrasting value orientation towards efficiency in work is repre-sented by the India Village Industry Association, whose organizing secre-tary wrote:[9]

> The culture of a nation does not develop when work is split into its component parts. If we are to derive full satisfaction from work, we have to keep as close as we can to the simple original form of work without dividing it up into its component parts.

He attacks the notion of technical efficiency, which in his view results in fatigue and demoralization of the worker, with loss of pride in workman-ship and skill. "Is it any wonder than in the most industrialized country in the world the United States of America, more people suffer from nervous disorders than from all other forms of ailments?" He presents the point of view that leisure should be an integral part of work, that work should be kept whole and production decentralized; that with over-emphasis on ma-terial production, we may be gaining the whole world and losing our souls.

Technical efficiency in the administration of social agencies, particu-larly the larger and more complex organizations, is generally a desidera-

---

[8] *Ibid.*

[9] J. C. Kumarappa. "The Philosophy of Work," *Indian Journal of Social Work,* Vol. VII, No.4 (March, 1947).

tum, and the techniques of industry are increasingly utilized. Yet, it is doubt-ful that in schools of social work much premium is placed on efficiency for its own sake, even where teaching of administration is given a prominent place. It is hazardous to generalize, but it may be fair enough to observe that neither the fruits nor the hazards of technical efficiency are exemplified in social work as much as they are in other sectors of American society, and that the idealogy of social work, while not averse to technical efficiency, gives it no high priority.

INDIVIDUALISM

Individualism has expressed itself in many forms of American life, and its roots lie deep. Some of these roots stem from the period of westward expansion in this country that lasted well toward the end of the 19th century, a period and a way of life that left an indelible stamp on America. In this way of life, each man stood or fell by what he was and what he achieved, not by conditions of inherited status. While there was cooperation, each worked and fought for himself and his family. Our folklore reflects the vividness with which these qualities associated with the "pioneer" and "frontiersman," epitomizing the American who "stands on his own two feet," still shine as dominant values.

In social welfare, individualism has been consistent with the development of voluntary associations and the growth of grass roots leadership. But it was also a factor in deterring the development of governmental programs of public welfare and social security.

In large measure, the Charity Organization Movement of the 19th century, ushering in the age of modern social work in the United States, sprang from the individualistic tradition which viewed personal success or failure as directly related to individual worth. The State had minimal responsibility for the economic or physical welfare of its citizens, and such responsibility was properly to be left to private initiative. Hence, well into the 1900s private benevolent agencies were, at times, opposed to social welfare legislation.

There were those who criticized the over-emphasis on individualism as a source of invention, progress, and wealth, and attributed to unhampered individualism, poverty, ugliness, and waste. Looking to social action by citizen's groups as well as government, they believed in the possibilities of directed social progress and improvement and received support for their position in the writings of some prominent sociologists and economists such as Lester Ward and Thorstein Veblen. Reforms in the penal system and the care of the mentally ill in public health during the 19th century were encouraged by this social humanitarian impulse which coexisted with individualistic humanitarianism.

Charlotte Towle[10] puts individualism into a professional social work perspective, when she considers the joining of "the science of human behavior as a humanizing force" with a deeper understanding of democratic values in social work practice, leading to the cardinal principle—and one perennially subject to re-examination—of self-determination:

> It is not surprising that the clients right to self determination was one of the first, if not the first, of our beliefs to become a banner around which we rallied. The turn of the century had marked a shift from "rugged individualism" to a more civilized concern with man's survival as a social being. This implied a concern to foster individuality rather than individualism. The right to self-determination prominent in the age of rugged individualism must now be modified to self-determination within the social limits implicit in democracy as a way of life. . . .

Miss Towle expands on the maturing concept of self-determination as social conditions changed and as concern with social responsibility was deepened:

> We accept the individuals right to help but we do not accept his behavior with a *laissez-faire* or protective response which connotes permissiveness. Instead we try to help him face the consequences and use them as motivation to cope with his unsocial behavior. Our responsibility to the community is not to be taken lightly.

The sources and meanings of individualism, and its derivative social work principle of self-determination, are many, and have been widely discussed. No attempt will be made here to develop this theme further, except to underline the relationship between individualism and the changes in American family patterns. Individualism in the United States cannot be seen as stemming alone from political democracy, the Protestant ethic, the

---

[10] Charlotte Towle. "Ethics and Values in Social Work" in *50th Anniversary Symposium on Ethics and Values in Social Work*, Chicago: Loyola University, April, 1965, pp. 17-18.

expanding westward frontier, and other massive determinants. It stems from the nature of family organization as well, a fact of special importance to social work.

The pattern of the modal American family itself has, of course, evolved as a resultant of the economic and social forces in American life and its inherent values, from Colonial times onwards.

> In spite of the tenacity of inherited English custom, the relative religious freedom and the economic opportunities of the New World worked radical changes in the spirit of the family institution. . . Puritans authorized the dissolution of the matrimonial tie for various reasons, including desertion and cruel treatment. . . .The ease with which youths could enter new occupations. . . tended to break the rigidity of the families' class status ... the abundance of cheap land. . . was always beckoning sons and daughters away from the parental roof, inviting them to make homesteads of their own in distant places. . . bonds of kinship were snapped; branches of families and emancipated individuals scattered themselves among settlements all the way from New Hampshire to Georgia. . . the individual in Colonial times began to emerge from the family group, as children commenced to cast off restraints of class and parents in the choice of mates, occupations, and careers.[11]

Talcott Parsons summarizes the essential characteristics of today's modal American family, located most commonly among the urban middle class. With all the variations of family patterns that exist in society, it remains "the family type" to which all such variations are compared:

> . . . in a peculiar sense, which is not equally applicable to other systems the marriage bond is, in our society, the main structural keystone of the kinship system. This results from the structural isolation of the conjugal family and the fact that the married couple are not supported by comparably strong kinship ties to other adults. Closely related to this situation is that of choice of marriage partner.

---

[11] Charles A. and Mary R. Beard. *The Rise of American Civilization.* New York: Macmillan Company, 1930, pp. 136-138.

It is not only an open system in that there is no preferential mating on a kinship basis, but since the new marriage is not typically incorporated into an already existing kinship unit, the primary structural reasons for an important influence on marriage choice being exerted by the kin of the prospective partners are missing or at least minimized. . . . Our open system. . . tends very strongly toward a pattern of purely personal choice of marriage partner without important parental influence. With increasing social mobility, residential, occupational and I other, it has clearly become the dominant pattern . . . .[12]

Within this family, the accent is on promoting individualism in the child and on encouraging individual achievement as the basis for success. "Parenthood in America has become a very special thing, and parents see themselves not as giving their children final status and place, rooting them firmly for life in a dependable social structure, but merely as training them for a race which they will run alone."[13] The accent is on individual fulfillment, not on family continuity or group solidarity. This salient emphasis, characteristic of much of American family life, is in sharp contrast to family and child-rearing values in many parts of the world, especially in developing countries.

The consequences of this direction in family organization include loss of reverence for the older generation and the loss of reliance on family ties as a keystone of economic security. An extraordinary premium is placed on the relationship between husband and wife, and particularly on the relationship between mother and child, as the context for the psychological and emotional development of the child. Where this structure breaks down through loss or separation of parents or through the inability of parents to rear the child with minimum standards of care, new arrangements have to be provided by the society to aid the family or care for the child. To a large extent, American social welfare developed its programs in response to the emerging vulnerabilities of the urban middle class family, with its ingrained individualistic values—values often severely questioned by social workers from traditional cultures, where forms of extended family remain the most

---

[12] Talcott Parsons. "The Kinship System of the Contemporary United States", in *Social Perspectives on Behavior*, Herman D. Stein and Richard A. Cloward, eds. Glencoe, Illinois: The Free Press, 1958.

[13] Margaret Mead. *And Keep Your Powder Dry.* New York: William Morrow and Company, 1942, p. 41.

general type, and where reverence for one's elders, family traditions and loyalties supersede objectives of individual self-fulfillment.

Where the extended family is strong, however, the role of the state in social welfare tends to be weak. Changes in family structure are inevitable with changing economic conditions and new patterns of urbanization. It has been pointed out, for example, that the extended family is less and less capable of coping with the human problems of poverty in developing Asian societies. Public assistance schemes are growing, but they are still rare in the Asian region. Ceylon, Malaysia, and the Philippines approach comprehensive schemes (along with Japan, which is not categorized as economically underdeveloped) but not many others.[14] The provision of professional help through family casework services may be seen in India, Japan, the Philippines, and Thailand, in agencies concerned with family counseling and guidance; these are generally restricted to the larger cities, where the "nuclear family" is on the increase and individualism emerges. Even in such situations, however, concepts such as "self-determination" may be recast in terms of family rather than individual self-determination.[15]

The improvement of social welfare training is still impeded in many Asian countries by the widespread impression that the entire field of social welfare is purely one for charitable and voluntary activity. In India, for example, private agencies have a long history and tradition. Social welfare is still perceived as being largely the business of the private charitable agencies, even though many of these receive subsidies from the state through grants-in-aid. There is, however, less and less response to state appeals for private resources, it being "generally accepted that in a socialistic pattern of society like India, the state should be responsible for expending a part of the national gain for social welfare."[16]

THE HISTORICAL BACKGROUND OF AMERICAN SOCIAL WORK

The origins of modern social work in the United States are commonly traced to the Charity Organization Society Movement in the latter part of the 19th century. Early developments remained potent influences, the two most

---

[14] *Planning for the Social Welfare Needs of Children and Youth in Asia.* Working Paper for UNICEF, sponsored Bangkok Conference on Planning for the Needs of Children in Developing Countries of Asia. ACCY/BP/11 September, 1965.

[15] See for example: *The Social Work Concepts of Self-Determination and Confidentiality Viewed Within Philippine Value Orientation.* Manila: The Philippine School of Social Work, 1965. "It is not proposed that self or individual determination be the one and only objective. Family-determination can precede self-determination," p. 110.

[16] Report from India, 10th International Conference, Rome: 1960.

important in Colonial America being the adoption of the English Poor Law and the development of charitable cooperatives.

The Elizabethan Poor Law of 1601 codified existing practices in the handling of relief and established three categories: the able-bodied poor, the unemployable and the dependent children. Almshouses were utilized for the unemployable and apprenticeship for dependent children.[17]

The principles which dominated the Elizabethan Poor Law were the following:[18]

1.   Charges were made to each parish separately

2.   Begging was repressed

3.   Employment was the chief means of assistance

4.   Care of the handicapped, old and blind who were poor and unable to work

5.   The apprenticeship of children for work[19]

6.   The free use of the House of Corrections for both the idle poor and the petty offender

The system of poor relief in Colonial America reflected the Elizabethan Poor Laws. The administrative unit was the town, corresponding to the English parish. Certain poor became the responsibility of the province, a broader unit of government. Poorhouses were erected for care of the indigent sick. (Over the generations, some poorhouses evolved into leading general hospitals.) Little distinction was made between problems of dependency due to physical and mental disabilities and the poverty of people due primarily to economic factors. Anyone in need of economic help was consid-

---

[17] Nathan E. Cohen. *Social Work in the American Tradition*, Chapter 2. New York: Holt, Rinehart and Winston, 1958.

[18] Sophonisba Breckenridge. *Public Welfare Administration in the United States. Selected Documents.* Chicago, Illinois: University of Chicago Press, 1927.

[19] While indenture and apprenticeship of children were commonly used, public institutional care and private "orphanages" also existed. The mixed "almshouse" was also in evidence, and legislation against this unfortunate means of "care" was not enacted until the 19th century. It should also be noted that in child care the colonies, and later the States, operated each in its own fashion, and certain broad national uniformities did not come into the picture until the Federal Government entered this field with the Social Security Act of the 1930's. See Hazel Fredericksen, *The Child and His Welfare*. San Francisco: W.H. Freeman, 1948.

ered a pauper. To be a pauper was to be a failure in an increasingly individualistic society. Provisions for "outdoor relief" and public welfare were of a generally punitive character.

There also developed voluntary agencies and charities, which changed their character from the Colonial period to the 19th century.

> From the beginnings. . . these early charities differed sharply from those of the Old Country. The charities of the New America were cooperatives—not the gift of the rich to the poor, but a happy sharing of small resources. Moreover, the early charities contained an element of mutual insurance, and they were considered a supplement to public aid. The essentials of a cooperative are seen in the records of these agencies: clarity of purpose, constant interpretation of this purpose to members in ways that made for understanding and loyalty, foresight in building a "stock," prudence in expenditures, the careful choice of trustees, integrity and sound business and social sense, discipline in rules and orders, skill in organization and administration, re-examination of purpose and methods in the light of changing times, and a fellowship which kept alive a sense of belonging.
>
> The cooperative aspect of the first charities faded away in the 19th century. Whereas the cooperatives were concerned with *us*, the 19th century agencies were concerned with *them*, the poor and the sinful. "The poor" came to be accepted as a class to be helped by moral suasion, not money.[20]

Charities emerged in profusion during the 19th century, and the Charity Organization Movement aimed at putting order into the business of private philanthropy, following leads begun in England and also in Germany and France. The essential rationale for the Charity Organization Movement was that it was more scientific, business-like and efficient than the sprawling array of overlapping and poorly administered charities which had emerged, drawing on charitable, humanitarian impulses from religious tradition and other sources, but without plan.

---

[20] Katherine D. Hardwick. "As Long as Charity Shall be a Virtue." *Boston Private Charities from 1657 to 1800*. Page Smith, 1962. Reprinted by permission of Doubleday and Company, Inc., p. 27.

The movement itself, however rational and attuned to the post-Civil War industrial mood, with its growing emphasis on efficiency, rested on a melange of philosophies, or moralistic preconceptions composed largely of Malthusian doctrine and social Darwinism. Its central preoccupation was with the moral condition of the poor and the separation between the deserving and the undeserving, the worthy poor and the depraved. The core doctrine flowed from the administration of the Elizabethan Poor Law, namely that relief by its nature was pauperizing and that work alone was redeeming.

The societies which became organized attempted at first to do everything but give relief. Eventually, most of them had to give some. It also became impossible to distinguish between the worthy and the unworthy poor in many cases, particularly with the influx of new populations into the cities in search of jobs which were presumably available. The rapid mobility of labor and irregular employment made it essential for some relief to be in cash or in goods, even if some "moral uplift" was to be done.

The underlying basis for "scientific charity" was the great understanding required of each case. The purpose of such understanding was the rehabilitation of the character of the individual. This was to be the objective of scientific charity, rather than an attack on social problems. The Charity Organization Movement had little to do with social reform.

> Like most Americans of comfortable means and good education, the founders of the charity organization movement had accepted the prevailing economic and sociological philosophies that attributed most poverty and distress to sinfulness, excessive reproduction, alms giving, or failure in the race for survival. . . .[21]

To begin with, it was the friendly visitor, the volunteer, who actually did the "treatment." The paid workers of the charity organization societies investigated and adminstered. The *volunteers* were, in the early stages of the Movement, the heart of the operation, and it was assumed that their most important requirement was "moral insight," not any special knowledge or skill.

Seen from the comfortably clear perspective of today, rather than in the context of the late 19th century, the Movement was naive in its assumption

---

[21] Milton D. Speizman. "Poverty, Pauperism, and Their Causes: Some Charity Organization Views," *Social Casework*, Vol. XLVI, No. 3 (March, 1965).

that the friendly visitors from the higher economic and social levels could, despite all the good will in the world, modify the attitudes, behavior, or life organization of the poor. The Movement stumbled very badly when the friendly visitors tried to work with the non-English speaking immigrants who came to the United States in large waves toward the latter part of the 19th century. The effort to "uplift" through paternalistic efforts, no matter how benevolently intended, was a failure.

Yet, some things were being learned about ways of helping and not helping. The need for facts about clients receiving help became increasingly evident. Gradually there emerged the concept of differential diagnosis which came to full bloom in Mary Richmond's *Social Diagnosis*. The roots of professionalism in American social work are represented in this classic work.

Toward the latter part of the 19th and early 20th centuries, voluntary agencies became increasingly occupied with social work training. The theme was no longer "not alms, but a friend"; it became "professional service."[22] First, the medical social workers, then the psychiatric social workers became professionalized, developing their own professional societies.

The long separation between the voluntary sector in philanthropy and public welfare stemmed partly from the fact that the Charity Organization Movement discredited public assistance when it chose for its major emphasis the rehabilitation of individual character rather than relief. While the development of casework diagnosis and treatment and an underlying scientific approach were fostered, the broad theme of public responsibility for meeting conditions beyond the control of individuals was neglected. This was in contrast with developments in England and in the Scandinavian countries where the major thrust was toward broad social legislation and less on individual rehabilitation. (It is, however, of interest to note that in these countries vigorous efforts are now being made to accentuate the values of individual casework and social group work treatment, as exemplified in North American social work.)

In the latter part of the 19th and early 20th centuries in the United States, there also emerged the Settlement House Movement with its strong reform interest, its political and social action, and involvement with the poor, particularly the immigrant poor. The Movement drew from pioneering efforts in England, and in the United States the names of Jane Addams of

[22] Roy Lubove. *The Professional Altruist*. Cambridge, Massachusetts: Harvard University Press, 1965.

Hull House, Lillian Wald of the Henry Street Settlement and Graham Taylor of Chicago Commons, are associated with this period.[23] It exemplified not only for settlement house workers but for social workers in other activities, the broad social purpose underlying social work.

SINCE THE 1920s

In Porter Lee's phrase, the shift in social work from "cause"—emphasis on social movement—to "function"—emphasis on method—was developing by the 1920s. At the same time, the volunteer had retreated into board or other activities and had become disassociated from the professional social worker who had the prestige and mark of professional skills at his or her command. American social welfare became increasingly complex. The sheer size of the welfare operation required both order and specialization. Both of these, in turn, had led to the same accelerated bureaucratization as has developed in the major sectors of all industrialized countries. The division of professional labor among many agencies and social work functions proliferated.

Social casework moved towards concentrated emphasis on method in the 1920s, but its theory and practice have progressed with all of social work, to a larger measure of balance between "cause" and "function."

> The full development of professional social case work has taken place within fairly recent times. It has moved from being a process utilized to give aid and advice to the poor and socially bereft to being a process for the enrichment of the social-personal functioning of all kinds of persons.[24]

During the 1920s came the impact of insights from Freudian psychology, the crystallization of social casework process and clarification of the social caseworker's responsibility to be concerned with massive economic pressures and with the establishment of governmental public assistance and social security programs. The dual accent on the individual and his social-economic situation was brought sharply into focus, then waned for a period and was revived in the mid-1940s.

---

[23] Arthur Hillman. "Settlements and Community Centers" in *Encyclopedia of Social Work*. New York: National Association of Social Workers, 1965, pp. 690-695.

[24] Helen Perlman. "Social Casework," in *Encyclopedia of SocialWork, op. cit.*, pp. 7-10.

The nature of the social situation gradually became viewed in more penetrating terms, with recognition not only of economic factors, but also of forces not as readily recognizable, such as the influences of social class and ethnicity shaping human behavior and life chances. Concepts from the social and behavioral sciences have become incorporated increasingly into the theory and practice of social casework. The relationship of individuals and families to their economic and social settings has become an essential perspective for the social caseworker. In addition, the necessity and patterns of cooperative relationship among all resources within social work, as well as between social work and other helping professions, have become clearer.

The directions in social casework have included "reaching out" to groups who need but do not actively seek help. The social caseworker has become steadily more aware both of the social environment of clientele and of the larger social needs which they may represent. If he cannot deal with these larger problem dimensions as a social caseworker, he may act on his awareness through his activities in his professional association or as a private citizen, but increasingly he can often also relate to the broad social needs directly in his capacity as a caseworker through affecting policies of his agency, enlisting the support of other community resources, and through other individual and group efforts. Social casework has become viewed less and less as a matter of "adjusting" the individual or the family to difficult life conditions. The casework approach has concentrated with increasing emphasis on mobilizing inner and outer resources of clientele towards constructive change in their life situation.

Social group work, with its strong base in the Settlement House Movement, had a potent history of "cause" but it too during the 1930s and 1940s became more technically oriented. Attempts made in the 1920s to discover common goals, methods and programs with casework led to the systematic study of group work early in the 1930s. By the end of the decade, 14 schools in the American Association of Schools of Social Work were offering courses in group work.

> Group work was moving from the early concepts of character-building to a conception of method and process for furthering the adjustment and development of the individual and preparing him for citizenship in a democracy. Thus, group work began to draw more closely to social work, and to explore the relationship of case work and group work. Group work, with its diverse body of knowledge

could well have been the channel through which the tendency in social work to emphasize one dimension, the psychological, might have been broadened to include the learnings of social sciences .... As group work drew more closely into the social work family, with casework playing the parent role, it tended to become more influenced than influencing.[25]

Social group work may be seen as deriving from three general orientations.[26] One is the concept of the contribution of small groups to maintaining a democratic society through furthering participation in democratic decision-making. This concept retains the active pursuit of social goals as inherent in social group work practice but it has, as Robert Vinter maintains, become a waning emphasis among social group workers over the course of the last generation. Related to this orientation is the concept of social group work as a way of serving developmental goals of individuals to help prepare them for responsible assumption of social roles. This is the most characteristic premise of group work practice in agencies with generalized citizenship-building and socialization functions. The third, and today the more dominant premise in social group work practice, is its utilization for the rehabilitation and treatment of people who are beset by personal and social problems.

Thus, Vinter defines group work as "a way of serving individuals within and through small face-to-face groups in order to bring about the desired changes among the client participants. This method of practice recognizes the potency of social forces that are generated within small groups and seeks to marshal them in the interest of client change."

The sources in social and behavioral science that have influenced social casework have also, and in some ways (such as the utilization of small group theory) more so, been penetrating social group work theory and practice. Similarly, the more pervasive and sharper view of the social environment of clientele which has emerged among social workers in all methods of practice, has drawn attention to the broader social conditions contributing to the problems of their clientele. The social group work practitioner may not, therefore, be any more "cause" or social purposeoriented in his

---

[25] Nathan E. Cohen. *Social Work in the American Tradition*, Chapter 2. New York: Holt, Rinehart and Winston, 1958.

[26] Robert D. Vinter. "Social Group Work" in *Encyclopedia of SocialWork, op. cit.*, pp. 715-724.

immediate practice with groups for whom treatment and rehabilitation are objectives, than the social caseworker, nor any less able to harness his experience to broader social purpose, and mobilize clientele to change through different utilization of outer as well as inner resources.

Community organization started as a "cause." Its basic idealogy reflected democratic popular interests and associations for the improvement of the common lot. With the emergence of the community federations, organized for joint fund-raising and planning of voluntary agencies in the 1920s, and their emphasis on coordination aid efficiency, community organization, in the judgment of many, became more "function" than "cause."

There is little question that the function of such community organization (since then greatly broadened) has been of great importance. The councils of social agencies and their equivalents have had a marked impact in creating rational mechanisms for ordering the operations and distribution of services in the voluntary sector.

> [T]he framework for coordination provided in most large communities are the council of social agencies (variously called Community Welfare Councils, Health and Welfare Federations, and so on). The council, of course, is a general social welfare planning organization, with coordination only one of its functions; and councils are only one of the many types of bodies devoted in whole or in part to welfare planning. The council, however, is the key coordinative unit at the community level; at its best it represents a high point in democratic participation in American communities. . . .[27]

The growing pattern of coordination has brought the professional social worker in community organization who works within councils and federations, into increasing prominence and influence in councils of social agencies and in planning operations, The businessman and other elite members of the community who rank high in prestige, power or economic means are generally more in control in the federated fundraising and distribution operations.

Community organization has moved through many stages in its history in the United States. Its current directions proceed far from its early

---

[27] Harold L. Wilensky and Charles N. Lebeaux. *Industrial Society of Social Welfare*, Chapter 10. New York: Free Press, 1965.

orientation in sustaining a democratic process at the grass roots level in small communities and neighborhoods, similar to origins of social group work, or its particular manifestation in planning via councils of social agencies or other coordinating and enabling mechanisms. The emerging accents have been on "community problem solving," social action management, leadership development, community development, and the concept of community organization theory and practice is also increasingly oriented to analyzing the impact of basic economic and social forces on different strata of the population, and of examining and formulating social welfare policies to provide "services and programs for all as an enduring part of the American social system."[28]

At the present time, while the major social work methods of casework, group work, and community organization are still being developed and taught separately, their interrelationship in the practice of social work, and increasingly in the teaching of social. work, is becoming more and more evident. Social work practice is, in part, becoming conceptualized as a complex of "strategies of intervention" into individual, group, small community, and larger collectivity "'systems." This way of thinking of social work practice emphasizes the various contributions of different modes of practice both to defined groups in society needing help, and more broadly, to participating in an attack on social problems along with other professions and groups. It also underscores the importance of drawing upon the insights of those whose practice is essentially therapeutic on individual or group levels, by those concerned with social policy and community development, as well as emphasizing for the former, the importance of seeing the social policy and community implications of the treatment situations in which they are engaged.

FACTORS IN THE BACKGROUND OF SOCIAL WORK EDUCATION IN THE UNITED STATES

The historical background of social work in the United States provides the backdrop for the development of social work education. Initially, such education began to be provided, at the turn of the century, by and for the voluntary agencies. As schools of social work developed, consonant with the growth of professionalism, their orientation was primarily to provide

---

[28] Meyer Schwartz. "Community Organization" in *Encyclopedia of Social Work*, op. cit., pp. 177-90.

staff for voluntary agencies, and teaching staff were recruited from these agencies. The initial impetus in teaching, as in agency practice, was on understanding individual behavior, and dealing with individuals, so that casework received a long "head start." There were courses in some schools that dealt with broad social problems, and one or two schools virtually began with the objective of improvement of social welfare service on a general scale. This, however, was not the central thrust of social work education, particularly in its early decades. While it paid a price in non-engagement with social policy, social work education, as it developed in the United States, also had an advantage—that of a close relationship to the needs of daily practice, and the application of imagination and academic study to the pursuit of more systematic and effective social work method, based on knowledge.

Dame Eileen Younghusband[29] contrasts the development in England and the United States as follows:

> In England, attention was increasingly focused on broad social and economic issues. . . . social work education began to move into university social science departments from 1904 onwards. . . teaching became more academic with less emphasis on the relation between the study of economics, social administration, political theory, and psychology and actual practice in social agencies. . . . It was left to the individual to apply general principles to individual situations. . . . The result was that much of the social science knowledge evaporated because it was not put to use, while practice was based more on giving agency services efficiently than on application of any consistent theory of human behavior and motivation. . . .

> The fact that in the United States of America social work education continued on these early lines of integrated theory and practice, absorbing material from the social and behavioral sciences and struggling to apply this in practice, as well as to feed back field observation into the theoretical structure, probably accounts for that country's leadership in this subject at the present day. . . .

---

[29] U.N. Department of Economic and Social Affairs. *Training for Social Work, Third International Survey*, pp. 117-119. New York: U.N. Department of Economic and Social Affairs, 1958. (Dame Eileen Younghusband was principally responsible for this report.)

What do we in the United States most represent in social work education?[30]

We provide an organized approach to the helping process in social casework, and increasingly in group work and community organization. We provide well-developed psychological theory, usually with a Freudian orientation. Increasingly, but still more sparingly than many of us would prefer, we provide relevant content from the social and biological sciences, background content on history and social welfare programs, exposure to the analysis of social problems, and some fundamentals in administration and research. In field work we offer a disciplined use of supervision to develop skills in one or more primary methods based on systematic concepts and principles, and increasingly are utilizing the field experience for perspective on other social work processes, and on administration and research.

Among the underlying values we communicate is the application of democratic attitudes and goals to helping processes with individuals, groups, and communities. We therefore emphasize the rights of the individual to determine his destiny within the broadest limits consonant with social responsibility, and, similarly, stress the values of self-direction for groups and communities. We try to develop a sense of professional self-awareness in order to minimize the extent to which the practitioner's problems and biases will intrude and interfere with his capacity to help. Our system of education increasingly tends to promote objectivity, a respect for scientific method and the uses of research, and we share with most of American society respect for competence, rather than friendship or family loyalties, as a basis for employment and promotion.

To a considerable extent these values and methods may be generalized for acceptance internationally. But due attention must be given to those aspects of our values and methods, if not our underlying knowledge base, that are peculiarly drawn from, and purposive for, the context of life in the United States, and may not be that readily universalized.

Family values present one illustration of the cultural system within which social work is ingrained. When social workers deal directly with families, whether in social security, health care, or marital counseling, the service is attuned to the country's modal patterns of family life. An egalitar-

---

[30] The paragraphs to follow reflect part of the author's discussion in "Issues in the Professional Education of International Students in North American Schools," *op. cit.*

ian relationship between husband and wife, for example, is not only the prototype for the urban, middleclass family, but tends to be the model most generally accepted by social workers.

The reference to casework and family life may also be applied to group work and youth culture, or to community organization in urban life. Group workers in our society concerned with problems of adolescents in youth programs characteristically find themselves considering approaches to helping youngsters establish social communication with members of the opposite sex. Such social contact is assumed as a desirable phase of heterosexual adjustment in our culture. Yet in many other societies, avoidance of such contact between the sexes is a predominant culture pattern.

The community organization student today learns the application of community organization method to many settings and problems, and increasingly to community development and social action milieux. Yet, the most common focus of attention for community organization is the urban setting, not the rural, as is the case of community development in most of the poorer countries of the world. Moreover, while private philanthropy represents an important sector in the social welfare programs of many countries, and value is attached to the participation of laymen, the extensive system of private philanthropy in the United States, and the special emphasis on voluntarism and the involvement of laymen in social welfare policy are for many countries, unusual.

The organizational matrix of social work in the United States also forms part of its inherent character and is not simply the array of settings within which social work operates. The fact that nearly all social work is carried on within agency auspices and these auspices are extremely ramified and increasingly bureaucratized provides a set of conditions not typical for social work practice, for example in Asian countries. There is the presence of relatively elaborate resources to draw upon in the United States either within the agency or elsewhere in the community; techniques are developed to draw upon them. There is an extraordinary development of voluntary agencies and a broad base of private philanthropic support, as well as government participation in the financing of services and unusual autonomy of voluntary agencies in developing their own direction. Technique and principles of lay involvement, of coordination of agencies, and of relationships of voluntary to public agencies have therefore emerged.

Moreover, the social work profession in the United States has a measure of status higher than almost anywhere else in the world and has a broad sense of professional loyalty and identification, no matter what agency is served. In these respects and others, the structure and setting of social work in the United States differ from those of many countries.

It is true that social work education in North America has been a standard-setter internationally for some time, and particularly since the end of World War II. Many of the hundreds of overseas students trained in the United States have assumed positions of leadership in social welfare and social welfare education in their countries, and have spread awareness of North American social work. In addition, North American consultants and experts have been widely used and sought by countries in all continents, by the United Nations and by national agencies in various countries.

The United States does represent advanced social work education in many ways. It includes the highest levels of education in social work, in its doctoral programs, and represents the most developed programs of master's degree professional education. It has produced the broadest resources for field instruction and for full-time faculty. Its schools of social work, as constituents of universities, occupy higher status than their equivalents in most other countries; and more educational resources to bolster social work education can also be drawn upon by virtue of such affiliations. American social work education has, as is widely recognized, pioneered in social work research and in the theory and practice of casework, group work and community organization.

To a considerable extent, however, the image of the United States as representing the pinnacle of social work education is illusory. Increasingly, the feeling among social work educators is one welcoming international reciprocity in the contributions to social work education, rather than demonstrating superiority. It is clear that United States social work education can learn much from abroad and has begun to do so, from social security measures to community development. It is also clear that in some areas, such as industrial social work, the United States has little to offer, whereas in the Netherlands and France, Italy, Latin America, India and Pakistan, in one form or another, industrial social work has developed. In the training of multipurpose workers, and social workers with considerably less than professional levels of education, many countries, particularly some of the developing countries, have pioneered in ways from which we in the United States have a great deal to learn.

In the development of basic economic and social programs for the entire population, the developing countries of the world can look to many other countries in addition to the United States for guidelines. The Scandinavian countries and Great Britain have, as has been noted, moved from a concentration on basic economic and social programs, to an accentuation of their development of social work method and technique, including more refinement in casework. In the United States we have been moving the other way, from a systematic concentration on casework, then to group work and community organizations, towards a greater concentration by the social work profession as a whole, and increasingly reflected in social work curricula, on the involvement of social work in broad social legislation and social planning.

THE CSWE CURRICULUM POLICY STATEMENT—AN INDICATION OF RECENT TRENDS IN NORTH AMERICAN SOCIAL WORK EDUCATION

The Curriculum Policy Statement of the Council on Social Work Education, representing the accredited graduate schools of the United States and Canada, is among the documents provided for this Seminar. The Statement was adopted in 1962 to replace the first Curriculum Policy Statement of the CSWE in 1952. The differences in these ten years may be more revealing than the actual content of the last policy statement.

The first difference is that the content areas of the 1962 curriculum statement do not require given curricular sequences. Great flexibility and latitude are, therefore, provided for the schools in devising their own curriculum so long as basic objectives are met, an approach more congruent with University values than is uniform curricular structure for all professional schools.

Equally important is that the content areas themselves have been changed. In the area of Social Welfare Policy and Services (replacing the former "Social Services") there is a heavier emphasis on the student's understanding of the profession's responsibilities to promote social welfare objectives, and to be prepared to participate in this development and in implementation of such objectives. In the second area, "Human Behavior and the Social Environment" (replacing the former "Human Growth and Behavior"), the social and behavioral science components are greatly reinforced, compelling a more systematic attention to the interaction of individuals and their social environment and to social processes generally that affect social work practice. There is a greatly heightened and more pointed recognition of the pervasive influence of the social structure in human needs and human behavior, drawing more heavily on theory and research in the social and behavioral sciences.

In the third area, "Methods of Social Work Practice," there are several departures from the 1952 statement. Casework or group work courses and field instruction do not have to precede preparation for community organization practice as was required in the 1952 statement. Moreover, the primary methods of casework, group work and community organization are no longer equated with the totality of social work practice. It is the entire curriculum which is used as the basis for practice, not only the "methods"; all learning, including research, administration, and other background knowledge content is viewed as part of the basic preparation for professional competence, along with casework, group work and community organization knowledge and skills.

The document stresses the importance of a basic professional education which will permit the student to grow throughout his practice career; to have a foundation in knowledge, fundamental skills and professional commitment that would provide a base for his further development and increasing contribution. Formal social work education is therefore not seen as an end in itself, but as a source of continued encouragement and stimulus for the social worker to learn and realize his potentials and strengthen his contribution to professional service.

Implicit in the document is the distinction to be drawn between professional education and training. Education provides the broad fundamentals; training, the techniques and skills for specific jobs. Some people are well educated and fully trained. Others are well trained and poorly educated. We naturally want our students to be both well educated and well trained. A competent professional practitioner in any field should be broadly prepared in the theoretical and practice ramifications of his profession as well as specifically competent in the tasks in which he is to be engaged. The problem, of course, remains "the mix" between such broad fundamentals and technical proficiency.

One of the central issues concerning curriculum policy, still not entirely resolved, is the relationship of graduate social work education at the master's level, to undergraduate education.

A second issue still being worked out is whether the basic professional curriculum should offer a primary concentration on administration or or research, similar to that now offered in casework, group work, or community organization. The 1962 Curriculum Policy Statement provided the latitude, but not the encouragement for this step. Attempts, however, are now under way in some schools to offer such concentrations. By now the 1962 Curriculum Policy Statement, consolidating advances of the time, is already in some measure out-dated partly as a result of the innovations it encouraged.

UNDERLYING EDUCATIONAL THEMES

Professional education in all fields shows many vicissitudes over time, but also certain underlying themes which are constant in their presence, and change only in the sense of becoming deepened and more refined in quality over the course of time.

Professional social work education in the United States reveals such themes. One is the concentration on the professional role of the social worker, the examination of the sense in which the role is professional, with its flexibilities, limits, and complexities in varying situations. While emphases have fluctuated from passive enabling, in all methods of social work practice, to more aggressive initiating, reaching-out and advising, the underlying theme has concerned itself with self-discipline and self-awareness. The objective has remained to equip the social worker, as far as knowledge could make this possible, with the understanding to perceive his role so that his own needs, his own shortcomings, his own personal biases would be least prone to get in the way of his helping function, whatever the professional social work context.

This awareness drew initially on psychological elements. The emergence of knowledge about the psychological and emotional makeup of the people one was helping created its own impact on self-understanding by the social worker himself. The growth of professional self-discipline rested for decades mainly on this understanding of one's inner psychic and emotional self, as well as on an intellectual understanding of one's duties in given professional settings.

More recently there has been added to this theme the importance of social and cultural self-awareness, an understanding of what one's implicit attitudes are that are affected by class position, religion, ethnic background or geographical origins. Again the emergence of this aspect of selfawareness paralleled the emergence of an emphasis on the social and cultural components in social work practice with individuals, family groups, and communities. This direction in self-understanding is still in the process of development and its relationship to the helping role still being clarified.

One price that professionals pay for greater self-discipline in their professional role is the accretion of value dilemmas, problems to be solved in theory, and often on the spot in practice, as to whether to act in relation to one's subjective predispositions or to retain objective detachment. The problem arises from the fact that the process of social work education is increasingly illuminating the area of potential subjectivity. Gone is the innocence of the days when the first paid workers could take their tasks as self-evident, and not have to be concerned about how their own idiosyncratic, psychological and emotional characteristics and their attitudes and predispositions, influenced by social and cultural background, might affect the clarity and effectiveness of their professional functioning.

A second major theme is the effort to develop a conceptual context for social work practice and so to educate for the profession rather than for specializations. As the ways in which social workers are utilized in today's society proliferate, and the field expands, the umbrella hovering over "professional social work" becomes wider and wider, and its edges less defined and more ragged. The years of basic professional education cannot be extended to incorporate all added knowledge nor reflect all added functions. Professional social work education has taken the route that education in other professions has taken, namely, to broaden the base of professional education and so to assume that a variety of specializations could follow after this period. Despite the vicissitudes of fragmented education during various periods in the 50 or 60 years of professional social work education in the United States, a long-range trend has been to try to teach a core of fundamentals while preparing students for practice in a given area. The conceptualization of social work practice in terms of "strategies of intervention" represents an effort at cutting across the separateness of method compartments.

A third major theme is the profession's development towards an increasingly more scientific and objective basis for social work practice. This has meant a steady increase in research carried on by schools of social work and the preparation of research practitioners. It has also meant the strengthening of a scientific, questioning approach, the utilization of scientific method more generally in the curriculum and the drawing of research evidence and theoretical developments from related sciences and professions.

A fourth theme is the relationship of the school of social work to research and to service as well as to teaching. These three functions, long accepted in social work education are, of course, also generally considered the functions of the university as a whole. Schools of social work are increasingly engaged in the production of scientific research, but the boundaries of what is appropriate for research in a school of social work, in contrast, for example, to research stemming from departments in the social and behavioral sciences, are as yet often ambiguous. The interpretation of what constitutes legitimate service beyond the educational function has broadened and also varies considerably. Some schools, for example, attempt to make a direct impact on social policy. Others would confine their conception of rendering service to initiating and demonstrating new modes of social practice in their communities.

A fifth theme has been the differentiation within social work occupations, of the place of professional education from other training. Most individuals engaged in social work occupations in the United States have for decades not had professional education, but have come to their positions, mainly in the public social services, directly from college or with less than college education. The proportion of those without professional education as compared with those with professional education has been increasing in the United States. Differentiations in status and rewards are made between the professionally educated and others, both within the profession and by employing groups. The issue of whether professional social work education (that is, on the level of the two-year Master's degree program) should be linked in any way with undergraduate presocial work programs, or with in-service training programs in social agencies, however, has become heated, particularly in the light of the severe social work manpower shortage which the United States shares with many other countries. Both organized professional education and the organization of professional practitioners have recognized the importance of developing links, and also the importance of differentiating social work responsibilities along lines of educational preparation, and in the light of potentially changing patterns both of the organization and the practice of social work.

Finally, the joining of classroom teaching and field instruction has been one of the hallmarks of social work education in the United States from its beginnings. The elaboration of this relationship and the diverse experimentation have not obscured the essential objective of field instruction for providing a disciplined opportunity for the student to put together in practice what he is learning in the classroom, to test this learning, develop skills. and have additional professional models for identification as part of the process of socialization into the profession.

These long-range themes in social work education in the United States provide a basis for some of the most salient of the current problems facing social work education, beyond those indicated.

One concerns the problem of relating the different methods of social work practice. How far can one go in preparing "the compleat practitioner" when developments in social casework, group work and community organization themselves have gone far beyond what they were a generation ago? To what extent should all in social work education receive the same fundamentals? To what extent should social workers be separately identified and educated, according to different methods of social work practice?

The concept of the "social worker role" covers the most therapeutic-clinical function within casework, at the microscopic end of social welfare, to the broadest social policy legislation, and execution, at the most macroscopic end. The distinction in emphasis may be seen even at the middle range of the continuum, when one contrasts treatment-oriented group work and the more social action-oriented aspects of community organization. Should one conceive of social work practice as having a common base but proceeding through two different routes—direct practice with defined client groups on the one hand, and social action and social policy influence and formulation on the other.

As the interest in expanding the scientific base for social work practice has extended, the absence of a consistent psycho-social theory to form the framework for practice has become more keenly felt. Neither the psychoanalytic view of personality, nor any other essentially psychological theory concerned with therapy, can suffice as a general theory for social work practice, since it deals essentially with a clinical model. Social work in the United States, as elsewhere, is concerned as well with a societal model and with the interaction between psychological and societal influences. Whether or not a general theory of social work practice can emerge, the search for theoretical formulations undergirding social work must take into account not only interrelationships of personality theory and social theory, but the practice strategies stemming from them. Social work education in the United States is increasingly concerned with the development of such theory for social work.

CONCLUDING OBSERVATIONS

Certain common trends can be seen everywhere around the world. There is a search for the essentials of social work practice and the basic ingredients of social work education, a search of which this Seminar is a reflection. There is also universally the fact and the recognition of the great shortages of personnel at all levels of knowledge, skill and experience. This recognition has brought more concentration not only on the development of high-level, education and training, but also on lower levels of training, on in-service and staff development programs, and on better utilization of volunteers.

Around the world, too, one sees an increasing emphasis on work with representatives of other disciplines and professions, whether it is in relation to community development, home economics or health programs. The interconnections between social work and other fields of work have their reflections both in social welfare programs and in social work education. Social work education is moving towards higher academic levels with an emphasis on stronger affiliation with universities; this is so both because of the need to direct and teach more people with minimum preparation for social work occupations, as well as the need to prepare for scholarship, research, teaching and administration. There are other trends common the world round, giving new evidence of similar international concerns in professional social work.

The Seminar for which this document has been prepared represents one step in seeking to determine the extent to which we can have more of an international profession, not in the sense of new international organizational arrangements, but rather in the sense of searching for underlying universals that we can all accept and build upon, and recognition not only of differences but common ways of analyzing and interpreting these differences. The effort in this paper has been to select certain strands in the background and current developments of social work education in the United States, to feed into this examination, with the hope, and an uncertain hope at that, that the strands selected are relevant.

6. Cross-National Themes in Social Work Education

Every international congress develops a character of its own. What is preplanned by way of program provides a framework, but what is molded to this scaffolding is generated by the live experience itself, arising not alone from formal presentations but from the interactions of people with diverse backgrounds and experience, yet with deep and shared commitments to their professional tasks. It is hazardous to predict in advance what these processes will produce. Still, they inevitably generate and reflect the salient themes of the times, themes which cut across the international scene in social work education. I am not referring to the major new developments of specific issues which have been presented, but to the ebb and flow of vital latent forces, some of which have the gossamer quality of abstractions. Each of us may develop an individual conception of what the most powerful undercurrents are, and my intention is to identify a composite of those I discern without claiming these as constituting the only or most perceptive vision.

The concepts which emerged for me out of the total context of formal and informal presentations and interactions at the Congress and which suggested directions, conflicts, and choices to which social work education, in all of its many forms, places, levels, and qualities, is subject, are: rationality, values and social responsibility, system and diversity, indigenization, innovation, and continuity.

RATIONALITY IN PLANNING AND POLICY

I am using the term "rationality" to refer to a respect for facts, for scientific method, for logical inferences. A mood of renewed respect for rational-

Reprinted with permission from *New Themes in Social Work Education, Proceedings of the 16th International Congress of Schools of Social Work, The Hague, The Netherlands, August 8–11, 1972* (International Association of Schools of Social Work).

ity appears to be emerging. This is in some distinction to pressures in recent years to play down the significance not only of conventional wisdom, but of continuities from past experience, careful research, and the building up of knowledge. The stimulus on the ideological front has had vital impact in shaking up the field, in clearing away the underbrush of static and perhaps trivial preoccupations, and in opening vistas of new objectives and new approaches, but inevitably the period of rapid acceleration of ideological concerns brushed past and submerged major concerns with rationality. What we appear to be seeing now is the re-emergence in fresher forms of regard for learning, reason, and research, without demeaning the importance of human feeling and value convictions. With respect for knowledge goes respect for competence, and a search for a new balance among these elements of ideology, knowledge, and technical competence is, in many diverse pathways, moving forward.

While rationality struggles once again to hold a central position in our concerns, the assumption that rational processes will necessarily lead to rational decisions is hazardous. To accept this assumption can lead to endless frustration. It is particularly troublesome in one of the fields which has become of great importance to social work, namely, social planning. The formula governing much teaching and learning in social policy and social planning goes like this: if there is a great deal of systematized data, and logical inferences are drawn and logical options spelled out, and if planners had all of these available and accepted the essential value premises of social work, then good and just things would be done. We need not be cynical to know that this has not been either the history of the world nor what necessarily takes place in the current conduct of organizations or nations. Rationality, even when it is respected, is not the sole basis—or often even the main basis—for important decisions. Non-rational (to be distinguished from irrational) factors intervene. These factors may concern politics and power, individual biases and subjective judgments of organization or government leaders, processes of conflict and accommodation among competing interest groups. The line between the rational and non-rational is not always clear, and non-rational considerations do not necessarily contravene wisdom and justice, but when major decisions are predominantly, dictated by non-rational factors, systematic analysis and rational planning become playthings, often conspicuously displayed but only a facade behind which the real decisions arc made.

The awareness of complexity and imperfections, the sentiments, human frailties, and seemingly extraneous forces which sometimes govern decisions in the field of social policy (as in urban planning and other fields) should not, however, be cause for dismay. For any profession that respects its knowledge and its competence, there must be an underlying assumption that the strengthening of its rational capacity in research, analysis, and systematic planning is essential and, in the long run, should and will increasingly influence policy and program decisions.

VALUES AND SOCIAL RESPONSIBILITY

It was with great interest that I observed that discussions of values and ethics were not confined to those sessions dealing expressly with such issues, but emerged in the Congress in the context of virtually every subject that was discussed. Concern with values, of course, and what are specifically social work values has preoccupied this field for many, many years. A great deal has been written about values, generally without precision about those discrete values which social work universally and peculiarly calls its own, but with some amorphous feeling that in the mix of humanistic values there is a special pattern which spells "social work." A vague discomfort with this approach has led some social work educators to invite philosophy educators to take a hard look at presumed social work values from the vantage point of the professional philosopher and to subject us to different kinds of probings. It is salutary to have our presumed values subjected to external examination, because when social workers talk of values, we are in a world of our own.

Underlying the consideration of values, principles, and ethics in the various subjects touched on in our sessions has been the issue of social responsibility. Such considerations, however, have not been confined only to the sessions designated for such explicit discussion.

Social work in many countries has had a longer history of concern with its social responsibility than have most other professions. One of the basic criteria in defining a field of practice as a profession is whether it has an enforceable code of professional ethics. Ethics, in this sense, has traditionally been interpreted as the ethics of the relationship of practitioners to patients or clients or institutions. What is emerging as a criterion of ever-greater importance is the responsibility of the profession to perform in its collective organization, as well as in the behavior of practitioners, in such a way that the interests of the society, and not necessarily only that of the professionals, are served.

How does social responsibility express itself? For one, through delineating the pros and cons of alternative courses of action facing society on issues in which the profession claims expertise, where the public directly or through its representatives is considering various options, so that the decisions take place through informed processes in which the professionals play a part but do not monopolize. Another approach is direct advocacy on behalf of those for whom social work speaks, based on the knowledge social work has gained.

Social responsibility also means turning expert attention to the possible broader consequences of decisions, beyond immediate professional concern. This is particularly important in those professions involved with technology and scientific development. It is no accident that we are now seeing for the first time conferences of engineers on "the social responsibility of the engineering profession," and "the social responsibility of the sciences."

How activist a profession is, how organized to advocate and best serve the interests of society in terms of its competence, how willing to engage counter-forces in society are not matters for which there are universal prescriptions. A refrain moving in and out of the values discussion in social work has been the caution about attempting to impose belief systems from one society to another. Beyond the level of shared humanistic values for social work, there are differences in the structure of belief systems from one society to another, the priorities of given values, the interpretation of how values are manifested, and the risks that could be undertaken in fulfilling these values in relation to societal needs. Sensitivity to cultural, political, and economic variations invariably is heightened through interaction in international meetings of the kind we hold. On this particular subject, such sensitivity is particularly wholesome, for it should make us less inclined to be simplistic in our judgments about the action possibilities of social work in other societies and more aware of how much we may not know about the complexity of their circumstances.

No professional body in one country can, therefore, legitimately instruct its counterpart in another on what risks or objectives to take. What we are learning is that the issue of the social responsibility of the profession must be built into the educational process and that it needs systematic and continuous attention in each society, although we recognize that these approaches will vary with different nations, different times, and differing professional organizations and capacities. Soft and amorphous statements of humanistic concerns will not suffice to define the scope, limits, and specific approaches for fulfilling the criterion of social responsibility.

On the International level, we are also becoming increasingly aware that just as the exercise of social work techniques without value underpinnings can be meaningless for serving social objectives, so ideology, however deeply felt, floating without the capacity to give service, devise programs, provide planning expertise—without competence, in short—is not harnessed to the hard realities of meeting social responsibility. Value convictions and technical competence must be joined and expressed through resources, organization, and program.

SYSTEM AND DIVERSITY

The search for organized systems of theory and practice is hardly new in social work, but at times it has the character of a virtual yearning for some kind of order. I suspect that if someone set up a little shop for social work educators offering "systems for sale," there would be many customers. it would hardly matter what the systems would be—educational, practice, analytical—any framework would do that could encapsulate or provide internal coherence for what social work is or ought to be. There has been no lack of systems of thought or action to which social work education and practitioners have been drawn—psychological theories and treatment systems, social change theories and ideologies, community analysis frameworks, practice methodologies, etc. But the range of social work concerns, under the large, ragged-edged umbrella that covers what is considered "social work" in different societies, continues to defy unified explanatory systems.

The very diversity of this field creates a measure of disorder, especially as the field grows and changes. When social work life was simpler, theoretical and practice frameworks were more restrictive and much smaller in scale, and what to know and what to do, based on such systems, were ever so much clearer. Those societies and those schools which prepared treatment and other service specialists who derived their knowledge and skills from particular psychological frameworks provided a relatively high measure of clarity and definition of role and purpose for their social workers. Do we, want, however, to return to that stance—or to any other comparable single-system approach?

We are now in the position of having a diverse and sometimes bewildering array of options about what social work is, or should be, or could be doing. Our propensity for rational internal consistency is jarred. Our impulse, therefore, is to put at least a semblance of a conceptual floor under it all, but the disarray defies our efforts at comprehensive order. Moreover, we are worried that nobody can possibly master it all. Just look at the possible sources of knowledge that now have relevance to social work education—and every year we seem to throw more into the mix. Sociology, social psychology, anthropology, economics, and political science hardly constitute all the disciplines from which social work now derives knowledge for its use. When we add to the knowledge sources the necessity for inter-disciplinary collaboration, which requires knowing the language and perspectives of professions from health, education, psychology, and many other fields, the range of knowledge sources gets broader and more diffuse all the time.

I see no early prospect of attaining unifying theory and clear-cut comprehensive systems, although the continuing search is merited and valuable. I also see no cause to be overly worried about the absence of such systems. If we can continue to work out increasingly defined practice and theory in discrete segments of social work, this is marked progress. We are, indeed, a fuzzy field. Few professions are content with the clarity of their functional boundaries, but ours are admittedly vaguer than most. I question whether this is a serious handicap. On the contrary, we can try to make a virtue out of this presumed limitation, which is more apparent than real.

Social work, because of the very looseness and flexibility in its human service potential, has opportunities to connect with wide varieties of activities, with other academic disciplines and professions, and with diverse institutions in society. In a given society, so long as there is a sense at least of what is at the core of social work—from which center of knowledge, purpose, and skills its diversity arises—there need be no absolute definitions about the entire circumference. The openness of social work boundaries permits us to connect all the more readily with such institutions as health, education, labor, and industry, and with such fields as urban planning and housing programs; to take every opportunity to draw on the wellsprings of humanistic values tied to rational pursuit of knowledge and skill, which characterize the social work contribution, and to develop increasingly effective lines of service.

INDIGENIZATION

One of the latent functions of an international congress is to shake us all up a bit and heighten our sense of the complexities and the unknown as well as to reinforce shared values and knowledge. If we go through an experience like this with all of our prior assumptions intact, feeling surer than ever that we have known what is right all along, we have missed the essence of the exposure. To have experienced the presentations and discussions on agology, animation, and conscientization—the latter now affecting an entire region of the world—is to be aware of the richness as well as the diversity of our field, and of the dynamic search for clarity and significance, and to see the confusion within a more balanced perspective.

It is more than instructive to realize that none of the proponents has urged that any one of these approaches become a worldwide formulation. Those who speak for "agology" as developed in the Netherlands interpret their confidence in its contribution to all fields of human services concerned with helping and leading, but with no effort at insisting on universal acceptance. The discussion of "animation" made abundantly explicit its relationship to the French social work history and milieu. The exposition of "conscientization" identified its sources in the social needs and conditions of life in Latin American countries, their political situations, the struggles of their schools of social work, the searches for new meanings by students and faculty and practitioners in the light of their realities.

That these are differential expressions of social work thought and action connected to given intellectual, social, economic, and political experience in given societies does not mean that other societies cannot adapt their views and methods to their own requirements. The field of social work is such that no country need accept another's formulation of specific function, conceptual framework, or method mix—and yet they will have a common base of concern with objectives, training, practice theory, and service delivery. It is doubtful that developments in one part of the world will not consistently enrich and influence what is happening in another, but not by way of automatic emulation.

We have entered the era of "indigenization"—of indigenous development based on the needs and resources and the cultural, political, and economic landscape of each society—and the schools of social work are taking the lead, as they must, in carving out such directions. The necessity for this process is most evident in developing countries, where Western models of social work education and practice have been transferred through nationals trained in the countries of North America and Western Europe, and through advisers and consultants. Change in these models to reflect more accurately the needs and opportunities of the respective countries in the developing world is not easy because leading educators have themselves been trained in the Western world, patterns of service have been developed in which organizations, personnel, and indeed clientele have their investments, and the resources needed for changed directions are not readily available. Nevertheless, such changes are in process in many of these countries. The Latin American developments have in particular been delineated at this Congress, but other developments are in progress in many Asian countries, and the newly created Association for Social Work Education in Africa is turning its attention to the African experience. What is also of interest is the indigenization of social work in Western countries, with new variations in emphasis based on their national situations. In virtually all countries there is also concern with training in relation to national manpower needs and possibilities of many levels of personnel contributing to social welfare, not solely those with so-called "professional" education.

CONTINUITY AND INNOVATION

Indigenization is closely related to the theme of continuity and innovation. Changing needs, new thinking, fresh insights from theory and research, the thrusts of activism directed to social change all create pressure to discard old patterns of teaching and doing and to start new approaches. Such dynamic pressure is essential to every field that must be alive to opportunities for progress and regeneration; there are periods when the pressure for change is more intense than in others and the conflicts therefore sharper. A historical perspective over generations nevertheless makes evident how continuous such development has been, even though in a shorter time scale it has a stop-and-start character and appears jaggedly discontinuous.

That change—including drastic change—has to occur is unquestioned, but one senses in this current period less inclination than in the immediate past to wipe the slate clean of previous learnings and experience on the basis that social work delivery systems must be altered, or because mass approaches, comprehensive developmental planning, and direct action programs are to be instituted to replace the monopoly of more conventional selective and individually oriented treatment or remedial approaches. What may appear to some to be archaic methodologies, including casework and group work, are being harnessed to new approaches, and learning in these methodologies continues to grow. The innovative and social action oriented directions we have been exposed to at this Congress do not disparage these methodologies. Because of changes in programs and goals, there is no inclination to give up understandings, for example, of resistance to change, of working with the strengths of people, of techniques to bolster human capacities for their own initiatives and problem-solving, of developing community leadership, of stimulating personal development related to social and cultural conditions, of identifying objectives for change and mobilizing people to work for such change, and of the many other understandings that have emerged and are still developing in social work practice.

The old obviously must be continuously re-examined, but not automatically discarded, even the old that was introduced at the wrong time, in the wrong way, for the wrong reasons—as in many developing countries—but has nevertheless become a part of the national social work experience.

There is necessary tension between the old and the new. If there were no tension, something would be wrong. When the novel is too easily accepted, we risk indulging in faddism. If nothing that is significantly new and different is accepted because it takes issue with prevailing norms and interests, we have the extreme of conservative rigidity.

As we move toward change, the continuities we experience in conserving what we can from what has been learned and what has been done are not smooth continuities in a steady flow. In the world of reality, they are marked with disagreement, conflict, and resistance, which may not altogether derive from differing perceptions of the merits of the issues, but from differing vested interests as well. No change of any significance comes without a certain measure of struggle. If the resolution of the conflict were too easy, or if there were no conflict at all, the chances are that the issue is not of great significance. The tensions between conservatism and innovation are at their best when they are related rationally to the issues and are most constructive when they provide a base for effective continuities.

We have other and related tensions which are necessary to keep the fabric of our field from becoming limp. The relationship between our educational systems and the world of practice reality is one in which tension is chronic but not necessarily unwholesome. The higher the level of education, the more strained such tensions tend to be. In other words, the more training there is at technical in-service or at lower levels of personnel, the less the tension between what somebody is learning to do and what job he is supposed to be doing. The more the training moves to higher levels of abstraction and conceptualization, generally the greater is the tension between education and practice. It is not necessary that the relationship between educational and practice systems be completely compatible at every point for there to be fruitful progress. At the highest levels of education, over-compatibility may signify too much of a "trade school" emphasis; professionals may simply conform without question to existing models of welfare practice, organization, and policy rather than gaining the capacity to raise questions and to pursue innovation. (In this connection, one might note that tensions at this level can be productive so long as the faculty teaching at such higher levels of training and education are competent to do what they teach in the world of practice.)

Education at its best raises questions about what might be changed in the world of practice and characteristically generates at least an element of skepticism about the validity of current patterns and functions in social work. The practice world, on the other hand, generally seeks personnel prepared for its tasks and socialized to its subcultures, and sometimes has its own significant innovations which are not yet reflected in the training centers. The struggle between conservatism and innovation takes place as much within the practicing milieux of social work as it does within the field of social work education.

CONCLUDING COMMENTS

This Congress has been of only a few days duration, yet, aside from the many months of previous planning by many people, it represents in its short span an input from hundreds of educators from scores of countries. What it has demonstrated above all is the capacity of our field to regenerate itself without destroying itself, often just as we appear to be at the disastrous edge of the cliff. Social work education is replete with confusion and perplexity, full of thorns, but it also has an inner excitement. Perhaps it is the thorns which stimulate the excitement.

Under all of the specific developments and issues at a given time, there runs the current of a field which tries to wed rationality to humanism, that tries to define and fulfill the ethical requirements of social responsibility. We are one part of those elements in society whose overriding values are to help expand the possibilities of the expression of human potential, of expanding freedom, and of social and economic justice. The struggle on all these fronts is unending. In addition to making even clearer the frustrating limitations under which we often work and the disappointing scope of what we can influence, along with the confusion and perplexities of often unsettling new ideas and approaches and information impossible to absorb all at once, the experience of this Congress also gives us renewed faith and confidence, revitalized energy, and fresh insights. On the whole, it is not a bad mix of products to take home with us.

7.   Issues in the Relationship of Social Science to Social Work Education

The purpose of this article is to consider the nature of the contribution required for social work education from psychology, anthropology, and sociology, and the problems inherent in making this contribution. It is intended to be more a statement of issues than of principles, of questions rather than of points of view.

Social work education has been thoroughly presented in the United Nations publication entitled *Training for Social Work: Third International Survey*,[1] which comprehensively reviewed the significant developments in social work itself, as well as in educational content and method. In addition, there are the reports of Training Seminars in Montevideo, in Athens, and Labote.[2] With these background documents available, it is not necessary to provide a detailed review of the nature of social work or trends in social work education. Certain general points, however, may be appropriate to set the basis for consideration of the questions involved.

DEFINITIONS OF SOCIAL WORK

Definitions of social work can be given in terms of its field of work, its methods, or of its characteristics as a profession. In none of these respects is there probably a completely satisfactory definition that would be both internationally applicable and precise. Indeed, there are often many current definitions within the same country. Where social work has begun to emerge as a recognized profession, its field of activity, its processes of help, and its

Reprinted with permission from *International Social Work*, Vol. IV, No. 1 (1961).

[1] Sales No.: 59. IV. 1.

[2] Seminar on Training for Social Work in Latin America, Montevideo, 20 July-2 August 1957; Southern European Regional Meeting of Experts on Training for Social Work, Athens, Greece, 6-16 April 1958; Asia and Far East Seminar on Training for Community Development and Social Work, Lahore, West Pakistan, 9-20 December 1957.

distinguishing characteristics can be more readily described than in countries where its characteristics in all these respects are even more tentative.

Among the definitions covering phases of social work that have received substantial acceptance are the following:

Social work as it is actually carried on has certain very general characteristics in all countries:

1. It is a helping activity, designed to give assistance in respect of problems that prevent individuals, families and groups from achieving a minimum desirable standard of social and economic well-being.

2. It is a social activity, carried on not, for personal profit by private practitioners, but under the auspices of organizations, governmental or non-governmental or both, established for the benefit of members of the community regarded as requiring assistance.

3. It is a liaison activity, through which disadvantaged individuals, families and groups may tap all the resources in the community available to meet their unsatisfied needs. . .[3]

It should be added that, in some countries, social work help is no longer restricted to groups that are "disadvantaged". Casework and group work services have been made available, for example, to middle income groups by many agencies in the United States of America and in Canada. Moreover, the preventive nature of much social work activity would today normally be included under a definition covering characteristics of social work.

At a meeting of experts on the social services, convened by the United Nations in 1959, social work was referred to as embracing the specific knowledge and skills used in the fulfilment of social service objectives. For purposes of their report, social services were defined as

. . . an organized activity that aims at helping towards a mutual adjustment of individuals and their social environment. This objective is achieved through the use of techniques and methods which are designed to enable individuals, groups and communities to meet their needs and solve their problems of adjustment to a chang-

---

[3] *Training for Social Work: Third International Survey, op. cit.,* p. 60.

ing pattern of society and through co-operative action to improve economic and social conditions.[4]

At a UN/WHO European Seminar on the Role of Health Workers and Social Workers in Meeting Family Needs,[5] held in October 1959, the emphasis was on health work and social work in the field of family welfare in European Countries; the following statements concerning social work which are taken from the Seminar Report, are, however, more inclusive:

> The basic task of the social worker is to help individuals and families to solve or mitigate social problems. For this purpose, the social worker must be able to diagnose such problems, to understand the personality of the individual, his family and his social milieu, and to build up a relationship with them through which they are enabled to meet their difficulties. In fulfilling this function, the social worker must also have an extensive knowledge of community resources and their appropriate use in particular cases. The social worker is thus concerned with problems of relationship within the family and between the family and the outside world—including its need for certain goods and services.

> The aim of the social worker in any setting is to help persons, families or communities to meet their social difficulties, to overcome handicaps, to enrich the quality of their daily lives, and to achieve better levels of social living. His essential function lies in helping individuals, groups, or communities with personal and social (including environmental, material and financial) problems or needs to mobilize their own and the community's resources to meet those. Such help may be required over a short period and may involve the giving of information, practical assistance or material help; or it may entail a continuing professional relationship lasting over months or even years. . . .

> The social worker includes in his purview, *a priori*, all of the community's social institutions or resources that might be of use to

---

[4] *The Development of National Social Service Programmes* (United Nations publication, Sales No.: 60.IV.1), p. 6. This group met at United Nations Headquarters from 9 January to 6 February 1959.

[5] Report not yet published.

the individual. Similarly, in working with families and groups, the social worker seeks to envisage them in the context of their social, economic and psychological relationships. A major aim is to maintain or to help in the readjustment of the family group. Social work also has remedial and preventive aspects. . .

The social welfare programmes in which social workers are employed in various countries include the following, which may be undertaken either under government or voluntary auspices: social insurance; public assistance; child welfare; family welfare; medical social work; psychiatric social work; marital counselling; parole, probation and social work in correctional institutions; social work with the aged; industrial social work; group work in clinical, recreational, industrial, hospital, juvenile and adult courts, children and old age institutions and other settings; community organization; community development (individually and in inter-professional teams).

It is generally agreed that the major helping methods in social work may be subsumed under individual, group, and community processes. In addition to direct practice, in which the overwhelming majority of the social workers in the world are engaged, a substantial number of social workers are also involved in administration, consultation, teaching and research.

PREREQUISITES FOR SOCIAL WORK EDUCATION

Social work training varies considerably, not only in its content, but in the educational requirements for the entering student. There is general acceptance, however, of the central objective of such training to equip the social work student to render service on at least a beginning level, for fulfilment of professional standards in a given country, by orienting him to the values of social work and by providing him with the knowledge and skills necessary for such practice, sufficient to enable him to continue his development as a social worker.

Typically, this preparation includes both courses and some form of field experience. In some countries, particularly where social work is given at the postgraduate level, this field experience consists of direct social work experience in an agency under the guidance of a qualified social work supervisor. Elsewhere it may consist of observation or elementary social work practice with varying degrees of educational supervision, or with considerable responsibility for service but with little or no teaching of supervision related to this field experience.

Educational prerequisites for social work training range from the equivalent of the completion of the secondary level, that is, twelve to fourteen years of education, to the equivalent of four years of higher education, or a total of sixteen years before entering social work training. There appear to be four distinct levels of social work training:

1. Following secondary school, as a technical programme of specialization, usually two to three years in duration and unrelated to a university programme.

2. Following the equivalent of two years beyond the secondary level, a two- or three-year programme, possibly leading to a bachelor's degree.

3. Following secondary education (up to ages seventeen to nineteen), a university diploma or degree programme of two to three years' duration, followed by one year of professional education.

4. Following four years of college, a two-year course on a post-graduate basis as part of the university programme leading to a Master's degree.

It is evident that the social work student training at level 1 would not be likely to have any significant background in the social sciences. Students training at level 2 may have had some social science orientation, but rarely any significant concentration. Students training at levels 3 and 4 would normally be expected to have had a concentration in the behavioural and social sciences prior to social work training.

In discussing the demands made by social work education on the social sciences, one cannot avoid the different implications in the selection and extent of social science materials, which are required at each of these different levels of educational preparation prior to social work training.

THE CONTRIBUTION TO BE MADE BY THE SOCIAL SCIENCES

Social work education requires knowledge derived from the social and behavioural sciences as part of the scientific foundation on which social work practice is based. One reason for this requirement, in addition to its liberalizing and intellectual influence is the necessity, which faces all social workers, of assessing as accurately as possible the nature of the needs of the people they serve. As with a member of any of the other "helping" professions, the social worker is compelled to make judgements about the people he helps, for example, in terms of their personality characteristics, attitudes, strengths and weaknesses, as well as of their social needs. For these judgements to be based on more than "common sense" criteria alone, or on the basis of the worker's own particular life experience, a grounding in the relevant sciences dealing with human behaviour is essential. Otherwise, the risk is magnified of making unwarranted assumptions about people and of having perceptions unwittingly distorted by bias. Moreover, the methods to be employed and the objectives to be sought by the social worker in his work with individuals, groups and communities, and in administration, should draw on the knowledge derived from theory and research in the appropriate behavioural science.

We are concerned with three of these branches of knowledge; each is vast, ramified in theory and exposed to diverse points of view. The problems of selection and adaptation to the needs of social work are complicated, particularly in view of the diverse educational backgrounds of social work students in the various national programmes.

Moreover, the separation of the three scientific disciplines is, for our purposes, artificial to a considerable degree. Not only do their areas of concern overlap, but in their usefulness to the social worker the lines of demarcation between sociology an anthropology and psychology are not significant. What is important to the social worker is the achievement of greater understanding of human behaviour and of society, an understanding which he will be able to utilize in practice, whatever may be the source of this knowledge. Indeed, one problem which should be considered is whether it is necessary to present social science content to social work students in the compartments of distinct academic disciplines, or whether it would not be best to bring together the most relevant material from the various social sciences and present them in one or more courses, at the same time interweaving relevant material into other courses and utilizing it in field instruction.

Perhaps the essential contribution that the social sciences can make to social work is to clarify and expand the social worker's understanding of the concept of social environment. The tendency in social work education in many countries has been to focus on a deeper comprehension of the individual personality, to learn to see in the individual more than meets the eye. With respect to the social environment, however, a much less sophisticated view has tended to prevail, and it is in this area that the central contributions of the social sciences lies—in providing the social worker with ways of understanding in more penetrating terms, the relationship of these being helped to their social environment, so that he can cope better with milieu as well as with individual factors.

The social environment may be seen as a range of systems of influence, all interacting and all affecting the individual in diverse ways. Thus social, class, ethnic, and regional patterns are transmitted through family and peer groups in various ways, and their norms are adopted or rejected by individuals, but inevitably affect their values, aspirations and behaviour. Such patterns and influences are not always easily observable or accurately perceived, yet they are necessary to our understanding of how best to help others, whether through individual, group, or community processes. Similarly, the nature of the setting in which help is given requires more than descriptive understanding—whether this applies to a hospital, a court, a settlement house, a factory, or a village; with such deepened understanding, the social worker can better evaluate not only the influences in the setting which bear on the individuals or groups being served, but his own role in relation to others in the setting.

A view of the social environment which takes such factors into account does not comprise all the understanding the social worker should have about the people he is helping or his own function in relation to them, but enriches his perspective so that key considerations are not ignored or misinterpreted.

CONTRIBUTIONS OF PSYCHOLOGY, ANTHROPOLOGY AND SOCIOLOGY TO SOCIAL WORK EDUCATION

With this general orientation in mind, and recognizing the interdependence in content and approach among the three disciplines under consideration, it may be appropriate to touch on the essential contributions from each to social work education.

Psychology

From the field of psychology we look first to an understanding of personality development. Not only in work with individuals, but in all the various branches of social service including the planning of so-called "mass programmes", the understanding of the needs and problems of the individual is basic. The psychological orientation most widely accepted in social work education is generally referred to as "psychodynamic" in character, and stresses the effects of the individual's life experience on his psychological and emotional development. In general, this orientation stems from psychoanalytic theory, whether Freudian and neo-Freudian (Fromm, Sullivan, Horney, etc.) or whether based on the systems of Jung or Peake. Differences among the systems notwithstanding, they share a view of evolving personality in the context of inter-personal relationships and particularly in the family setting. While, with any of these theoretical approaches, knowledge of constitutional and hereditary factors is essential to an understanding of personality, the emphasis is on the effects of life experience and on the understanding of these elements in personality and environment that may be modified in the solution of individual and family difficulties.

With such an orientation, the social work student would normally be instructed in the various phases of the individual's life cycle, on the types of pressures the individual is likely to face in relation to each, the nature of the satisfactions he tends to seek, and the nature of his physical development and its implications. The norms of emotional development generally serve as the basis for viewing pathology. The individual is seen in relation to his social milieu and particularly to what he has absorbed in the way of values and sentiments from significant figures in the course of his development, as well as from the point of view of the relationship of these values and sentiments to those of the larger society.

Particular attention would naturally be paid to, such areas of interpersonal relationship as kinship ties from childhood to parenthood and old age; school and occupational adjustment; and friendship groups. Intelligence is perceived as a function not only of natural endowment, but in relation to the emotional factors freeing or limiting the use of the individual's intelligence and to the pressures within his milieu bearing on the presence or lack of incentives for the development of intelligence. Abnormalities in intelligence would be perceived in terms of all of these factors. In this kind of assessment, as well as in other connexions the social worker should be equipped to make appropriate use of the services of psychologists.

It is necessary for social workers to learn the scope within which they can be helpful in individual treatment (to the extent they are called upon for such work), and to recognize where the services of other disciplines, if available, should be utilized (as in the case of psychologists in the assessment of intelligence). All social workers require the capacity, drawn in large measure from the contribution of psychological thought, to assess the strengths of individuals as well as their weaknesses, and to understand the ways in which they can build on these strengths. It is clear that, for these purposes, the particular theoretical basis which provides the framework for the social worker's activity is of crucial importance.

The level of previous study and experience which the students bring to their social work education, and the particular practice programmes in which they are likely to be engaged, will determine in large measure the emphases to be provided in the social work curriculum. Where social workers are to be engaged, to an extensive degree, in individual treatment for counselling, and have considerable previous background to draw upon, close attention to at least one psychological theory is necessary, as well as possible exposure to diverse theoretical perspectives. Where these background conditions are not present, the academic depth. of theoretical preparation may have to be lessened, and instruction may deal more with the inferences to be drawn from theory and research for social work practice than with theory itself.

It is, of course, not only in individual terms that the study of psychology is important for the social worker. The psychology of group behaviour forms a necessary underpinning for the social worker's practice in the utilization of group processes. The development of indigenous leadership in groups including, for example, modes of resolution of group conflict, stimulation of motivation for group development, awareness and use of group behaviour in administration, and utilization of group process for therapeutic objectives, depends on an understanding of the psychology of groups. In countries where social workers are being trained for such special programmes as those in industry, industrial psychology should be taught.

No small part of the contribution of psychological thought to the preparation of social workers is represented by the material presented to the student, which helps him understand his own psychological needs so that these do not get in the way of his being of help to others. Education in social work is education and is not designed to be therapeutic for the student; it is natural, however, for students to examine themselves critically as they become exposed to psychological techniques. In field practice, it is not uncommon for a student to recognize how his own particular psychological needs may be interfering with his work. It is, of course, not only the understanding of formal psychology, but the training in the methods of social work practice and the supervision the student receives in the field that aid him in developing professional self-discipline. However, the organization and presentation of materials in psychology form a necessary part of this effort.

The study of psychology should also help to equip the social work student to comprehend the ways in which people may be motivated to change given behaviour and the ways in which change is resisted; such study should also enable him to gauge progress towards constructive change in individuals and groups. Above all, perhaps, the contribution of psychology

should enable the student to grasp the essential concepts of the meaningful-
ness of behaviour, including seemingly irrational behaviour.

Anthropology

The contribution of cultural and social anthropology in the training of
the social worker also rests partly on his developing self-understanding in
cultural terms. Such preparation should minimize his natural ethnocentrism, and help him to see cultural patterns of groups dissimilar from his
own, seeing them also, as far as possible, from their point of view. Just as in
the course of his learning about psychology he should be aware of the fact
that individual behaviour is meaningful if its pattern can be traced, so it is
equally important for him to understand that there is meaning behind various types of cultural behaviour, even those that strike him as bizarre.

An understanding of the student's own culture is basic; he must understand the culture in which he has been raised, and the variations that exist
among the various segments of the society in which he will be living and
practising social work. Thus it is essential that he should learn the sub-
stance of the regional, rural-urban, religious, class and ethnic patterns of
groups within his own society with which he is most likely to be working.
While it may be difficult for him to obtain a thorough knowledge of all the
sub-cultural systems in a given society, he should acquire the basis for
examining differences in customs and in values, to learn where to go for
more information, and to recognize that, if he does not scrutinize his cultural premises carefully, he may be proceeding from a basis of distorted
perceptions of the values of others.

A study of social anthropology should also assist the social work student to understand social change processes; to locate not only the sources of
resistance to change, but also to discern the nature of the changes already
implicit in the society and the direction in which the culture is moving.

In many areas of social work practice, particularly in community organization and community development, the social worker is an agent of social change. As such, he should be alerted to the concept that, in attempting
to induce change in one part of the social system, one may be affecting other
systems and inducing effects over which one has no control. On the level of
individual psychology, the student learns that a significant change in one
member of a family may affect the stability of the entire family, and that in
certain situations the entire family becomes the object of help and not one
individual alone. On a larger scale, the student should be aware that efforts

in an urban area to develop indigenous neighbourhood improvement through better sanitation and housing inspection may run counter to the existing political power structure; or that efforts in a rural area to increase literacy or agricultural productivity may have consequences affecting the family system.

In addition to an understanding of the culture of his society and those of the major ethnic groups comprising it, it is important that the student should be aware of the culture of smaller sub-systems within the society—in the factory, the hospital, the prison, and so forth. While this area borders on sociology (and, as indicated previously, it is difficult to make sharp distinctions between the various behavioural and social sciences in terms of the content covered), an anthropological view of cultural sub-systems is most relevant to the basic perspective from which the social worker views those individuals and groups which he will be serving.

Where the training programme of social workers is designed to help prepare them for community development programmes in regions from which the students themselves may not have come, the content of cultural anthropology is quite crucial. Religious values, the nature of family structure, the kinds of roles in community life acceptable in the community, the relationship of the economic and political systems to the cultural system—all must be understood. While the need for understanding anthropology is perhaps most dramatic in this instance, it should be clear that a cultural orientation is essential to social workers who practise in urban settings with individuals, in educational and therapeutic settings with groups, and in larger community programmes at any level in the society. The capacity for empathy which social work education attempts to develop requires a capacity on the part of the social worker to put himself as far as possible in the cultural perspective of those whom he is helping, in order more fully to understand their problems, their needs as they see them, and the directions for development and change that would permit the greatest possibility of integration with their underlying values and patterns of living.

Sociology

In considering briefly what sociology can and should provide for the social work student, one is again faced with the overlap both with psychology, particularly the psychology of groups, and with anthropology. In general, sociology should provide the social work student with a picture of the major institutions of his society and the way in which they are articulated, as well as the strains that are operative in the society. The relationship between economic, political and social institutions should be considered, so that the student can locate himself and social work programmes within the context of the larger social system. He should be helped to have a clear idea of the gaps and difficulties existing in the social order to the removal of which social work is expected to make a contribution: these include, for example, the critical social needs of poverty, unemployment, disease, illiteracy, and the extent to which they exist.

Sociology can provide the social work student with a comprehension of the social sources of various types of , pathology, including various forms of physical illness, crime and delinquency, mental illness, suicidal tendencies, alcoholism, and so forth. Sociological content should be employed, not to give the full answer to the nature of these forms of deviant behaviour, but rather to underscore the factors influencing their development which may be amenable to change by social as well as by individual programmes. The study of sociology is particularly important in locating deviance within the social structure, and not in viewing the social structure as an intropsychic phenomenon.

The student should also gain a comprehension of the different levels of the society in which he will live and practise, the nature of the power system in the society at large, and the authority systems governing the programme in which he is likely to be working. By the same token he should develop perspective in terms of useful concepts for analysis of the administrative structure of the setting in which he will be practising, whether this is a public assistance programme, a court, a voluntary family agency, a mental hospital or a factory.

In order to distinguish between patterns of life in rural and urban areas, a student is naturally brought closer to cultural anthropological material, but perhaps the sociological emphasis can be distinguished in the sense that it concentrates less on the patterns of behaviour than on the social forces which tend to produce and fortify certain patterns of behaviour, and on the strains most likely to develop in the interaction of these sources of influence.

All the social sciences should contribute to the student's heightened sensitivity to a scientific view of human behaviour. The materials and the ways in which they are presented should enhance the student's appreciation of the value of research, and enable him to understand and critically examine relevant research undertakings. While the methodology of research in sociology has, perhaps, proven most appropriate to the research needs of social work, certainly research methods in psychology and anthropology have also been employed and, to a certain extent, common research approaches have been developed.

PROBLEMS IN MAKING USE OF THE SOCIAL SCIENCE CONTRIBUTION

Schools of social work throughout the world are concerned with the task of how best to make use of the necessary contribution from the social sciences. Problems of various kinds complicate this task, and have been met in various ways. While the specific ways in which the problems arise vary, and the problems themselves are rarely separable from one another, for our purposes they may be classified into: role, administrative, and curricular problems.

Role problems

The most critical role problem is whether teachers who are not themselves experienced in social work may, by their background or by their mode of presentation of their material, provide confusing role models for social work students. A specific variant of this problem occurs in the field of psychology. One point of view has it that, whenever possible, the teacher of psychological materials should himself be in, or at least from, clinical practice rather than from the field of academic psychology. The inference to be drawn is that, where the instructor has himself engaged in psychological treatment, he would be able to bring to his teaching a necessary clinical orientation; and that otherwise the material might tend to be too theoretical and unrelated to the specific needs of practice. By the same token, however, the question arises whether, if the instructor is a psychiatrist or a clinical psychologist, his therapeutic role will not be that of the social worker; it may therefore be confusing for the social work student to have such instruction serve as a model for clinical performance. Particular objections have been raised to the use of psychiatrists or clinical psychologists as supervisors for social work students in their field work.[6]

A different kind of problem arises when the instructor in social science is a teacher from an academic department of the university. The issue here is whether, aside from the relevance of his material, the point of view likely to

---

[6] Such objections were raised, for example, during the discussion of the WHO/UN Seminar on the Role of Health Workers and Social Workers in meeting Family Needs, October 1959. The reference at this meeting was to the supervision of paid staff, but would presumably apply even more strongly to students.

be expressed would not be of necessity an academic rather than a practitioner's point of view. In other words, the emphasis could be confined to the study of society and human behaviour rather than on dealing with the problems arising from the society itself and from human behaviour. Since every instructor during the course of social work training serves in some measure as a person to be emulated, the question arises whether emulation in this regard might not tend to underplay the professional and practitioner orientation, while maximizing the more detached perspective of the academic prototype.

In some schools, particularly in North America, it has been possible to meet this problem in part by having social workers who are also trained in one or more of the social sciences teach courses in the integration of these materials into social work practice. More often, both in North America and elsewhere, the instructor in these materials tends to be a sociologist, anthropologist, or social psychologist. In the latter cases—and it is evident that this will continue to be the dominant pattern for a long time to come—the issue arises whether the academic teacher should attempt to change the nature of his approach to his material to adjust to the practice orientation of the social work students, or continue to teach as he would in his courses at the university, where there is more apt to be an emphasis on research objectives.

Administrative problems

In many social work schools throughout the world where social scientists are employed, little time is allowed for the social science instructor to re-plan his courses to meet the needs of the social work curriculum. Frequently the instructor does not have the time; in some cases, this problem is met by payment to the instructor for such planning. Similarly, the problem of relating the course materials to other courses in the curriculum requires time for discussions, and unless special provision is made the time simply is not made available. A related problem is the payment for the course teaching itself. Frequently payment is at such a low level that the servcies of qualified instructors cannot be obtained or qualified instructors tend to regard such teaching as of much lower priority than their equivalent courses in the university. Turnover in instructors is likely to occur in such circumstances and this absence of continuity can create severe problems in planning, dubious standards of course instruction, difficulties in removing inadequate teachers because the low remuneration limits the number of qualified instructors available, and the relegation of the social science segments of the curriculum to part-time instructors unrelated to the total programme. Note should also be made of problems of work-load and programme planning in cases where the university social science teacher is regarded as a full-time instructor within his own department; in addition to administrative complications that may arise, relationship and role strains may also attend such a teaching pattern.

Curricular problems

The principal concern in the curricular area is whether the social science material should be given separately, or should be integrated into the teaching of social work methods in course and field work instruction. A related problem is whether psychology, sociology, and anthropology should be taught separately as distinct knowledge areas. A third phase of this issue, as noted above, is whether the course or courses in this area should be the same as for students elsewhere in the university or should be completely revised in an attempt to meet the special needs of social work students.

In general, the direction of movement in schools of social work is towards emphasizing the necessity of selecting and adapting materials for social work use. This requires, however, a great deal of re-thinking of the subject matter by the instructor and makes it important for him to have a sound orientation to social work objectives, programmes, values and processes. As indicated, all of this requires time and investment by the school. Without such investment likelihood is strong that the academic social science materials will be indifferently related to the social worker's perception of his practice needs. Another danger is that the social work student who comes upon social science materials for the first time in the course of his social work training is apt to become so intrigued with this area of content that he develops an overly academic as against a professional approach to his social work interests.

A recurrent issue is the extent to which the materials and perspectives provided for in the social science segments of the curriculum can be interwoven in the field training programme. This is a problem which has hardly been satisfactorily met anywhere, even where qualified field supervision is provided in the routine course of training. Many of the insights of the social and behavioural sciences, particularly those of sociology and cultural anthropology, are only now coming to the fore in social work training, and supervisors, by and large, have not been exposed to these theoretical currents. How a school can ensure that its students see the various approaches they are learning in courses reinforced in the field experience is not a simple matter. As a way of meeting this objective, some attempts are being made to bring supervisors back to the school for course training. In countries where there is not adequate field supervision, the problems are of course intensified in all areas of social work learning.

This is not to say that the problem of integrating background knowledge into methods teaching in the classroom has been solved. It, too, is a serious problem since there is often a tendency for methods teaching not only to be divorced from materials in the social and behavioural sciences, but to be restricted to administrative or procedural detail rather than to develop concepts for practice. However, the solution of this kind of difficulty lies more directly within the control of the school than does the more prevalent equivalent problem in field supervision.

The existence of diverse schools of thought in the various branches of the behavioural sciences also gives rise to complications. In personality theory, it has been usual to begin by selecting a particular theoretical orientation, minimizing or excluding consideration of other approaches to the understanding of behaviour and personality. Which orientation to select is then a critical matter, and the view represented by the instructor becomes quite important. The situation is less likely to be critical in sociology and in cultural anthropology, where it may take the form of particular theoretical predilections of the instructors which may or may not be the most appropriate to the school's conception of the needs of its students. A school of social work which does not have a curricular point of view on these matters, and does not have a faculty sufficiently conversant with social science, will find it hard to exercise proper selection of social science faculty or content, assuming it has room for choice.

Most basic of all problems, of course, is the extent to which theory *per se* is taught to students. Here the educational background of the students is most important. Where students come with virtually no previous knowledge of psychology, sociology or anthropology, the question of selectivity of content, always complicated, is most aggravated. Obviously, social science courses cannot overwhelm the curriculum. One method of resolving this problem is not to dwell on the history of the science and not to treat theory in depth, but rather to draw as far as possible on inferences from principles which have been established through theory and research, and to demonstrate their application. Where the student has a fairly solid background in the academic materials, it may be possible to expand the treatment of theoretical implications of the subject matter, and also to attempt to interweave such content much more thoroughly in the teaching of basic social work methods since it would be possible to draw on concepts with which students are familiar and to show how they apply to practical situations.

Yet the problem of selectivity in theoretical orientation, even for students with the most concentrated undergraduate preparation in the social sciences, is ever-present and cannot be minimized. The range of personality theories alone is vast. Even if one decides to restrict the teaching in this area to one basic orientation, there remain: social change theory, stratification theory, role theory, reference group theory, culture theory, organizational theory, small group theory, family organization theory, and many others, and a claim can be made for the significance of each.

It is hardly feasible to attempt to cover all possible theoretical directions at once, or even to cover a few in depth within the already broadened social work curriculum. One approach is to minimize theoretical coverage and to attempt to concentrate on concepts instead, with the recognition that these concepts are based on theory. Thus, the concepts of class and caste, social mobility ascribed and achieved status, can be discussed in their relevance to social work without necessarily going deeply into stratification theory. Similarly, the various types of role strains can be described, so that students can be made aware of such areas of difficulty, without penetrating into all the highways and by-ways of role theory. This would also apply to such concepts as bureaucratic structure, ethnicity and change agent.

Where one can draw on previous academic background, and where the student is at a stage where he is concentrating on one of the primary social work methods, one area of theory might reasonably be developed, such as small group theory for the group worker, or social change theory for the community organization student.

SUMMARY

The practice needs of social workers involve, *inter alia*, knowledge derived from the social and behavioural sciences. Such practice needs include the assessment of individual personality; the selection of appropriate helping methods; an understanding of group behaviour; an orientation to social class and ethnic systems and to other aspects of the social environment of those being helped; a perspective of social needs in relation to the social order; a sensitivity to modes of resistance to individual and social change;

and an awareness of the processes and consequences of change efforts in individual, group, and larger collectivity terms.

Efforts to include relevant content for such purposes in the course of social work training are complicated by several factors. One is the uneven character of the students' prior academic preparation, ranging from no social science instruction to considerable instruction at university level. Another is the difficulty of integrating such content into the social work curriculum. Role problems in instruction, administrative problems in making proper planning and orientation possible, and curricular problems affecting the forms which course content are to take, the weight of social science in the curriculum, its reinforcement in field work instruction and the critical issue of selection of content, have been among the problems specified as appropriate for consideration in this context.

Part Three
SOCIAL WORK PRACTICE

8.   Social Science in Social Work Practice and Education

Social work in recent years has recognized the need for an increasing investment in the social sciences. The purpose of this paper is to examine this relationship—to identify its values and its risks and to discuss some means for developing a more fruitful, reciprocal relationship between social work and the social sciences.

In the early days of organized social work in this country, the two fields were closely related. The first national conferences of social work, in the 1870's, were sponsored by the then "American Social Science Association." Although the Conference was established independently in 1879, social work continued until about 1920 to draw heavily on sociology, economics, and political science. Since the early twenties, however, while social work has never lost interest in or contact with the social sciences, we have been largely concerned with incorporating the insights of dynamic psychology into our theory and practice. As one effect of our dose alliance with the behavioral sciences—particularly Freudian psychology—the problem of defining our role as practitioners loomed large for many years. Today, however, the issues related to function are no longer uppermost. Although questions continue to arise, we have succeeded to a large extent in establishing our role and have developed security in it. We know the kind of material that is relevant to our purposes and have had extensive experience in working with psychiatrists, psychoanalysts, and psychologists. We are now in a position to assimilate, without great commotion, the research findings and the new insights that emerge from the behavioral sciences.

Reprinted with permission from *Social Casework*, Vol. 36, No. 4 (1955). The article also appeared in Howard J. Parad, ed., *Ego Psychology and Dynamic Process* (New York, Family Service Association of America, 1958) and is based on a paper presented at the Massachusetts Conference of Social Work, Boston, December 1954.

The social work profession has not, however, developed the same close relationship with the social sciences. We have not kept abreast with the marked technical and theoretical advances made during the past thirty years by the various fields, particularly those of cultural anthropology, sociology, and social psychology. We can no longer afford to ignore these contributions, but we are in the position of trying to restore a relationship that has been weakened by neglect.

A trained social worker, for example, can read with understanding a highly technical psychoanalytic paper, but would probably encounter difficulty in comprehending the average article in a journal of sociology; the issues, the concepts, or even the very language itself may not be understood by him. To some extent, the social worker's lack of interest in, and unfamiliarity with, social science literature are related to the nature of its content. Unlike psychoanalytic writing, which is directly applicable to clinical practice, the subject matter of social science is not generally oriented to application. Social science is concerned with demonstrating what is true—why it is true and to what extent-and with raising hypothetical questions for theory and research. Social workers, on the other hand, tend to seek answers to the problems of practice and therefore are disappointed when the social sciences fail to provide answers in such terms.

Nevertheless, with the current emphasis on putting the "social" back into social work, we are turning, naturally to the social sciences for help in providing knowledge on which to base our theory and practice. The social sciences can contribute to the development of this base in three main areas: (1) substantive knowledge, (2) theoretical contributions, and (3) research methods.

Substantive knowledge includes information about the nature of a particular society, an ethnic group, or a social class sub-culture; it also includes facts about the social structure of specific communities, the significance of distributions of incomes and occupations, the behavior of groups under stress, and an endless variety of data which can be drawn upon for social work use. The large-scale study of the relationship between social stratification and psychiatric disorders which is being conducted at Yale University is an illustration of such efforts to discover new knowledge.[1] Indeed, the tie-

---

[1] August B. Hollingshead and Frederick C. Redlich: "Social Stratification and Psychiatric Disorders," *American Sociological Review,* Vol. XVIII, No. 2 (1953), pp. 163-169; "Social Stratification and Schizophrenia," Vol. XIX, No. 3 (1954), pp. 302-306, A. B. Hollingshead, R. Ellis, and E. Kirby, "Social Mobility and Mental Illness," Vol. XIX No. 5 (1954), pp. 577-584.

up of social science and psychiatry may quicken the interest of social work in social science.[2]

Theoretical contributions include concepts with which social work is becoming increasingly familiar, such as the relationship between culture and personality; and explorations which are less familiar, such as the nature and implications of bureaucratic structure and reference group theory.

Research methods for studying social and behavioral phenomena have been developed largely in the social sciences. Social work has drawn on these methods for its own research purposes. The growing interest in research should bring social work in closer alliance with the social sciences.

In this connection it may be noted that the scientific skepticism characteristic of the social science researcher may touch our sensibilities as we move closer to the social sciences. Doubtless we shall encounter a questioning attitude about many of our basic assumptions. Our most cherished notions are likely to come under the chilly-eyed scrutiny of the scientist who maintains his inalienable right to ask, "How do you know?" In our attempt to answer, we may be able to enlist the help of the social scientists themselves. Out of such joint scrutiny we may gain a better perspective of our own theoretical position through distinguishing between (1) knowledge that has been arrived at empirically, (2) premises that are provable but have not been properly tested, (3) assumptions that we accept on faith but have no way, as yet, of proving or disproving, and (4) values that we simply affirm.

DIFFERENCES IN FUNCTIONS

Twenty-five years ago, Robert M. MacIver said: "The relation of sociology to social work is that of a science to an art. . . . An art manipulates, controls, and changes the materials with which it deals; a science seeks only to understand them. An art individualizes' a science generalizes. . . . Social work can never can on social science to justify its aims. The justification of these lies not in the logic of science but in the hearts of men."[3]

---

[2] An example of cultural knowledge put directly to social work use is the book, *Socio-Cultural Elements in Casework: A Case Book of Seven Ethnic Studies*, Council on Social Work Education, New York, 1953. This work is the product of a group of cultural anthropologists and social workers who met together at the New York Cultural Project, under the leadership of Katherine Spencer, an anthropologist. This publication summarizes relevant material about different ethnic groups, applying the data to case records. The Russell Sage Foundation co-operated in this Council project.

[3] Robert M. MacIver, *The Contribution of Sociology to Social Work*, Columbia University Press, New York, 1931, pp. 1-3.

Here we have a statement of the fundamental element in the relationship. It follows that social work is not applied social science; it is not even applied social, psychological, and biological science. Social work derives its knowledge from science but its spirit from philosophy, religion, ethics, moral values; and its method is derived, at least in part, from unexplored—or unexplorable—subtleties of human relationships. There is art in social work method precisely because it is not all science, and while we must strive constantly to enhance the scientific base of our work, we would not wish to, even if we could, eliminate the aesthetic or the ethical components.

The heart of the distinction between social science and social work lies in the difference between the function of an academic discipline and the function of a professional discipline. The underlying function of the academic discipline is to acquire and to disseminate knowledge—even if it is knowledge only for its own sake. This is the overriding purpose of all science. The professions have as their major function the application of knowledge for the rendering of services. The central objective of social work is to help people—through social planning and through preventive and direct services. In order to further this objective, knowledge is necessary and much of that knowledge comes from the social sciences. But the task of developing knowledge for its own sake belongs properly to the academic, and not to the professional, disciplines.

It would be false, of course, to state that social scientists are not concerned with applying what they learn. Today it is perhaps the rule, rather than the exception, that social scientists are concerned about values which they wish to strengthen through their scientific efforts. The ivory tower has been invaded by the headlines of tile world we live in, by the bread-and-butter problems of daily life, by issues of good and evil, and by the force of the scientist's own convictions about promoting what he believes is good.

In this country, for example, cultural anthropologists have contributed to governmental deliberations on the problems of war and peace. Social psychologists have pooled their knowledge and utilized it effectively in such instances as the recent Supreme Court ruling on school segregation, by submitting supplementary briefs. Sociologists have studied the problems of interracial housing with little ambiguity about their position on the social issues at stake. Economists have used their skills in policy formation in the field of social security.

At no time has all of social science been wholly "pure" or unentangled with social reform. Social scientists have frequently translated their knowledge into social action, but we should not confuse these activities with the essential function of social science—which *is science*. The fact that many scientists have interest in a wide range of human affairs and a concern about social values brings them in close harmony with the objectives of social work. We should not assume, however, that the productions of the various branches of social science will be consistently oriented to human betterment, nor should we expect that the individual social scientist will be interested in the *social work* application of his findings.

A relevant question has been asked by Henry Maas: "Is it essential that social scientists compartmentalize research and service, knowing and helping?"[4] His answer was in the negative, with which I agree. It is not essential that the functions of "knowing" and "helping" be rigidly separated. I also agree with Mr. Maas's suggestion of establishing service-linked research—where a service is rendered in conjunction with research, largely in the interest of accumulating knowledge. I should like to stress, however, that social work should retain a firm hold on its own function, which is to render service. The search for knowledge in social work, in contrast to that in the academic field, must always be a means to an end.

NEGATIVE AND POSITIVE IMPLICATIONS

The social sciences can contribute knowledge on which social work may draw for its purposes, but the social scientists cannot teach social workers how to accomplish their ends, or even what findings to use. This is an obvious point, but it is an important one to remember. If we forget it, and follow social science as a shining new lodestar, we are likely to repeat the mistakes of the past generation when social work developed its alliance with psychoanalysis. A hierarchy of status developed, based on the proximity of the social worker to the psychiatrist. This prestige stratification in our profession is only now being dissolved and its marks on the field remain. We should be careful not to let the same thing happen in relation to social science. It should not become necessary for a social worker to become a "little social scientist" or for an agency to jump on an esoteric "band wagon" of social science research, for example, in order to achieve recognition in the profession. We may decide to do research in our schools and in our social agencies on straight social science subject matter. There is noth-

---

[4] Henry Maas, "Collaboration Between Social Work and the Social Sciences," *Social Work Journal*, Vol. XXXI, No. 3 (1950), p. 106.

ing necessarily wrong with this, provided we are clear about what we are doing. We must be clear that research is *not social work research* unless it is oriented to the development of social work theory or practice.

Another risk in the new relationship is that social workers may accept everything that appears under the name of social science as sacrosanct. We should remind ourselves that the social sciences are still groping for answers to their major problems, and there are at least as many schools of thought in social science as there are in social work. Let us not assume that there is any less chaff among the kernels in social science literature than there is in social work literature. We should develop the capacity to pick and choose for our purposes—not only what is relevant but what has worth. We may not all make the same selection but we should have some basis for making a discriminating choice. We do not all have to belong to one school of social science thought, but we should be able to distinguish between the schools.

Moreover, the elaborate and necessary specializations within the total social science field should caution us against assuming that any one scientist can speak authoritatively on all aspects of social science, any more than a social worker can be expert in all areas of social work. Therefore, in seeking the resources and skills of any given social scientist, we should be prepared to appraise his areas of special technical competence, as well as his more general social science perspective. It is fair to assume that social scientists themselves would be the first to want us to do so.

These admonitions imply that social workers need a high level of sophistication and this requirement, in turn, means that we cannot expect the whole body of social workers, already hard-pressed in doing their daily tasks, to encompass and evaluate the staggering amount of social science knowledge that is available. It seems likely that we shall develop "specialists" within our own field, that is, social workers in particular areas of practice with sufficient grasp of relevant social science subject matter to be able to feed in and relate data to their area of practice. The advanced educational programs, particularly the doctoral programs, should help provide us with social workers who can exercise this essential middle-man function. Interpreting, social science findings for social work use is a task that we cannot assign to the social scientists, for it is we who will use, or not use, the knowledge. We, therefore, must be responsible for the choice of what is significant.

But such an essentially one-sided relationship—where social work is the "taker" and social science the "giver"—is bound to change. Because of its basic role of meeting the needs of people, social work has much to contribute to social science. Social workers, in both the governmental and voluntary fields, are constantly exposed to human distress and are in a strategic position to see the effects of changing social conditions, even if the conditions themselves are not clear. Social work, therefore, should be able to offer to the social sciences help in the following ways: (1) identifying significant problems, (2) presenting evidence from social work experience related to hypotheses developed by social science, (3) expanding social work research that utilizes and tests concepts developed by social science and applies them in relation to problems of social work, and (4) making available the raw data of our experience for social science research purposes, in as organized a form as possible and with due protection of the client.

These potential contributions of social work to social science will be increasingly realized as we continue to involve the social scientists in collaborative study of our problems. Already, after only limited experience in working with us, many social scientists have come to sense the richness of our resources—in data, ideas, and approach. With further experience we should gradually overcome both our diffidence in asserting our knowledge and our other problems of communication. We shall learn both how to frame questions for study and how to organize our information for appropriate use by the social sciences. This closer relationship will develop as the social scientists interest themselves in our problems and in our data, and seek better communication with us, just as we now seek it from them. It will develop particularly as more social workers become informed on the subject matter of the social sciences.

PATTERNS OF COLLABORATION

Appropriate channels are required to make the contributions of social science available to social workers. If we recall our premise that we should start with the needs of social work, and apply this principle to an agency, we can envision the following steps. For example, an agency in a suburb—either a casework or group work agency or a community council—may decide that it is important to know something about changing family patterns in suburban life in different social class groupings. If the interested group explores the sociological literature, it will learn that some sociologists who have examined "the urban fringe" are of the opinion that a new family form is emerging in this setting. Among other trends they have found: a tendency toward fixed social stratification, with higher education and membership in a profession becoming a badge of acceptance; a prominent functioning of the kinship system with a strengthening of parental roles, the associated roles of siblings, and particularly the role of the father; increased control by parents over the courtship process, which represents a compromise between arranged marriages and the, theoretically, completely free choice implied in the dating pattern of urban youth; a higher rate of family participation in social institutions; more solidarity in the family role of the aged. In brief, what is suggested is that the historical functions of the family—including the economic, educational, recreational, religious, and protective functions— are becoming reconstituted and better retained in these "urban fringe" areas.[5]

The agency may then ask: How do these trends, if true, affect our clientele? What do these findings suggest for our program? What do they suggest for over-all community planning, of services? The agency may feel that the information from current social science literature is insufficient to help answer the questions, and may wish to call on an expert who knows the trends and who can relate his knowledge to the problems of the specific community. Or the agency may question the trends and hypotheses suggested in the literature and may decide to embark on research of its own, with or without the help of a social scientist.

In such instances, we can see that each field may make reciprocal contributions to the other. Social work agencies—through appropriate participation of board and staff—are in the position of raising problems that are of interest to social scientists: they can react to hypotheses, undertake research of their own with the help of the scientists, engage in independent research, and make data available for the use of the social scientists.

To use another illustration, cultural anthropology has a good deal to offer agencies that have sizable numbers of clients belonging to ethnic groups about which the staff members have little knowledge. An agency may gather whatever information it has on a particular group and have it discussed in board or staff meetings. Some agencies have done this. The Puerto Rican migration, for example, into New York and other cities on the eastern seaboard, has stimulated study of the Puerto Rican culture, its internal variations, and the strains placed on these families as they are exposed to our way of life.

---

[5] E. Gartly Jaco and Ivan Belknap, "Is a New Famfly Form Emerging in the Urban Fringe?" *American Sociological Review,* Vol. XVIII, No. 5 (1953), pp. 551-557.

Social workers may feel the need, however, for more information than they can obtain from their own sources. A series of questions may be raised: What are the best ways of preventing family disorganization in those Puerto Rican families where the position of wife and mother is affected by her going out to work; where control over the social life of young women in terms of Puerto Rican standards becomes difficult; where the man of the family cannot maintain the traditional patriarchal role? What strains are placed on interpersonal relations when members of this group are exposed to racial or cultural prejudices? How do these clients visualize the functions of the various social agencies? Is it true, for example, that they tend to want only practical and concrete services? The social scientists, obviously, cannot change the social environment or provide the resources needed to cope with such problems, but they can provide us with certain important information if we raise the questions and they also can help us develop methods for dealing with these problems.

An agency may be concerned about a specific group of clients or it may raise more general, and therefore more difficult, questions such as: What is our clientele like in terms of significant social and cultural factors? The question, when answered, leads to the more significant one: Does this information indicate the need for changes in policy or program? The development of a sociocultural profile of a caseload may not be an easy task, but it offers real possibilities for improvement of services.

What does this task involve? It means identifying a current caseload in terms of such factors as occupation, social class position, residence, nationality, generation in this country, and comparing the caseload and the total community with respect to the distribution of these factors. This analysis should serve as a basis for inquiry along two lines: (1) What is already known in social science about the ways of life, attitudes, and values of the groups represented in the clientele which will be of help in diagnosis and in treatment? (2) What may be learned about the differences and similarities between the caseload and the population of the community being served which will enable the agency to identify needs of particular groups, as an aid in agency planning and interpretation, and also to generalize about the problems being faced in the community as a whole? These questions may lead the agency to social science source materials and may also motivate it to seek the co-operation of social scientists in analyzing and interpreting the materials. New questions of special interest to social scientists themselves may also arise which, if explored by them, will further illuminate the problem and thus enable us to serve our clients and our communities better.

Whether the questions are simple or complex, they cannot be studied unless people are interested in the task and are given time to do the work. Conviction about the value and importance of developing such information must be present, not only among the practitioners, but among administrators and supervisors. The conviction must be translated into assignment of the personnel and the time for staff meetings; that is, concern for such study should have a measure of priority in an agency program. Since it is at the agency level that integration of social science subject matter takes place, social work agencies have a particular responsibility to initiate inquiries. Obviously some questions are of mutual concern to several agencies in a community, or to agencies in a particular field on a national basis. Some problems "cut across the board" and require the resources of many agencies for proper exploration.

CURRENT STUDIES

It may be relevant to make brief note of a few of the current social science studies that have particular relevance to social agencies, councils, and professional and national associations.

The work being done on sociocultural approaches to medical care in many settings, giving rise to an expanding stream of publications,[6] should be of direct interest to social workers. The studies cover such subjects as the response of different cultural groups to pain, to medical care, to problems of rehabilitation; the effects of the social organization of the hospital on personnel and on patient reactions; and role interaction among the professions in medical settings. The findings of these investigations are becoming increasingly familiar to certain segments of our profession, particularly to workers in medical settings.

Reports of studies of the attitudes of foreign students to the United States and to their educational experiences in this country are also now

---

[6] Otto Pollak. "Cultural Factors in Medical Social Work Practice," *Medical Social Work*, Part I, Vol. III, No. 3 (1954), pp. 81-89; Part II, Vol. III, No. 4 (1954) p. 139-152.

Lyle Saunders, *Cultural Difference and Medical Care*, Russell Sage Foundation, New York, 1954.

Leo W. Simmons and Harold G. Wolff, *Social Science in Medicine*, Russell Sage Foundation, New York, 1954.

"Sociocultural Approaches to Medical Care" (special issue), *Journal of Social Issues*, Vol. VIII, No. 4 (1952).

available. This research project is sponsored by the Social Science Research Council with the assistance of the Rockefeller and Ford Foundations and the Carnegie Corporation.[7] The material published has considerable bearing on problems encountered by schools of social work in planning training for their foreign students. The reports still to come of these studies of cross-cultural education will undoubtedly be as relevant.

Studies of national character, several of which have been sponsored by Columbia University Research in Contemporary Cultures and by UNESCO, have direct relevance to the understanding of social work in other countries and have particular value to those who take on social work assignments abroad. The study of national character—a field that now engages the attention of psychoanalysts and anthropologists as well as tourists—is yielding illuminating insights about the characteristics of many societies, including our own.

The research that has been done in the field of mass communication and public opinion has also produced information useful to social work in its public relations program. Such subjects as the suitability of various media for particular audiences, evaluation techniques, the relative effectiveness of different methods in influencing public opinion have all received attention. Often even our public relations specialists are not aware of the extent of the social science information available for our use. Some effort, of course, may be required on our part to translate the material into a form suitable for social work purposes.[8]

The study of social stratification—the field in American sociology in which there has been extensive research and reporting—has produced considerable material of direct relevance to social workers. Between 1945 and 1952, some 333 articles and books on social class were published.[9] Of this total, at least 17 are of direct interest to social workers, and perhaps twice as many are of peripheral interest. This selected list deals mainly with questions of child rearing, family life, and mental illness in relation to social class.

---

[7] Reported in part in *The Annals*, "America through Foreign Eyes," Vol. 295, September (1954), *passim*.

[8] Herman D. Stein, *Measuring Your Public Relations*, National Publicity Council, New York, 1952, pp. 36-45.

[9] Harold W. Pfautz, "The Current Literature on Social Stratification: Critique and Bibliography," *American Journal of Sociology*, Vol. LVIII, No. 4 (1953), pp. 391-418.

The work of Robert Merton and others[10] in analyzing bureaucratic structure should be of help to us, not only in increasing our understanding of social organization in general, but in applying sound organizational principles to various social work processes, including administration and casework. Also, reference group theory is adding new dimensions to the understanding of human behavior. Much of the research in the field of group dynamics is, as group workers know, directly applicable to group work practice. The work of Talcott Parsons[11] and others, in analyzing American family structure, provides many new insights which should be of value in diagnosis and treatment, as well as in social planning.

IMPLICATIONS FOR SCHOOLS

Schools of social work have an important function in establishing a closer relationship between social work and the social sciences. They should take leadership in developing a conviction, in the whole field, about the usefulness and relevance of social science materials. They should be in a position to help agencies translate the academic material into suitable form for use in their professional activities. The schools, however, cannot meet the objective of bringing social science back into social work simply by accumulating social science information, or even by engaging in research. Somehow the social work practitioner must be given the impulse to keep abreast of these developments and must be trained in the capacity to use the knowledge. The scientific outlook must be incorporated into the profession as a whole.

A single specific course in the application of social science to social work, which now is given in some schools, has certain merits but it should be considered only a supplement to the basic educational responsibility of integrating pertinent social science material into all parts of the curriculum. However, such a specific course[12] can be a vital influence in promoting positive identification on the part of the students with a social science point of view. The objectives of such a course are: (1) to develop in the student an awareness that certain concepts and findings from the social sciences are

---

[10] Robert K. Merton and othen (eds.), *Reader in Bureaucracy*, Free Press, Chicago, Ill., 1952.

[11] Talcott Parsons, "The Kinship System of the Contemporary United States," in *Essays in Sociological Theory*, Free Press, Chicago, Ill., 1949, pp. 250-274.

[12] The writer is familiar with two of these courses, given at the New York School of Social Work, Columbia University; and Smith College School for Social Work.

important to social work practice and theory; (2) to broaden the student's understanding of the social and cultural aspects of human behavior; and (3) to help the student be selective and judicious in his future use of social science material and of social scientists.

The emphasis in these courses is on applying relevant content, from cultural anthropology, sociology, and social psychology, to social work purposes rather than on delineating theoretical subject matter for its own sake. Considerable attention is focused on "group membership determinants"—ethnic, religious, social class, and so forth—and their use: in casework, as an aid in diagnosis and treatment; in group work, as an aid in defining objectives for particular groups and in clarifying the group worker's role; in community organization, as a way of examining community structure in order to define need and to plan services. The instructor, naturally, can assume that full-time students have a basic minimum grounding in the social sciences and can refer to content taught in other parts of the curriculum. Some allowance must be made, however, for students whose previous school experience dates back several years and for those who come from other countries and therefore are not abreast of the social science concepts or vocabulary of this country. Throughout the course the instructor must help the students maintain a balanced point of view, avoiding the temptation to ride the hobby-horse of social science to the neglect of social work learning.

It is important, also, not to have such a course focused entirely on cultural differences of ethnic groups. It is true that social workers have a particular interest in this area and want to learn more about the cultural differences of Italians, Jews, the Irish, Puerto Ricans, Negroes, and so forth. Although this is an important content area and one in which social workers are responsive because of social work's emphasis on accepting differences, the course should not be limited to this one theme. In this connection, note should be made of the dangers of developing stereotypes, particularly in the discussion of ethnic materials. Although the value of generalizing about cultural patterns, on sound evidence, should be recognized, we must take care not to exaggerate the usefulness of these generalizations and forget the individual and his uniqueness.

It is not possible to predict at this time how this part of a school curriculum will ultimately develop. The current objective, however, is to instil in the student a social science point of view, with full awareness that we are training him to be a social worker. Gradually, we should succeed in strengthening the intellectual and scientific content of our teaching, both in class and field, with the help of the social sciences, and give the student a sound conceptual grounding in social work theory, practice, and research.

SUMMARY

Social work is rapidly strengthening its ties with the social sciences. We have much to gain from this relationship. To make the most of it, however, we must be careful to retain a firm grip on our professional function, which is a helping one. It must be distinguished from the academic function of the scientist. We can do this best by utilizing the social sciences in relation to our needs for theory and for collaboration in developing new knowledge and improving social work methods. The relationship between the two fields should be developed by professional associations, agencies, and schools. We shall have to develop increasing sophistication in order to make the best use of social science materials and of social scientists themselves. Such sophistication can most logically be achieved by working on special problems related to areas of service of social agencies, and by developing social science competence in certain practitioners—by means of basic courses and advanced programs. Social work has its own contributions to make to social science. These can be specified; they will grow out of interaction based on the needs of each field requiring the help of the other, rather than by social work seeking to aid social science without reference to its own purposes. The schools of social work have a vital stake in strengthening the social science content of their curricula, in class and field, in order to aid in the further development of social work practice and theory in the whole field.

9. Socio-Cultural Concepts in Casework Practice

By this time the renewed relationship between social work and the social sciences is quite apparent to everyone in our field. Our national and state conferences, our journals and books, and our teachings in schools of social work continue to give increasing recognition to this development. There is every reason to expect that this rapport will become even stronger. Since World War II the relationship between social work and the social sciences, which had lain dormant since the 1920's, became reactivated. Among the reasons have been the growing availability of "middle men," such as social workers with advanced training in the social sciences, who could bridge both fields; the interests of foundations, such as Russell Sage, in promoting social science for the professions; the availability of funds for demonstrations and collaborative research; developments in social science theory and research providing ideas and knowledge of increasing relevance to social work practice; and the growing interest of social science in the practice and data of social work.

Not least among the factors responsible has been the fact that psychiatry has taken up social science theory so that it has become a bit more respectable for social work through that avenue of influence. I refer here to such collaborative research between psychiatrists and social scientists that have been published: for example, the work of Stanton and Schwartz,[1] and that of Hollingshead and Redlich.[2] There are some basic approaches in the use of social science material that I think we ought to be aware of. The develop-

Reprinted with permission from *Smith College Studies in Social Work*, Vol. 29, No. 2 (February, 1959), a version of this article was delivered as an opening presentation at the Supervisors' Conference, Smith College School for Social Work, July, 1958.

[1] Alfred H. Stanton and Morris S. Schwartz. *The Mental Hospital* (New York: Basic Books, Inc., 1954).

[2] August Hollingshead and Frederick C. Redlich. *Social Class and Mental Illness* (New York: John Wiley & Sons, Inc., 1958).

ment, first of all, is not a fad; when content is relevant and important, it has to be studied and not brushed on lightly. We should have no interest in substituting one jargon for another, or adding a new jargon. This is content to be mastered and not a bundle of impressive terms and phrases to be added to our vocabulary. It is content to be approached with respect for its complexity and its contribution, and also its limitations.

Moreover, in dealing with this content we should have our professional practice in mind and not look at it from an academic point of view. As social workers we are not interested in becoming sociologists, nor in schools of social work should we be interested in training sociologists. For that matter, our primary concern is not social science theory for its own sake, any more than we should be interested in psychological theory for its own sake. Our problem is to select out of the vast body of knowledge in the various social sciences that content which is most relevant to practice. Unless the material makes a difference sooner or later to ways in which people can be better helped by social workers, the content is not appropriate to social work. It is important also that we keep in mind that social science deals in generalizations—in terms of trends and tendencies. It does not attempt to explain any given individual. The data of social science are mainly concerned with variations in behavior among groups in different locations in society. These data do not explain why Mr. X. behaves the way he does, but they should help us to understand Mr. X. better in the light of his particular social environment.

When we speak about the social environment we mean more than the traditional use of the term "social." We have characteristically thought of the environment in terms of what meets the eye: housing, jobs, etc. These concerns are very important and I hope they will always remain important to us. When we look through the perspective of social science, however, we should have a view of individual and group behavior which also takes account of more underlying influences of the social and cultural systems at work. The operations of these influences are as subtle and as potent and as requiring of the same kind of disciplined learning as are the inner psychic and emotional experiences of the individual.

It should be clear that one of our chief problems is selection—just what is most appropriate to our use? I am going to run through some basic concepts which I feel are central for our purposes. I am not going to try to present these concepts in highly concentrated and intensive fashion, but rather to indicate their general significance and the nature of their relevance to casework practice.

FAMILY STRUCTURE

First, let us take the concept of family structure. There are many patterns of family organization in the world and there are many varying patterns within our own country. The fact is that the kind of family we regard as most typical in the United States—mother, father and children—is actually a minority among the family patterns in the world. In many parts of Africa, Asia and South America, and in rural societies elsewhere, what is most common is some variant of the extended kinship family. Characteristically, this kind of family includes many relatives in the household and the kinship relationship is a highly significant one and remains significant throughout life. Most extended relationship groups are patriarchal, that is, the father is the source of authority in the household and he keeps this position throughout life with respect to his children. These are authoritarian type families, and in the more authoritarian the marriage partner and the future occupation of the child are determined by the parents. Even from these brief characterizations one can see the contrast with the more typical American family, which is the urban, white, middle-class family. Here we have a family which starts with the marriage of husband and wife. This is a new family, and when children come they are part of it. When they grow up and marry, however, they start families of their own, and they are actually reared towards independence as the ideal. We have come to think of this family as more democratic than authoritarian. In other words, husband and wife tend to have more equal authority than in the extended kinship type, and children are groomed for independence, rather than for lifelong acceptance of the parental will. Our type of family is characterized by a strong emphasis on individualism. The marriage itself is the union of two individuals rather than, in the extended kinship type, more nearly the union of two family lines.

What is significant for us is to see the various patterns of family organization that are possible, and the fact that they make for different kinds of family balance. While we all probably understand the virtues and the difficulties in the kind of family we have grown up in, we are less likely to see the consequences of somewhat different patterns of family structure. In the urban middle-class family, which we call the "nuclear" family, we can note the inherent strengths in its adaptability to our economic life, in its mobility, its stress on individuality, and its intense relationship between parents, and between parents and children. There are characteristic strains, too. The very intensity of mother-child relationships creates considerable vulnerability in this regard: "When it is good it is very, very good, and when it is bad it is, if not horrid, at least not so good." There tends to be an accent on achievement to attain status. Anxieties are generated by the very choices to be made in the absence of traditional standards. To find guide-lines in child-rearing, parents search for authority and expertness outside of their own upbringing. By contrast, the extended kinship family structure has a good deal of stability in terms of values, clarity of roles throughout life, and family interdependence, but it is much less adaptable to rapid economic and social change, and it is not oriented to independence on the part of the children. It is, furthermore, a family system in which power tends to be invested in the father and women do not have equal rights with men.

By understanding the concept of family structure and the consequences of different types of family arrangements, we can see the various ways possible for family interaction. The kind of family we know best, as well as families in diverse ethnic groups and different social classes, can become much more easily understood. We should be able to see further that there is, perhaps, not any one ideal type of family, that the kind of family that tends to develop in a given society is one that has been strongly influenced by the larger social structure. We should be able to understand not only the existing social patterns in the Puerto Rican and Negro families and Eastern European Jewish families and Italian families in various social classes, but also the kind of changes in progress and therefore the kinds of strains that are being generated. An understanding of family structure should enable us to comprehend more sensitively the meaning of grandparents and other relatives in various types of families. In the American nuclear family the special problems of being wife and mother, or husband and father, are illuminated through the perspective of family organization—why it is, for example, that the American middle-class mother relies so heavily on the expert in family life and child-rearing, her constant search for "what is right," her inability to depend on her own mother for guidance. There is a kind of built-in anxiety, which has its values as well as its risks, although in clinical practice we usually come across the seamy side of this pressure. Finally, we should have a much more perceptive insight into the positive values of the so-called authoritarian families as well as awareness of the negatives.

ROLE

The second concept I would like to deal with is that of role. This is an important notion and one which has been given a great deal of study. To some extent it may even be over-stressed with our behavior seen exclusively through the medium of role theory. There is not much question, however, that social role belongs in our armament of essential concepts.

Role refers basically to the way in which an individual perceives himself and is perceived in relation to the expectations of society. I know that isn't a very helpful way of putting it, but it may satisfy the need for a quick definition before the term is further discussed. Sometimes the fact of a definition is more reassuring than its content.

Every individual, of course, occupies many roles in life: family, age, friendship and occupational roles. These may all be in harmony with one another, or there may be various types of strains arising through the attempt to meet the diverse demands of these roles. One type of strain is *role-conflict;* that is, the successful fulfillment of one role is seen as making it impossible to fulfill successfully another role. When the pressure to meet the demands of both is equally intense, then such efforts are seen by the individual as mutually incompatible and the individual will suffer from role conflict. For example, a husband who feels he must work late at his job in order to be a success and also to be home in order not to disappoint his wife, again is experiencing distress induced by the strains of conflicting kinship and occupational roles. Or one may see role-conflict in occupational terms alone where the role is defined differently by different groups, and the attempt by the individual to meet all the definitions induces strain. Thus, in the article by Ohlin, Piven and Pappenfort[3] on the social worker in probation and parole, the varying definitions of the social worker's role from the standpoint of the court, the community, and the social work profession, all combine to develop conflict in the probation worker.

A second type of strain is *role confusion.* Not knowing just what is expected of one, the absence of role models with whom to identify, can make it difficult to find a clear self-image with respect to a given role. For example, the father's role in the modern American family is subject to considerable role confusion. Just what is masculine and what is not? What does it mean to be a good father to children? Is one head of the family or is one not? Is the father supposed to help with the housework and wash the dishes? Is the father the "autocrat of the breakfast table" or a congenial "pal" to his children? Role confusion tends to set in as roles are changing, and unless there are inner resources to help the individual develop guides that are sound *for* himself, role confusion may be experienced as a very potent strain.

---

[3] Lloyd E. Ohlin, Herman Piven and Donnell M. Pappebfont, "Major Dilemmas of the Social Worker in Probation and Parole," *National Probation* and *Parole Association Journal*, Vol. 2, No.3. (July, 1956), 211-225.

A third type of strain *is role discontinuity,* and this refers to the lack of preparation for succeeding roles, particularly age and sex roles. In extended kinship type families, young children know what is expected of them in later ages because they have role models available with whom to identify. What it means to be a younger or older sister, a younger or older brother, an adolescent working into adult occupation, a girl preparing for later house-wifely duties, a husband, father, wife and mother, an elderly man, or elderly woman—what it means to be all of these—is clear to a child in the process of growing up. In our country we experience role discontinuity very strongly. Boys may have had no previous experience with wage earning or with the total view of the father's role, and may enter marriage without adequate preparation for its responsibilities. Similarly, a girl may never have experienced any of the responsibilities of taking care of a home or having managed young children. Old age is seen as a role for which there has been little preparation in our society, and the lack of such preparation in terms of previous life experience can induce very severe strain.

The implications for casework in its consideration of role theory are quite wide. Client problems often involve role conflict, role confusion, and role discontinuity. Much of our work lies in the area of helping clients to resolve such kinds of strains. When we see the problem in role terms as well as other terms, we can get a larger view of the client's problem and see it in much deeper social context.

SOCIAL CLASS

The concept of social class has until recently been almost totally neglected, if not avoided by social work. This has been so despite the fact that there has been more research in this branch of sociology than in any other, and a significant part of this research is concentrated on class differences in child-rearing, parental relationships, behavior in voluntary associations and other areas of direct interest to social work. I think it would be fair to say that psychiatry has been far ahead of social work in recognizing the implications of an understanding of social class. The Hollingshead and Redlich study on social class in mental illness[4] is a reflection of this recognition within the field of psychiatry.

---

[4] Hollingshead and Redlich. *Op. cit.*

Let us make clear that the concept of social class has nothing to do with democracy or non-democracy. The concept basically involves the fact that in every society that we know of there is a ranking system, a system of inequality based on one or more criteria by which the particular society differentiates among people, whether the criteria include wisdom, strength, beauty, riches, or whatever. Every society distinguishes among its members on the basis of those characteristics which it holds to be most important. When one groups individuals into "the highest," the next highest, and so on through the lowest ranking levels, one has been working with a concept of social stratification.

In our culture *social prestige* has been the dominant conception behind stratification theory and research, while *power*, particularly in economic terms, has been the prevailing conception in European sociology. Prestige and power do not necessarily go together. There are individuals of high prestige and low power such as main-line aristocratic families whose fortunes have ebbed but nevertheless rank high in prestige, or union leaders who may have considerable power but relatively low social prestige.

Our interest in social class is primarily in the area of differences in behavior or personality related to differences in social class position. For example, the studies by Davis and Havighurst[5] on the comparison of Negro and white children in lower class and middle class positions demonstrated that there were striking class differences with respect to toilet training, discipline, handling of sex, aggression, educational achievement, etc. Furthermore, the contrast between lower class and middle class was greater than between Negro and white. In other words, Negro lower class and white lower class had more in common in child-rearing patterns than did Negro lower class and Negro middle class. We have considerable material of this kind available, some of it verified, some of it only suggestive; a good deal of it is available, however, for research in social work terms and with the use of social work data. I think it should be evident that this kind of information can be very helpful to us diagnostically.

---

[5] Allison Davis and Robert J. Havighurst, "Social Class and Color Differences in Child Rearing." *The American Sociological Review,* Vol. 11, No. 6, December, 1946, 698-710. Also, Havighurst and Davis, "A Comparison of the Chicago and Harvard Studies of Social Class Differences in Child Rearing." *The American Sociological Review,* Vol. 20, No. 4, August, 1955, 438-443.

One of the concepts now associated in part with social stratification theory is that of the *reference group*.[6] One view of reference group concerns where in the social structure the individual actually identifies himself rather than where he may belong by empirical indices such as occupation or education. A lower-class mother whose reference group is in the middle class may tend to try to behave as though she were in a middle-class position. If this becomes impossible for her, we have the phenomenon known as *reference group conflict*. Sometimes in marital problems we find a father and mother identified with different reference groups. This can induce very severe strain since the expectations of each other would be incompatible.

We have considerable evidence about the consequences of rapid *social mobility* and the kinds of reference group strains that are thereby generated. Let me make clear the fact that when a given situation in general tends to produce strain it doesn't *necessarily* do so, and that different individuals can react quite differently to similar kinds of pressures. Thus, Mr. A. may be rising rapidly in the social scale and coming through fine, while individual B., who was doing the same, is experiencing all kinds of heartache. Knowing the types of dislocation which rapid mobility can induce does not tell us what the reactions are going to be for a given individual, but it should tell us where the areas of weakness are which *tend* to make for trouble. For example, in this upward mobility development we often see individuals who find themselves having to adjust not only to a new neighborhood but to a new educational level, new recreational and cultural interests and, in general, a new way of life, often to a new set of friends. The loss of familiar landmarks of behavior can be quite disorienting, and the search is sometimes to outdo one's neighbor in order to prove that one has "arrived." Here we have the familiar phenomenon of the nouveau riche and "keeping up with the Joneses." Such mobility change, however, can be experienced with relatively little stress under different conditions of preparation and where certain personality features are present. In either case, however, the caseworker would have some idea of where to look for the spots in which tension is likely to appear.

Occupation is, by all odds, the most important single index of social class position in our society. We haven't got the time now to consider why this is so, but some brief reflection, even without a mass of evidence, would

---

[6] The term "reference group theory" has been recently coined (by Herbert Hyman), but researches bearing on the concept of reference group have preceded the term, particularly those in *The American Soldier*, by Samuel Stouffer, et al, Princeton University Press, 1949.

indicate the validity of this notion. When one tries to place someone for the first time, the question "what does he do for a living?," or "what does her husband do for a living?," is likely to be the first approach for locating someone in the social structure. The importance of occupation as the standard bearer for the family, especially in middle-class culture, must be understood if one is to be sensitive to the attitudes of family members towards the father's occupation or to those conflict situations where both mother and father are working.

Among the other implications of social class for social work is the general issue of *social class values.* The question is being increasingly raised as to the values social work implicitly holds and whether these are not influenced by the position in society which social workers normally have. For example, what is our position regarding achievement or our concept of success? This has been an issue particularly in group work, but it affects casework as well. Do we tend to pressure lower-class individuals, who may have high achievement potential, to middle-class aspirations, or somehow feel they have failed if they do not aspire to "do better"? By the same token, do we judge people by middle-class standards and are we not more moralistic than we claim? Some introspection as to the ways in which our attitudes are shaped by social class influences would be a boon. We try to keep out own psychic needs from interfering with those of the client, but there may be social class influences of which we are not cognizant which are also in danger of intruding on the treatment situation. Let us keep in mind, of course, that the term "middle class" is not a naughty expression. The values included under middle-class values are standards of propriety, postponements of immediate gratifications, restraints on physical aggression, thrift, cleanliness, etc. Middle-class values are nothing to be ashamed of. What is important is not that we discard them but that we come to some secure position in using them or not using them with respect to those clients who may not share the same values or not share them to the same degree. Most important is that we be conscious of the fact that social class influences pervade the individual environment; that they are transmitted largely through the family, that they are the source of deeply held values, and that they are internalized and are as much a part of us as our psychosexual development. To ignore social class patterns related to ethnic, regional and other considerations can affect accurate diagnosis. Naturally, to repeat and underline the caution specified at the beginning of this discussion, one should not ever get into the position of stereotyping individuals on the basis of their social class backgrounds or present location in the social structure. One cannot know anyone's personality or pattern of behavior solely by knowing his social class position, but one can know what general influences he has been subjected to and often there are clues, in terms of reference group, for example, as to what to look for as critical indices in his life adjustment.

ETHNIC GROUP

The last concept that I would like to take up this morning is that of the *ethnic group.* The term ethnic has replaced such unsatisfactory terms as race and nationality. It refers to any group with a core of cultural homogeneity and would include the Irish, Negroes, Jews, Puerto Ricans, Italians, Kentucky hill folk, etc. The ethnic component is probably the easiest for us to understand. It has almost become synonymous with the term "cultural" although it is too restricted a use for this term. As social workers we tend to be accepting of difference and interested in ethnic differences. However, there is more to this ethnic component than meets the eye. We are beyond the superficial differences of dress and food preferences. Social workers have, for example, begun to note differences in family structure among ethnic groups. Studies have given us more insight to differences in relation to authority, to seeking help, to attitudes towards discussing personal problems, to responses to illness, and the like. The implications for diagnosis are extensive. When the client is not of the same ethnic group as the worker, it becomes most important systematically to raise such questions as, from an ethnic point of view, how does the client see the agency, the worker, and his problem? Would he tend to see the agency as authoritarian, as a political outfit, as essentially hostile, as belonging to him? Would he tend to see the worker as a possible friend, as in impersonal official, as someone who must be placated? Would he tend to define his problem in a way that would meet his perception of the kind of place he is in? In some ethnic groups it is much more customary to put one's request in material terms than not, even if the essential problem is not material. In those ethnic groups with modified extended kinship types of family systems it is rare to find individuals who would naturally discuss personal, intimate family problems with strangers, even professional strangers. In the American middle class this is quite common because of our reliance on the outside expert.

It is not necessary that social workers know every possible ethnic group. There is a good deal, in fact, that can be found out from the client. What is important is to know what to look for and where information is available. Where an agency has extensive clientele from a given ethnic group, it would be most important, of course, for staff to get a thorough orientation to the patterns and variations within that ethnic group.

Are not ethnic differences naturally taken into account? Isn't that simply good casework? It is true that a good caseworker would intuitively pick up differences, but why rely on intuition? How about those competent caseworkers who are not especially wired along intuitive lines? A profession is built through systematization of knowledge and an understanding of ethnic factors should be approached systematically.

I referred earlier to situations where workers do not come from the same ethnic groups as clients. Actually, an understanding of the ethnic factor is quite important even where the worker and client do come from the same ethnic groups. While the worker may have a rich understanding of given ethnic patterns there may be other problems at work. For example, if there is a class difference between the worker and client within the same ethnic group, this may pose special relationship problems. The worker may find himself demanding too much of the client, especially if they both come from a minority group. The client may view the worker with hostility or suspicion. There is no need to develop this here, but suffice it to say that a consciousness of the ethnic factor is as important when the worker identifies with the ethnic background of the client as when he does not.

May I emphasize that one should not confuse ethnic or "cultural" with "normal." Ethnic patterns, for example, may be interwoven with personality disorders. A sadistic father who happens to have been brought up in an ethnic group characterized by a patriarchal family structure remains a sadistic father, and to say, "Oh, that's ethnic," as if that explained him, is silly. Furthermore, it need hardly be stated that conforming to ethnic norms is not necessarily the same as being mature and "well adjusted," and conversely, not conforming to norms is hardly the same as pathological.

One might add that the *direct* use of cultural material with a client in a casework relationship can be dynamite, and like dynamite it can explode dangerously, or it can be used constructively. We have far too little systematic consideration of this matter and it is an issue to be carefully examined. What is important is that we realize that the ethnic dimension is a most profound one in the shaping of personality and behavior.

Among the other concepts one could discuss would be that of bureaucratic structure, but it is of less immediate concern than those considered previously. Since you will be hearing this term frequently, let me simply say that bureaucratic structure in the sense that we use it in social science is not the same as its newspaper meaning, but refers to a special type of organization with which we are very familiar in modem life, and there is no negative connotation to the word. An understanding of this area is particularly important in terms of administration and organizational behavior, and to some extent can help us also to see clients more clearly in terms of their special occupational settings.

I hope this rather informal presentation has at least suggested that to absorb appropriate social science content does not mean forgetting what one has learned as a caseworker. On the contrary, it is rather a question of building on what we have with additional knowledge and ideas that have become available to us. Our need is to incorporate some of these insights as a field, just as in the 1920's we began to incorporate the concepts of psychoanalytic theory. The real test of the implications of the kind of thing we have been talking about will come as it affects practice. The significance of these understandings should lie in the difference they make to treatment. As our field becomes more sophisticated in these areas we will have greater experimentation in practice, and the implications of social science content will become much more visible to us. Right now we can see quite readily the diagnostic implications of many of the concepts we are concerned with, but not as readily what to do about them.

It should be clear that there is no "case" without sociocultural content. There is always a social environment. There are social class factors, cultural factors, occupational factors, role factors, etc. in every case. I am not saying that these are always the crucial considerations, but they should be increasingly examined in a systematic manner and not taken for granted.

I hope we avoid taking either of two extremes in our attitude toward this social science content, either that "we have been doing it all the time" or "we cannot possibly master all this." There is content to be mastered; many social workers have already done so, others gradually are building it in to what we have developed in casework theory and practice all these years. Social science content is far from being the last milestone to be crossed. As our profession grows, we will have new knowledge and new kinds of ideas facing us to be mastered, and a hard-headed, objective, unthreatened position would, I think, be the most sensible one for us to have.

In a sense this meeting is a milestone for Smith since it is a formal recognition of the importance of this area for development in casework. I am sure the meetings we will have this afternoon and evening, and particularly the opportunity for open discussion, will help both to produce and to define questions and hopefully to dispel unnecessary concern or confusion. I hope I have not been responsible for adding too much to the latter.

10. Implications of Social Change Theory for Social Work Practice and Education: A Discussion Based on Dr. Irwin Sanders's Paper, "Approaches to Social Change"

Theories of social change have occupied not only sociologists but historians and philosophers for many centuries. Indeed, it is difficult for most people to avoid having if not a full-blown theory, at least some tacit assumptions as to why change takes place. Predestination or fatalism, sheer chance, invention, manipulation, devil figures or great men, metaphysical and materialistic explanations have singly or in combination roamed the imagination of mankind in attempting to explain the past and present, or predict the future. The search to explain, to interpret, has been part of man's attempt to locate himself in some rational way in the ebb and flow of human history, rather than to regard himself as a speck of dust blowing in random winds.

Today many professions are attempting to draw on these efforts not only to understand but to direct change. Dr. Sanders takes pains to remind us of the many different kinds of approaches towards change that there are within sociological theory alone, in his review of major theoretical perspectives. It is true, as he wrote, that the sweeping, grand theories are not easy to put to use, but they do represent more than intriguing intellectual explorations. These theories each have their value premises and individual philosophic orientations whose acceptance or rejection is of no small importance.

While we should be reminded of their vastness and the abstractions which they include, we need also to be cognizant of the fact that from many such seeming abstractions have come ideas, organizing concepts, that have proven quite utilitarian in character. Many of the concepts that we are now employing, such as anomie and bureaucratic structure, in turn have their

This chapter is based on a presentation delivered at the Council on Social Work Education Annual Program Meeting, Oklahoma City, January 21, 1960.

roots in larger theoretical systems. We tend to see the concept, the *point of contact* with utility in practice, but should also recognize the large area of theoretical exploration from which it emerges.

In terms of values we need only to turn to the contrasting theoretical positions of William Graham Sumner and Lester Ward, the former a proponent of an evolutionary school of social change, Social Darwinism, the survival of the fittest as applied to mankind. Ward, on the contrary, stressed man's capacity to control his own destiny and his obligation to do so in the light of democratic and humanitarian objectives. Ward's accent on purposive change, on the importance, as well as the potentiality of improving the welfare of mankind, represents an underlying value assumption which social work has carried forward to the present day.

Dr. Sander's review of other approaches to the understanding of change—acculturation, technological change, analysis of selected change processes and systemic change—make clear, if we had any illusions about it, that the understanding of change even within the discipline of sociology alone has been and is being attempted through very diverse directions.

The emphasis that Dr. Sanders has selected, that of change in social relationships, is in many respects a most congenial approach for social work. "Social relationships" constitutes a terrain which we cannot only grasp within the framework of much of our practice, but where we can and do see ourselves actually being able to achieve change. This area, as Dr. Sanders uses the term, includes not large social systems, such as nations, but would include communities, groups, organizations, and smaller structures, such as families. In all of these it is relationships between people that are ultimately affected.

It should be noted, parenthetically, that in the larger sphere of social reform we are related to more than social relationships, but rather to subsystems, in Sanders's definition "networks of groups which are functionally articulated," such as government bureaucracies and educational sub-systems.

In selecting this theme, Dr. Sanders has presented us with a conceptual framework which defines where change takes place within the context of social relationships; connected statuses, status hierarchy, role repertoires and normative patterns. He has not attempted to develop an entire theory, but to clarify one approach with which he has worked directly in the field. To illustrate certain of his concepts: in leadership development in a small town one can see new *statuses* emerging as a consequence of change efforts.

Agencies that have passed through a stage where professionals gain control of service activities rather than lay volunteers have seen change in *status hierarchy*. *Role repertoires* in many boards of voluntary agencies are in the process of change where the status of board member has not been altered but where the role of the board member has begun to minimize or even to exclude fund raising; a search for a new role repertoire is, therefore, in the picture. *Normative patterns* may be seen as the locus of change when in educational work with parents the attempt is made to change child-rearing attitudes and beliefs.

With respect to sources of change Sanders emphasizes particularly the importance of determining whether the change came from within or without the system that was eventually changed. In this area of sources of change we have too little knowledge, and it is one of the places where we look to social science for far more clarity.

In regard to the threefold division of cataclysmic, socio-cultural drift, and directed change that Sanders refers to, it is, of course, directed change that we are primarily interested in. Cataclysmic change in terms of wars, floods, and other disasters, represent eventualities that social work can hardly do much about controlling, preventing, or re-directing. As for "socio-cultural drift," I gather this refers to long-term secular changes. These are important to us since we should recognize trends, the direction of movement, whether it is in changing family systems and courtship practices, or in recreational patterns, in order to interpret for ourselves more clearly both the advantages and strains such trends induce, and where directed change would fit in or run counter to long term trends of these kinds. Parenthetically, may I note that the term "drift" in this connection seems rather questionable, as if such changes have no recognizable etiology and are sheer happenstance.

Sanders emphasizes and interprets the stages of directed change in terms of:

1. Confrontation—preceded by initiative and planning.

2. Evaluation—by those who are on the receiving end of the change in terms of their own values and existing social relationships.

3. Decision—where the innovation is accepted.

4. Elaboration—where the change is fitted into other relationships.

It is of interest to contrast this process of analysis of stages of change with that of Lippitt, Watson and Westley, in their study of "The Dynamics of Planned Change."[1] The Lippitt group deals with what they term four "client systems": the individual, small group, large organization, and community systems. While Lippitt and his colleagues use "client systems" to cover all individuals and groups with whom professionals deal in a context of change, my own disposition is to dispense with this term. While I am a firm believer in the necessity of concepts and abstractions, I am a bit uncomfortable at having a caseworker seeing a troubled mother conceptualized as a change agent in inter-action with a system. Moreover, the whole notion of "client" with respect to communities may be stretching the term somewhat beyond the bounds of utility. If one is referring to social change theory I believe both the term and the concept of "target system" as utilized by Charles Loomis, and others, is preferable to "client system."

In the course of their analysis Lippitt and his colleagues define the sequence of the change process as follows:

1.   Devlopment of a need for change.

2.   Establishment of a change relationship.

3.   Working towards change through:

    a.   Clarification or diagnosis of client systems problem

    b.   Examination of alternative routes and goals

    c.   Transformation of intentions into actual change efforts

4.   Generalization and stabilization of change.

5.   Achieving a terminal relationship.

If one compares the two sets of sequences—the approach Sanders has outlined and that of the Lippitt group—and ignores differences in terminology, one notes an essential similarity between the two. The major differences lie in the Sanders model being more highly generalized and applicable to self-directed, internal change—as well as to change from outside the system; while the Lippitt approach is related to external change efforts, or change as applied by an external agent. What the Lippitt model supplies, however, is the attribute of relationship between the change agent and the

---

[1] Lippitt, Ronald; Watson, Jeanne; Westley, Bruce. *The Dynamics of Planned Change*, Harcourt Brace and Co., New York, 1958.

"target system." For social work purposes this aspect of the process is often essential, since change efforts with which we are occupied are most typically those induced by a professional outside the system being changed.

There is, however, another context of relationship in which the change agent may be seen as closely involved with the "target system" In the presentation of systemic change theory that Charles Loomis projects, and to which Sanders refers, Loomis lays particular emphasis on the relationship of the change agent to the "target system." At the risk of over-summarizing and over-simplifying his thinking, Loomis' position[2] is that in certain contexts of change, where there is a directed or planned approach, the change agent attempts to win the confidence of the "target system," builds up his own prestige and power, and later may manipulate what he has gained in prestige and power in order to bring about the change, much as a parent may manipulate the love and respect which he has gained from a child, as well as his power position, in order to affect and influence the behavior and character of his child. In this context the change agent attempts to present to the target system an opportunity to adapt to new ways of behaving which are represented by the change agent as being more desirable or effective. In Loomis' terms, the change agent then becomes part of the target system by "systemic linkage." In other words, the system with which the change agent is personally concerned becomes combined with the target system. In this connection, the relationship is not simply a relationship of a disinterested professional helper whose own life and activities are uninvolved in the target system to be changed, but rather one whose values and behaviors are definitely engaged with the values and behaviors of those to be changed.

One of the clearest illustrations of such engagements is that of the work being done by the Cornell anthropologist, Allan Holmberg[3], and his colleagues in a hacienda in Peru. They have been attempting over the course of several years to modify the patterns of the Indian peons in this community, to help them assume more direction for their own affairs and to achieve improved social and economic organization. In this effort the Cornell group has engaged in what Holmberg calls participant intervention," as contrasted

---

[2] Loomis, Charles. "Toward a Theory of Systemic Social Change" in *Interprofessional Training Goals for Technical Assistance Personnel Abroad*. Council on Social Work Education, 1960, pp. 188-189.

[3] Holmberg, Allan. "Participant Intervention in the Field." Human *Organization*, Vol.XIV.No.1 (1955). Also, "Land Tenure and Planned Social Change: A Case from Vicos, Peru," *Human Organization*, Vol. 18, Spring, 1959, No. 1.

with both participant observation and non-participant intervention. They are not apart from the group being helped but their activities have been rather thoroughly interwoven with those of the area's residents. The objective of the Cornell group is actual change as well as the study of change, but they do not dissociate their own lives and activities in this process from the group to be affected. This concept is of importance to us, since we tend to see the professional helper as having a "hands off" relationship with those to be helped. But similar involvement with the "target system" may be seen in much of community organization in general, and community development in particular; and may also be seen in current experimental efforts to reach lower class clients where they live and through less depersonalized relationship than we normally assume.

The accent on *social change processes* which Sanders's paper highlights, is most important to us in social work. It alerts us to the fact that in attempting to induce change in one system the change agent may be affecting other systems, running counter to their influence or otherwise inducing effects over which he has no control. We have learned that changing an individual will bring repercussions to his family, and the very definition of our change focus has been altered to take these relationships into account. On a larger scale, efforts to increase productivity in an agricultural system may affect the existing political power structure or the family system. An attempt to develop neighborhood improvement through better sanitation, housing inspection, and more recreational centers may run connter to the activities of the local political machine. A plan to develop seemingly more efficient and rational administration procedures in an organization may have unforeseen consequences in the resistance of the informal group sub-structure within the staff.

The more we can perceive the manifold reactions set in motion by our change activities, the more effective our professional efforts can be in defining more clearly our objectives, anticipating resistance, and in mapping strategies of intervention and change that can include oblique as well as head-on directions. The better, too, will we be able to work with professionals in other fields and draw on their fields of competence. Among these fields, incidentally, we should not forget the agricultural extension agent, whose experience has much to teach us and who shares many approaches in common with social work.

At this point, it is important that we recognize that the social sciences have not yet provided us with a combination of theoretical depth and action prescriptions in the area of social change comparable with the psychoana-lytic model, or its major theoretical variants, in the area of individual change. We look to the social sciences for an ever-increasing contribution to our understanding of the sources of change, the processes of change, and the consequences of various modes of intervention. This is not to minimize the importance of the contributions to date or to suggest that we have fully made use of them. What it does suggest is that our own efforts to induce change are important as data to be examined systematically. They should be recorded and examined in the light of existing concepts, without wad-ding ourselves as yet to any particular scheme. We can ourselves contribute to social science theory in this area if we make our practice experience available for analysis, and undertake our own research into change pro-cesses in the social work field.

HELP, CHANGE, AND CONTROL

There are two general problems in change theory as applied to social work, both of which I should like to pose and tentatively answer, but both merit, I believe, more concentrated exploration.

One problem arises if we accept an all-embracing conception of social work as constituting change. It is the general question of whether all help-ing is change and whether we may not be in danger of forcing our concep-tion of practice too uniformly into this concept. Great skill is often involved in helping a person stay just where he is without breaking down. A process of helping has nevertheless gone on. Must we conceptualize this also as a change process? Public assistance involves in many cases essentially meet-ing economic need. It is help. It is important. Does it also *have to* be change? Similar analogies can be drawn from all fields of social work practice. One can maintain that by and large directed change in individual, group and community properly represents one underlying function of the profession, and one that requires much more emphasis, but still only one. Every profes-sional activity does not, therefore, have to be gauged against the yardstick of change.

The second problem has to do with the relationship of social change to social control. As one of the institutions of society, social work serves an integrative function and adds not only to human potential for social pro-ductivity, but helps keep the larger social system in balance by rectifying ills and providing remedial measures. The major norms and values of society are, after all, represented by social workers who serve as models for identification in many practice contexts. Moreover, some social work roles are defined by society at large as peculiarly in the control area, as in protective services, such as probation and parole. The question becomes, can one simultaneously serve as an agent of change and an agent of control?

At the risk of seeming to raise a straw man only to have something to punch, if not knock down, may I suggest that the seeming paradox may to a large extent be a matter of relating to different objectives, immediate and long range. To work intensively with a delinquent in order to help the individual become a non-delinquent and thus conform to social norms, is to serve a latent function of social control, but also a manifest and immediate function of individual change, To attempt to change social conditions in a community that are contributing to delinquent behavior, is likewise to serve an ultimate social control function, but an immediate social change function. The concept of social control in this sense tends to recede into the general backdrop of what is functional for social organization. The issue of change versus control becomes less of an issue if change is seen as related to the direct and manifest objective and control constituting a latent indirect function for social organization. In the case of the protective services, control is more visible, even where there is an accent on individual change, and here at times a conflict may indeed exist.[4] Thus, in all of social work, change and control functions are both present at any one time, in social work, not necessarily in conflict, but one tending to be in the forefront, the other in the background.

Change need not, of course, actually serve to bolster the social system in which it is introduced, even where it is so introduced. Colonial powers who provided education to groups of so-called natives because literate manpower was needed to help man their organization, found that literacy did not stop with reading instructions and obeying orders. The expansion of education helped give rise to an intellectual elite who eventually moved into positions of power and changed the system. Nevertheless, it may still be maintained that the latent social function of professional change efforts is towards enhancing the effectiveness of the larger social system. Both of

---

[4] Such conflict is vividly illustrated in the case of the prison where an individualized treatment orientation is included in the program. Cressey, Donald R. "Limitations on organization of Treatment in the Treatment-Oriented Prison," in *Theoretical Studies in the Social Organization of the Prison*, Social Science Research Council, March,1960. An effort to harness the control to the change functions, and minimizing conflict between them, may be seen in the "therapeutic milieu" approach in certain mental hospitals.

these issues—change in relation to help and to control—merit more analysis than we have yet given them.

SOCIAL CHANGE AND INDIVIDUAL CHANGE

The accent on dispassionate analysis of social change has not, and should not, obscure the persistent concern for social reform, which is simply another way of referring to planned social change towards the fulfillment of humanitarian objectives. For some years the expression of this concern has been coupled with the argument that the concentration on individual psychology in social work is to a significant extent responsible for restricting the professions' energies that are directed to social reform and to the fulfillment of the broad social objectives of social work. Implicit in this argument, and occasionally quite directly expressed, is the equation of casework with concentration on individual personality. The critique then settles down essentially to the proposition that the preponderance of casework values, as well as casework activity within the field of social work, has been a deterrent to the development of active professional responsibility in stimulating change toward social reform objectives.

By inference the other two segments of our social work methods triad—group work and community organization—are at least innocent bystanders to the spectacle of casework holding back social action, or at most, protagonists of change fighting an uphill battle against the passive resistance of hosts of caseworkers engaged actively in individual help but apathetic to social change.

It is time, I think, that we reconsidered this somewhat too convenient diagnosis of any institutional malaise we may have in the area of planned social change. It is important to distinguish first the different systems with which practitioners are most directly concerned. The range of systems include: personality, interpersonal organizational, and larger collectivity systems. If we view these as a continuum from individual to societal systems, we can identify the primary (but not exclusive), professional concentration of the caseworker as traditionally on the personality and interpersonal systems; of the group worker on the interpersonal and organizational systems, and of the community organizer on the organizational and larger collectivity systems. Over the past years sound emphasis has been given in curricular development as well as in social work objectives to prevent a too parochial concentration of any method in relation to one given system, and to enhance understanding of the inter-relationship of all of these systems.

This has meant both that the caseworke his practice should not ignore the community, nor the trends and the strains in society at large that would add to the understanding of individual personality or interpersonal relations, any more than the community organizer should ignore personality and interpersonal relationships in working towards change in organizational or inter-organizational community policies and programs.

Awareness of the inter-relationship of these systems does not, however, alter the necessity of having at any one time a primary focus of change for the practitioner. If there has been no growth or change or increased resourcefulness on the part of the individual client the caseworker cannot deem her activity in that case as successful, even if, during the course of the case, the intake policy of another agency was altered for the better. Neither can the administrator or community organization worker consider his work effective when the program he is interested in promoting is completely bogged down, even *if* one of his lay committee members has "grown" or gained increased individual capacity and satisfaction as a result of his participation. In the first instance the caseworker should be trained to see the possible effects of agency policy on the welfare of individual clients, and definitely try to affect them, but from the vantage point of his proper and primary focus on the welfare of individual clients and families. In the second case the community organization worker needs understanding of individual motivation and may note or even indirectly affect the individual "growth" of a committee member, but do so in order to fulfill the primary objectives of his practitioner role, which is to influence policy, get a program under way, or otherwise affect an organizational or larger social sub-system.

It is as unsound from this point of view to accuse a caseworker of unconcern with larger social issues because he is primarily concerned with individual and family relationships as to accuse the community organizer of unconcern with individual values because he may be primarily interested in developing a more rational plan of inter-agency cooperation. Each practitioner has a primary focus of activity on the basis of which the effectiveness of his work is primarily evaluated.

Furthermore, the group worker and community organizer, while dealing more directly with organizational and societal problems are not, by virtue of that fact, necessarily operating within the framework of social reform or directed social change. They may be concentrating on limited aspects of program or process, and not necessarily to definable social objectives. Thus, a community organization worker who sees as his function the servicing of a lay committee as a resource person and facilitator, without the power or the intent to influence the direction of its activities, is no more a social change agent than the clinic worker engaged in play therapy with a child. The community organizer may be involved in the necessary work of committee change and development, but this is hardly the same as being a social reformer or engaging in social change.

It may be maintained, rather, that if there is any one serious deterrent within social work to social change it is the emphasis on technique and process for its own sake, in whatever method, with an under-emphasis on social values, on purpose and objective, and not the spurious conflict as between an individual and a social emphasis in the practitioner's primary role.

It must be conceded, however, that a practice context which puts a premium on the personality system as the object of change does provide conditions which can support a conservative view of social change, or simple lack of interest. When etiology of individual problems is seen exclusively in intra-psychic or inter-personal terms the social milieu can be more readily ignored as the object of change and the entire emphasis placed on individual adjustment. This can be true, incidentally, of the community organizer as well as the caseworker, depending on his training and orientation; and it should in this sense be emphasized that it would be handicapping to the community organizer if his role model as a change agent were a caseworker, since this practitioner role is in key respects inapplicable to the demands of community organization.

To those not interested in modifying any aspects of the social structure, either out of conviction or out of apathy, an exclusive concentration on psycho-dynamics can provide a safe retreat, but this is hardly equivalent to saying that concentration on individual or family needs *means* that there is a necessary disinterest in the larger social environment. The point need hardly be documented that outside of the practice context, caseworkers have, after all, been among those most active in the promotion of change in social welfare policies, and one would be hard put, without much better evidence than we how have, categorically to assume that caseworkers, by and large, have attitudes to social change more or less different from those of social workers in other practice disciplines.

Outside of their immediate practitioner relationships, there are change target systems in which virtually all social workers can be involved. One is the very setting in which the worker operates. Organizational change partakes of all of the facets of social change analysis which we have been addressing. A public welfare agency, a community council, a child guidance clinic, changes as any social system must change. Our professional curriculum, it may be noted, should include an understanding not only of the responsibility for policy control residing in the Executive and Board, but also to the relevant modes of staff participation in influencing change.

Our professional organizations also provide channels for social change activity not necessarily provided for within the practice context. For all of our students, an understanding is necessary of the purposes and structure of professional organizations as related to social change objectives. The NASW social policy statement of 1959 should be required reading in this connection.

Social workers can also function within their communities in civic organizations, drawing on their professional expertise to carry forward activities in the broad public interest.

MANIPULATION AND CHANGE

Perhaps the concentration on directed and planned change will enable us to rethink the implications of some of our cherished concepts which serve to deny to the practitioner the prospect of specific goals. Thus, the concept of self-determination sometimes has the effect of inhibiting the social work student from conceiving of definite objectives for client or client groups. Instead, the student is led to think of process which "enables" the client to perceive his own best interests. The aversion to manipulation, in the sense of tricking a client into superficially accepting a worker's preconceived objectives, is well founded. The fact is, however, that social workers in all walks of social work life find themselves moving their clients, or "target systems," toward objectives which are considered professionally in the best interests of those who are served. This does not mean compelling people to accept what they do not wish to or are not ready for, or preventing choice. On the contrary, it can mean maximizing choice and self-determination but without tossing aside the professionals obligation to influence the direction of change when he is sure of what it should be. To accept the role of change agent is to accept the responsibility of knowing where change should take place, if such knowledge is possible while understanding that there remain, of course, situations in which we can rely chiefly on process when the end is not clear or within our professional responsibility.

SOCIAL CHANGE THEORY AND THE PROFESSIONAL CURRICULUM

It is difficult to comment on curricular implications of social change theory without reference, at least briefly, to a general consideration of the relationship of social science theory to social work education.

As we approach areas of knowledge and theory that offer new promise of utility for social work we are tempted to make room for it by squeezing the rest of the curriculum a little tighter, if we can, giving a hypodermic injection into an existing oourse, or replacing one piece of content with another. If we cannot slip it in somewhere at the Master's level we might do so at the Doctoral level, and if we can do none of these things then frustration is the order of the day. Sometimes we treat our curriculum like a stew which rests on a warm burner, and every once in a while we toss in another content bone, hoping it will enrich the stew. I tried that once—with a stew—and it was no enriched concoction. It was just a mess.

The question of how much theory in what disciplines can and should be included in undergraduate education is being considered by our field in other connections. It is fair to say that by and large thus far we have depended on such undergraduate preparation for the students' exposure to orientations in the social and behavioral sciences, as part of his basic background education, to the extent that we have required such theoretical background at all.

Assuming this premise, the problem at this point is how much of what theory the budding social worker really needs, particularly in the existing professional curriculum. If we are talking about theory in the basic sciences from which social work draws we have quite a list. Even when we restrict ourselves to the social and behavioral sciences alone, and exclude all psychological theories and theory in the biological sciences we have: social change theory, stratification theory, role theory, reference group theory, culture theory, organizational theory, small group theory, family organization theory, and the list can be prolonged—sometimes you can't tell which theory is at bat without a score-card and, as we all know, some of these areas, as in the case of social change, have complex stores of knowledge included and many sub-divisions.

Our current and basically justified enthusiasm for utilizing social science theory in social work should not blind us to the fact that a generalized push in all social science theory directions at once can have not an energizing but a potentially disorienting effect on social work practice and education. This may seem a strange emphasis to make on the part of one who for some years has been, and continues to be, an advocate of including a socio-cultural perspective in our basic professional curriculum, but I do not believe it is an inconsistent position.

We are faced with an enormous range of theory from which to draw and we have the need to develop our practice theory as well. If we insist that social work students have to know—really know—all such theory in addition to learning "practice theory" and method, we can be in for an endless chain of frustration, and our practice can become so over-conceptualized that social workers wouldn't know which theoretical end was up.

Yes, our students need theory, actually more theory than they now get, but not *all* theory in equal doses. Social workers deal with practice situations, which do not conform to neat theoretical models. It is rare that practice situations require only one theoretical orientation, but it is rarer still that they would require, let us say, a score of theories to draw upon. We need to apply extraordinary care in selectivity, both in order not to overwhelm students and to make sure we are offering something they can make use of. While a range of concepts is necessary for all students, as we are all aware, to understand the elements of individual and social behavior and the disciplines of helping, concepts are not theories. They are the building blocks of theory. We can regard the concept, as I have indicated previously, as the *point of contact* between the theory and the practice need, and students should be aware of the fact that salient concepts are usually the result of laborious theoretical development.

Depending on the primary method of practice field in which a student is engaged a given theoretical orientation should be more substantially developed, but they need not be equally developed for all. The range of potentially relevant concepts lies outside the scope of this discussion, but we may note illustratively social role, bureaucratic structure, ethnicity, social class, deviant behavior, as well as change agent, target system, the social relationship systems that Sanders has developed, and other concepts in the area of social change. All of these concepts should be related to their practice connotations so students can draw upon them and build upon them, and all students should be aware that there are theoretical roots to these concepts, but only sparingly and judiciously should be in the basic professional curriculum develop underlying academic theories beyond available undergraduate preparation. In the Doctoral curriculum it is a different matter. There, theoretical depth should be the focus of concentration.

I realize that these observations lie to some extent in controversial areas, but it seems to me that this issue of relevance needs continuously to be addressed even if different schools decide on different approaches, so that we as a field can equip ourselves to absorb and react to social science developments in our curriculum without the harrowing feeling that our back is constantly to the wall.

With this as a general position my basic comment on social change content in the curriculum can be very brief: basic concepts and an orientation to individual and social change for all students, selected theoretical development for group workers in, for example, small group theory, and for community organization in broader fields of social change theory, and for administration majors, if there are any, in organizational theory.

Building in more emphasis on the analysis of social change should not be impossible within the existing framework of our professional curriculum. The concept of a change process is hardly new to any of the social work methods, even if the terms "change agent," "client system" and "target system" have not been part of our vocabulary.

The possibilities of more refined analysis of basic change processes are exciting. Such an approach could serve to tie together more firmly the primary social work methods in a more inclusive frame of reference. Equally important, the concept of directed or planned change in which professional social work is engaged through its particular sets of functions makes more possible the utilization of knowledge of other professions and disciplines similarly occupied with individual and social change. Expanded areas of research are also opening up for the study of change processes add the effects of different approaches to similar objectives.

Attention likewise should be focused more intensively than heretofore on different change agent roles that social workers occupy, and the different consequences for strategies of change and for the extent and nature of the involvement with the system to be changed. The traditional casework practice setting provides a well defined stage for interaction with clients, highly specified and differentiated roles, and minimizes involvement between worker and client outside of this concentrated interaction. The stage is broadened, the lines less clear, the roles are more diffuse and less segregated in group work. And in community organization the struggle is often to maintain any recognizable professional boundaries at all, while the worker engages in practice activities where he is interacting with numbers of people in varying relationships with the practitioner. Similarly, non-traditional casework roles in neighborhoods and in residential institutions may require greater involvement with individuals and groups who are the recipients of service.

In addition, there is the consultant role which is often ignored in social work education, even though many of our graduates will find themselves in consultant positions. This role provides its own complexities. How active should a consultant be as a change agent? Can one be a consultant within the system in which one is consulting, or must it be an external position? How does one define the consultant's status and role in situations where a consultant has not previously been included? These and similar questions should be raised and referred to our curriculum.

CONCLUSION

Consideration of the area of social change has led to the suggestion that we should be building in the following themes to our course and our field teaching:

1. In social work we are dealing with individual, interpersonal, organization, and community, or larger collectivity systems of change. The practice situation will define the most appropriate target system, but the relatedness of the other systems should be understood by the social worker through training in both class and field.

2. All planned change involves both process and direction, both means and ends. An exclusive concentration on process and technique, in whatever practice context, evades responsibility for defining objectives. An exclusive concentration on achieving ends, even where successful, may make the achieved end spurious and short-lived, and can create effects more pernicious than the problem originally to be met.

3. Directed or planned change tends to follow given phases, from initiation to acceptance, to generalization of the change. Acceptance of change cannot be assumed until it is integrated within the total target system involved, whether the system is the personality in a single individual, the inter-relationships within the group, or given behavior or beliefs in larger collectivities.

4. Consideration should be given to inducing change when one is involved with the target system, as well as when one is essentially segregated.

5. All directed or planned change should be evaluated both in terms of process and achievement of objectives.

6. Basic concepts related to the sources of change, the processes of change, and the consequences of different ways of inducing change, should be

the common property of all students. Community organization students and group work students should have selective grounding in relevant aspects of social change theory.

7.   All social workers have a stake in social change. For some this will lie more directly within the practice context, for others it will be related but not central. Outside of the immediate practice context, however, channels for affecting social change exist, among them being organizational change, and working through appropriate professional and civic organizations.

8.   The relationship of help to change, and of social control to social change, needs further examination. It is suggested that not all help is change, and that in social work change functions and control functions can exist simultaneously, without necessarily being in conflict.

Finally, it is part of the merit of Dr. Sanders's approach to the analysis of social change that he deals with a context of social change which permits change to be directed, and that there is an implicit optimism in relation to man's capacity to control his own destiny.[5] Moreover, he has taken a utilitarian, pragmatic position which is timely for our purpose, rather than advocating at this time a single, all-embracing theoretical system. The interest of social work in theories of social change is not confined to a generalized concern about human affairs or to the esthetic pursuit of intellectual issues, but to the fact that social workers are substantially in the business of change, whether working with individuals, groups, organizations or communities. Whatever we can learn about the processes of change that can make us more effective in carrying out our professional task is worth knowing. The general theme of this meeting and the contribution of Dr. Sanders serves to highlight for us the richness of the concepts involved even when limited to aspects of change in the context of social relationships, and permits us to examine whether we have been as attentive as we should to the implications of concepts in this area in our curriculum.

---

[5] In this connection, it may be noted that Sanders's approach departs from the conservative ideology represented in sociology by the concern with "system maintenance," "equilibrium," and "homeostasis." His approach thus conforms to the expectation voiced by Lloyd Ohlin in a paper delivered at a previous CSWE meeting, to the effect that "the growing collaboration between sociologists and social workers may be viewed as a beginning step toward the development of systematic theory and practice methods for achieving social change." Ohlin, Lloyd, "The Development of Social Action theories in Social Work," proceedings, Annual Conference, CSWE, 1958.

Part Four
ORGANIZATIONS

11. Organization Theory—Implications for Administration Research

In this discussion we are concerned primarily with research stemming from organization theory that may contribute to our professional needs in administration, rather than to the development of organizational theory per se, recognizing that these objectives are not mutually exclusive. Absent from our present consideration are the researches, many valuable, that serve to answer specific problems in administrative practice and planning, but are not essentially oriented to theory.

The problems involved in addressing this subject are several: (a) the difficulty in classifying organizational theory; (b) the lack of definition of the issues in social work administration to which research is appropriate; (c) the paucity of research in social work administration that is not purely operational and specific to a given agency.

The student of organizational theory is confronted with a vast array of materials from diverse organizational sources, including governmental, industrial, political, labor, military, educational, general hospital, mental hospital, correctional. The theoretical concepts have been derived, in turn, from a variety of professional and academic disciplines: engineering, political science, public administration, economics, sociology (in several branches), social psychology, anthropology, history. It is not the function of this paper to review and assess theoretical positions or to arrange them systematically. The task of classifying this array of organization theory and interpreting it in some systematic manner does need doing.[1] It is a difficult

Reprinted with permission from Leonard S. Kogan, *Social Science Theory and Social Work Research* (New York: National Association of Social Workers, 1960), the following article includes comments from the book's author on the chapter discussion, as well as response to the comments from Dr. Stein.

[1] A recent effort in this direction was made by March & Simon, largely as an introduction to their own formulations. March, James G. & Simon, Herbert A., *Organizations*, John Wiley & Son, 1958.

enterprise and should be undertaken, perhaps, from a variety of analytical vantage points. In the absence of a definitive classification some framework, however limited, may be of some value in seeing the relationship of present and potential research in social work administration to the major themes of organizational thought. For our present purposes—without attempting a genuine typology—such orientations in organizational theory and analysis may be grouped in the following way:

1. Efficiency principles—the "scientific management" school, with its focus on maximum efficiency of production operations;

2. Administrative management principles emphases on rational structure and formal administrative systems, including executive functions and systems of delegation, departmentalization, authority, and control in large organizations;

3. Supervisor–work group and small group theory and analysis, including productivity and morale, leadership, interpersonal communication, supervisory roles;

4. Bureaucratic theory, including functions and dysfunctions of bureaucratic structure, relationships between formal and informal structures, power and authority systems, organizational change, role dilemmas, organizational conflict.

It should be emphasized that these four general headings and their subdivisions hardly exhaust the major emphases of organization theory. Moreover, there is considerable overlap among them, as well as continuity, and a specific piece of writing or research is not necessarily to be placed exclusively in one of these categories. These groupings may provide us, however, with a preliminary framework for the consideration of administrative problems in social work to which research has been or may become relevant.[2]

For present purposes, only brief consideration need be given to theory stemming from the earlier "scientific management" group, with its strong engineering emphases. The Taylor[3] approach of finding "the one best way"

---

[2] E.g., Chester Barnard's *The Function of the Executive* and other of his works may be seen both in relation to administrative management theory and bureaucratic theory.

[3] Taylor, F. W. *The Principles of Scientific Management*, New York, 1911.

to do things (in terms of cost and time) has, of course, left its mark (or made its contribution, if one prefers), particularly on industrial organization and to some extent on public administration. In its basic form, this approach would seem at present to have limited applicability to social work organizations, because of its central concern with the routinization of manual labor, and its governing view of personnel as adjuncts to machines (a view, in its premises of behavior, not inconsistent with the psychology of the pre-World War I period). The "efficiency" emphasis in mechanical and physiological terms (*e.g.,* in time–motion studies) conforms currently neither to the modes of social work activity nor to its ideology.[4]

Efficiency in nonmechanical terms, however, remains a legitimate object of investigation in social work settings for the purpose of developing rational planning procedures and bases for evaluation. The Hill–Ormsby study, for example, by providing a method for ascertaining cost and time equivalents for various agency activities, provides a means for certain kinds of agencies by which to develop criteria for efficiency. In a sense, therefore, this kind of study may be placed in the "engineering–accounting" framework of organizational analysis, without, however, necessarily imputing to it any of the psychological preconceptions of the earliest "efficiency" school.[5]

The "administrative management theorists" have had a potent influence not only on public administration, where this influence seems most strongly manifested; they have seen their formulations diffused throughout all fields of administration. Here we are in the tradition of Luther Gulick, Mary Follett, L. Urwick, and others who have been concerned with such concepts of organization and management as Division of Work, Coordination, Span of Control, Technical Efficiency, Executive Functions (POSDCORB),

---

[4] Because of the theories of behavior implicit in this approach, March & Simon, (*op. cit.* pp. 12-22), have termed it "physiological organization theory." In their conclusions, they observe that organization theory in the first quarter of the century was concerned with management principles in which personnel was essentially viewed as impersonal instruments of production; in the second quarter of the century, the "human relations" approach endowed human beings in organizations with feelings and motives; and that the next stage should be most concerned with their reasoning and adaptive properties.

[5] Hill, John G. & Ormsby, Ralph. "Cost Analysis Method for Casework Agencies," Philadelphia Family Service, 1953. "Administrative research" that is purely operational and related only to a particular agency's problems is, of course, not uncommon. The present discussion pertains to more "basic" social work research in Ernest Greenwood's use of the term. ("Social Work Research; A Decade of Reappraisal," *Social Service Review,* September 1957, pp. 315-316).

Decentralization, Line and Staff.[6] The concept of professional management received strong impetus from the work of these spokesmen for "underlying scientific principles" in administration.

The contribution of this body of work has been primarily in its concentration on the rational blueprinting of formal organizational systems. While it has been criticized for its "tendency to view the employee as an inert instrument performing the tasks assigned to him" and to ignore the motivations of individual behavior,[7] one cannot put this system of thought in the same class as the earlier Taylor school (in terms of the latter's underlying mechanistic psychology). Moreover, while "the tendency" to ignore motivation exists, the literature in this area makes frequent reference to attitudes and responses[8] to the psychology of leadership, to interpersonal relationships, and the like. If anything, there is an overly simplified view of motivation rather than an absence of concern with individual behavior, and a naive premise (by today's thinking) that if all is rationally conceived, then all will be well with organization and people.

There has been a considerable production of conceptual writing by these influential theorists, but it is difficult to locate empirical research associated specifically with this school. There would appear to be a connection, however, between the emphasis on the science of administration, particularly in the public service field, and the development of a research program in public administration. This program, with its slogan of "capture and record" (directed to administrative crises and processes), has resulted in a series of valuable monographs and volumes of case presentations, and also in the definition of professional issues in public administration

---

[6] See, for example, "Notes on the Theory of Organization," by Luther Gulick, in *Papers on the Science of Administration*, ed. by L. Gulick & L. Urwick, Institute of Public Administration, Columbia University, 1937.

Courses in administration stemming from this general emphasis have given much attention to POSDCORB (Planning, Organizing, Staffing, Coordinating, Reporting, Budgeting), the development of organization charts, etc. (See Waldo, Dwight, *The Study of Public Administration*, Doubleday, 1955, pp. 45-47).

For an adaptation to social work of some of the concepts in this body of work, see Aronson, Albert H., "The Application of Business Techniques to the Administration of Social Agencies," from *Administration, Supervision and Consultation*, Family Service Association of America, 1955.

[7] March & Simon, *op. cit.*, pp. 29-30.

[8] *E.g.*, Follett, Mary Parker, *Freedom and Coordination*, Management Publications Trust, 1945, *or Dynamic Administration*, ed. by Metcalf & Urwick, Harper & Bros., 1942.

worthy of research interest.[9] It may be noted, parenthetically, that a case reporting program may not be amiss for those concerned with the progress of social work administration, particularly in view of the relative lack of more systematic types of research.

With respect to the theory and research involved in the supervisor–work group relationships, one may note that there has been significant research as well as theory, and hazard the impression that administrative thought in social work has been relatively unaffected by either. The relationship between productivity and morale, so often a theme in this area of organizational research, does not appear to have influenced appreciably either concepts or research in social work administration. One element is undoubtedly a problem of defining productivity, outside of those social work organizations (or divisions) where there is considerable routinization of work. Yet social work has a set of "morale" problems peculiar to professionally staffed agencies; for example, the conflict of loyalties among professionals, as between the organization (which seeks to gain their loyalty) and their larger professional reference group.[10]

In contrast to theory directed to the total structure of an organization, morale studies in industry have largely centered on the work group and the supervisory relationship, along the lines developed by Elton Mayo and stimulated by the Western Electric studies, and drawing also on small group theory, as in the work of George Homans. It is of interest to see the potential bearing of morale factors in the social work agency context. Thus, in one study,[11] morale was defined as being composed of five satisfaction dimen-

---

[9] Anderson, William & Gaus, John M. *Research in Public Administration,* Public Administration Service, Chicago, 1945. Much of the writing in public administration, and the evaluation of case studies, is related to value considerations—e.g., making the organization more responsive to democratic processes. By contrast, Herbert A. Simons, in works like his *Administrative Behavior,* separates values from the scientific study of administration, and places values themselves as objects of study.

[10] Gouldner, Alvin W. "Organization Analysis," in *Sociology Today; Problems and Prospects,* ed. by Robert K. Merton *et al.,* Basic Books, 1959; particularly in his discussion of the "cosmopolitanism" of experts. Note might be made here of the problem of staff turnover, which is affected by this problem as well as the more usual contributing conditions.

[11] Kahn, Robert L. and Morse, Nancy S. "Relationship of Productivity to Morale," *Journal of Social Issues,* No. 3, 1951.

Another perspective on what may be construed as the morale dimension is the relationship of the *socializing process* of the organization (where the individual is an agent for the realization of organizational objectives) to the *personalizing process* (where the

sions," or classes of dependent variables: (a) intrinsic job satisfactions, (b) involvement in immediate work group, (c) identification with the larger organization, (d) satisfaction with immediate supervisor and employees, (e) satisfaction with reward system of the company (including non-monetary rewards).

This line of analysis can be quite suggestive in terms of social work agency studies. The problem arises in the definition of the independent variable, for productivity in the industrial situation can be defined (as in the above case) as "the number of units of work in a given time interval," whereas such a concept has at present only limited applicability to social work organizations.

Difficulty with the concept of productivity is also one, but only one, of the problems that helps explain the absence of research on organizational effectiveness in social work. There is apparently a paucity of concepts that can be operationalized and insufficient methodological development in the study of organizational effectiveness in all fields, although interest in this line of attack has been growing.[12] The difficulties in the way of devising measures of effectiveness, even when confined to supervisor–employee work groups alone, are considerable, as Pfiffner has pointed out.[13] They are even more complex in the context of social work settings, not only because of the lack of agreement on productivity standards, but also because of the evanescent criterion of quality of service. To approach the area of organizational effectiveness requires a concept of organizational goals in terms which

---

individual tries to make the organization the agent for the realization of personal objectives). The simultaneous operation of the two, in Bakke's terms, is the *fusion process.* Argyris, Chris, "Fusion of an Individual with the Organization," A*merican Sociological Review,* 1954, Vol. 19, pp. 267-272.

[12] Of 75 pieces of sociological research in social organization reported in 1950-51, four were considering the question of effectiveness, apparently the beginning of a breakthrough. Cuber, John F. "Current Research Activity in Social Organization," *American Sociological Review,* Vol. 17, 1952, pp.477-479.

[13] Pfiffner, John F. "Research in Organizational Effectiveness." *Public Personnel Review,* Vol.14, April 1953. It may be of interest to note that his preliminary findings supported the notion that there was more "effectiveness" where there was the democratic concept of the consultative, communicative and helpful supervisor, but that being a good supervisor required something more than simply being humane, considerate and communicative. Further, that good human relations was apparently not antithetical to maintaining the formal policies and credos of the organization.

Pfiffner's *Supervision of Personnel* (Prentice-Hall, 1951), while concerned with supervision primarily, stresses the location of supervision within the framework of the formal organization, utilizing concepts developed in the "administrative management" school.

can be so specified as to permit analysis of the extent to which organizational ends are being achieved. To reduce organizational goals in social welfare agencies to operational terms is far from simple. In terms of method, if the stratagem of expert raters of effectiveness should be employed, the difficulty should be noted not only of what they should be rating, but even of gaining consensus as to who should rate. Pfiffner, in his preliminary methodological study which compares organizational effectiveness in a variety of public service organizations, used expert ratings, recognizing the shortcomings of this approach. While Pfiffner's work was focused on the supervisory group, he expressed the need for study of total structure and procedures. He suggests that the hypothesis to be tested is: "Other factors being controlled, the more effective organizations are those which are better structured, have an optimum of formalization, and are well 'tooled up' procedurally." This hypothesis leads us naturally to the general area of bureaucratic theory.

It is bureaucratic theory that is now being looked to as the major source of understanding of organizational problems stemming from the experience of social work administration, and it is this area of theory that is now providing a growing source of research ideas. Undoubtedly, the increasing interest of social work educators, researchers, and leading practitioners in social science theory and research, particularly over the past decade, has laid the groundwork for the specific interest in bureaucratic theory as it applies to administrative practice and process. While social science has not given organizational theory and research high priority, the work of Max Weber, Robert Michels, and other theorists in this field has been essential to the general understanding of social theory. The researches of Selznick, Gouldner, Blau, *et al.* have developed the theory further, albeit from different points of view, provided methodology for empirical investigation, and yielded fresh insights into the consequences of administrative decisions for organizational behavior.

Beyond the growing intellectual concern with the relationship of social science theory to social work practice have been the specific problems of the field in its organizational development. These have in turn led to the increasing importance within social work of the "rational model" of organizational analysis, in Gouldner's terms,[14] i.e., viewing the organization as an instrument in which planned control is directed toward organizational

---

[14] Gouldner, Alvin W. "Organization Analysis," *op. cit.*

ends. The emphasis on purposive formal structure and its consequences is not surprising in the light of the fact that social work is an agency-centered profession. This is so, whether the agency is professionally staffed exclusively by social workers, whether it is staffed by social workers and members of other professions, or whether social work, as in a hospital, constitutes an ancillary service. In addition to the large public welfare agencies, the voluntary agencies and institutions in which the social work function is based tend increasingly to be large, departmentalized, with a hierarchical form of organization, formal policies and regulations, and so on, conforming to the classic Weberian[15] conception of bureaucratic structure.

The contribution of Gouldner[16] in distinguishing between the "representative bureaucracy" and the "punishment-centered" type of bureaucracy is of special significance to social work, because of the assumption within the field—to the extent the question is raised—that social work administration should and would militate toward the former, rather than the latter type. Whether this is indeed so, to what extent, and the consequences when it is not so would be of considerable importance. Here, case studies of individual organizations, as well as comparative analysis, could reveal implications of "bureaucratic type" for board, executive, staff, and clientele. This kind of study may very well be of the kind that social work encourages the sociologist to make, rather than the social work researcher.

Emphasis on the general process of bureaucratization in social work is reflected in Wilensky and Lebeaux's[17] stimulating discussion of the relationship of this process to the professional subculture, and some of its consequences in terms of agency objectives.

---

[15] Weber, Max, *The Theory of Social and Economic Organization.* Translated by A. M. Henderson and Talcott Parsons, Oxford University Press, New York, 1947, esp. pp. 333-341.

[16] Gouldner, Alvin. *Patterns of Industrial Bureaucracy. Glencoe,* Ill.: Free Press, 1954. Also, Gouldner's "Organization Analysis," *op. cit.* The term "Representative Bureaucracy" was borrowed from J. Donald Kingsley's study (by that title) of the British Civil Service (Antioch Press, 1944).

[17] Wilensky, Harold I., and Lebeaux, Charles N. *Industrialization and Social Welfare,* Russell Sage Foundation, 1958, esp. chapter on "Agency Structure and Social Policy," pp. 233-282.

A further extension of this discussion and review of the literature is presented in Robert D. Vinter's article on "Social Structure of Service," in Kahn, Alfred J., ed., *Issues in American Social Work,* Columbia University Press, 1959.

Selected theory, related specifically to community organization, is referred to also in *Executive Responsibility,* by Ray Johns, Association Press, 1954.

The fact is that while social work agencies are increasingly conforming to Weber's "ideal type" of bureaucratic structure, and speculation is, therefore, possible about functional and dysfunctional consequences, little is empirically known about the factors (a) maximizing bureaucratic "strengths" in social work agencies (economy and efficiency, stability, role security, democratic impersonality of policies), or (b) giving rise to bureaucratic "strains"—the possible tendencies toward ritualism, overconformity, inadaptability to change, resistance to public accountability, depersonalization of clientele.[18] Research into the policies and procedures that serve to minimize or to prevent dysfunctional strains is also not apparent.[19]

A study in this general area that comes very close to social work interest is Blau's research [20] into two government personnel departments, and the consequences of different procedure for staff and clients. While the administrative action implications were not within Blau's purview as a sociologist, such implications can be drawn. Were a similar study applied to social work settings, directed to the consequences of typical social work procedures, we would have theory-based research related to professional concerns.

Sills's study of the National Foundation for Infantile Paralysis, *The Volunteers*,[21] takes its point of departure from Selznick's emphasis[22] on the

---

[18] Cf. Merton, Robert K. "Bureaucratic Theory and Personality," in *Reader in Bureaucracy*, ed. by Merton *et al.* Glencoe, Ill.: Free Press, 1952. This essay has probably been the single most important statement regarding dysfunctional strains in bureaucratic structure.

[19] Some students of organization concentrate on the negative implications of bureaucracy, and view both the structure, and the process of bureaucratization, as inherently inimical to the interests of the organization and its clientele. E.g., Dimock, Marshall E. "Bureaucracy Self-Examined," in *Reader in Bureaucracy*, ed. by Merton, *et al., op. cit. In* the context of my discussion, of course, the term is used without invidious connotations.

An illuminating and provocative analysis of strains for the individual in large organizations is provided by Chris Argyris in developing his thesis of the basic incongruency between the needs of a mature personality and the requirements of a formal organization, Argyris, Chris, "Some Propositions About Human Behavior in Organizations," in *Symposium on Preventive and Social Psychiatry*, 1957, Walter Reed Army Institute of Research, Washington, D.C. See also, "Professional Persons in Bureaucratic Organizations," by David M. Solomon (in the same *Symposium*) where the thesis of basic incompatibility between professional and bureaucratic ideologies is discussed.

[20] Blau, Peter M. *The Dynamics of Bureaucracy*, University of Chicago Press, 1955.

[21] Sills, David L. *The Volunteers*, Free Press, 1957. This study probably supported the decision of the National Foundation to expand its function, but was not designed as a problem-solving study for the organization.

[22] Selznick, Philip. "An Approach to a Theory of Bureaucracy," *American Sociological Review*, February 1943, Vol. 8, pp. 47-53. The concept of co-optation is fully developed in Selznick's by now classic study *TVA: The Grass Roots*, University of California Press, 1949.

unplanned, necessary modifications of the formal structure through the process of co-optation, with the emphasis on the effects of this process on formal organizational objectives. This study directly concerns significant social work interests. Its major themes bear generally on issues confronting national agencies which depend on volunteers, and on the effects of various modes of volunteer participation on organizational policies and effectiveness. This study could stimulate research into structural relationships in other national organizations that have different relationships between the professional hierarchy and the volunteers, or differ in some other significant way, in order to clarify further some of the administrative implications in various arrangements for involvement of volunteers.

It may be noted that Sills's research utilizes to some extent the "natural system" model of analysis (in Gouldner's term), examining closely the unplanned, adaptive responses within the organization. This line of conceptualization and research, however, is much more evident in the area of the effects of agency structure on clientele, without this relationship always being seen in terms of *administrative* implications. For the most part, the "clientele" in such studies to date have been resident populations, and with few exceptions the studies have not engaged social workers nor have they been stimulated by the needs of social work, although affecting social work activities.[23]

Thus, *The Mental Hospital*[24] and *The Psychiatric Hospital as a Small Society*[25] have called attention to the subtle but penetrating influences of such seeming abstractions as staff relationships and administrative organization on the well-being of mental patients, indeed, on their very symptomatology and chances of recovery. Similarly, the English experiments on the "open hospitals" have raised questions about the implications of current hospital structure for the treatment of the mentally ill. Settings featuring the

---

[23] Institutions having such resident populations have been characterized by Goffman as "total institutions." In analyzing such institutions, Goffman concentrates on ways in which "staff " and "inmates" define their reciprocal roles and develop institutional devices for "role release." Goffman, Erving, "The Characteristics of Total Institutions," in *Symposium on Preventive and Social Psychiatry*, Walter Reed Army Institute of Research, 1957.

[24] Stanton, Alfred H. & Morris S. Schwartz, *The Mental Hospital*, Basic Books, New York, 1954.

[25] Caudill, William A. *The Psychiatric Hospital as a Small Society*, Harvard University Press, Cambridge, Mass., 1958.

"therapeutic community"[26] have been observed assiduously by American students and, to some extent, specific features have been applied and evaluated in this country.

During recent years considerable interest has similarly been evinced in "patient self-government" in mental hospitals, with research directed to this end. The general theme of such research has been the "use of the social environment of the hospital for therapeutic purposes," focusing attention on the structural context within which patients live, and utilizing concepts from organization theory and role theory, as well as psychiatry.[27]

More recently, research in which social workers, as well as social scientists have been engaged, has been directed to the social systems of inmate groups in correctional institutions for both adult prisoners and juvenile delinquents. The researches of Cloward and Ohlin,[28] for example, are concerned with the relationship of the informal inmate structure to the formal custodial and treatment structures. Although this research is still in progress, the tentative findings disclose a telling impact of administrative policies and arrangements on the ways in which inmates define their own goals and relationships within the institution. While developing theory, this research is clearly related to long-range professional needs of social work for developing more effective use of institutional settings for delinquents.

Very little research has actually been done, as far as one can gather, on the relationship of administrative policies and arrangements to nonresi-

---

[26] Jones, Maxwell. *The Therapeutic Community,* Basic Books, New York, 1953.

[27] Greenblatt, Milton; York, Richard H.; Brown, Esther L.; Hyde, Robert W. *From Custodial to Therapeutic Patient Care in Mental Hospitals,* Russell Sage, 1955, especially Chapter 6, pp. 132-146. The term "milieu therapy" is avoided in this work because of its specific psychoanalytic connotation. It may be noted that part of the beginning process of the development analyzed in this book (in the Boston Psychopathic Hospital) consisted of a piece of research by a Simmons School of Social Work student for her thesis (at the request of the hospital) on patient attitudes towards the hospital. Hatch, Mary E. "An Inquiry into the Attitudes of Patients Towards Their Hospital Environment," 1958.

[28] A number of inter-related publications of Cloward and Ohlin bear on the general problem of the relationship of formal structure to inmate norms in correctional institutions, viz., Ohlin, Lloyd E. *Sociology and the Field of Corrections,* Russell Sage, New York, 1956; Cloward, Richard A. & Lloyd E. Ohlin. "Normlessness and Children's Cultures in Correctional Institutions," (New York School of Social Work, mimeographed); Cloward, Richard A., *Social Control and Anomie, (Ph.D.* Dissertation, Columbia University, 1959); Cloward, Richard A. & Lloyd E. Ohlin, "Individualization Re-examined," New York School of Social Work, (mimeographed) 1959; Cloward, Richard A. "Social Control in the Prison," in *The Organization of Containment* (New York: Social Science Research Council, to be published).

dent client populations, as in casework or group work agencies, although it would appear, particularly in the latter, that the extent to which the formal agency objectives are accepted is appreciably influenced by the nature of the sentiments, attitudes, and loyalties engendered in the groups served. Problems have arisen in the effects of professionalization on the administration of group work services, problems which may be explored from the standpoint of the functional and dysfunctional consequences of bureaucratization and the impact of the informal structure on the formal. Cloward points out, for example, the absence of an organized body of knowledge concerning the relationship between different modes of agency organization and types of responses among members.[29] He characterizes the variations in member response to agencies in terms of recruitment, turnover, demographic characteristics, program participation, and social distance (between members and agency); the major structural variables are agency size and degree of formalization of agency structure. No systematic comparison of different types of agencies is available, Cloward notes, for making the relationship between these two sets of variables better known.

There is evidence that theory-based research in social work administration, however scanty, is on the increase. Thus, the roster of dissertation abstracts as of June 1958 and the listing of dissertations in progress as of that date would suggest (on the basis of titles) that eight of the total ninety-five titles in both groups concern some form of administrative research.[30] Three concern supervisory and consultant roles and processes; two, leadership and morale; one, the area of formal procedures (personnel principles); one, administrative aspects of multi-agency co-ordination; and one, the relationship between formal and informal structure within an institution. Placing them in the context of major organizational approaches would be difficult without knowing their theoretical orientations.

These efforts, and others that are appearing, suggest, however, a gradually growing interest in social work administration research that is not entirely operational and specific to one agency. At the present time, it should be re-emphasized, the actual amount of such research that is available is quite sparse. One can debate the question of whether new research of this

---

[29] Cloward, Richard A. "Agency Structure as a Variable in Service to Groups," in *Group Work and Community Organization*, Columbia University Press, 1956.

[30] *Social Service Review*, September 1958, "Doctoral Dissertations," pp. 303-310. Three of the 18 completed dissertations, and 5 of the 77 in progress would seem to be in this general area.

kind should be a priority for social work administration, or whether the investment might better be made in trying to absorb and utilize what is already known. Both objectives are necessary, of course, and few would hold that everything about social work administration is so specific to social work that one could not draw on the pragmatic experience, as well as theory and research in other fields, for application to social work.

There would seem to be certain characteristics of social work organization, however, that do present research needs, if not unique to social work administration, at least peculiarly relevant to it. There are, first, the principal research areas cited above, namely, (1) factors maximizing functional attributes and dysfunctional strains in social work agencies; (2) the effects of various types of agency setting on clientele; (3) measures of organizational effectiveness. To these may be added a number of others, without attempting an exhaustive list: the general issue of delegation of authority, particularly with respect to supervisory functions;[31] problems of organizational change[32] peculiar to our field as agencies move, for ninety-five titles in both groups concern example, from small structures with emergency-based objectives to large settings with more permanent objectives, or as mergers occur; problems of developing normative standards without overroutinization in non-bureaucratic settings; the dilemmas (and their resolution) for executives in their relationship to the informal structure of their organizations; the effect of the size of the unit providing service on the kind of client service given;[33] the relationship of social work staffs to the formal and informal systems within essentially nonsocial work institutions;[34]

---

[31] Note, for example, problems in admixture of supervisory and consultative roles implicit in Lucille N. Austin's paper, "An Evaluation of Supervision," *Social Casework*, October 1956, and Frances Scherz's paper presented at the National Conference on Social Welfare, Chicago, May 1958, "A Concept of Supervision Based on Definitions of Job Responsibility."

[32] Bavelas, Alex. "Some Problems of Organizational Change," *Journal of Social Issues*, Summer 1948, Vol. 11. Bavelas considers two groups of changes: 1) where the social system can be expected to adapt the change to fit itself or where the change can be adapted to fit the system, and 2) where the change is too fundamental to be assimilated into the established system.

[33] See Vinter, Robert D., *op. cit.* pp. 252-257.

[34] Hospitals are the chief illustrations. E.g., Wessen, Albert F., "Hospital Ideology and Communication Between Ward Personnel" and Harvey L. Smith, "Two Lines of Authority: The Hospital's Dilemma," in *Patients, Physicians & Illness*, E. Gartly Jaco, ed., The Free Press, 1958, pp. 448-468; 468-477.

modes of participation in administrative policy at various staff levels in different types of bureaucracies; professionalism and staff turnover, and so on.

The difficulties in the way of doing organizational research in such areas, even on a very small scale and on limited problems, should not be minimized, despite the success of several studies in single organizations. Aside from such endemic concerns as conceptual clarity and the need for appropriate methodology, not the least of these difficulties are gaining access to the organization, and specifying the terms under which the research relationship is to be established with the organization, whether or not the organization is involved in the support of the research.[35]

It should be recognized, too, that research into organizational phenomena is still in a relatively early stage. In general, in and out of social work, there seems to be relatively little field research in proportion to the literature on theory. March and Simon state: "Not a great deal has been said about organizations, but it has been said over and over in a variety of languages."[36] They point out, while emphasizing the complexities of such research, that there has been more speculation than evidence.

Nevertheless, it is up to those social work practitioners, executives, teachers, and researchers who are particularly concerned with issues of administrative policy to become aware of what has been said in theory, in at least some "language," and of at least some of the evidence for what has been said; and to stimulate, if not themselves carry out, the kinds of research that are professionally appropriate. We should bear in mind the many distinct fields of activity and different types of experience from which organizational theory has been developed. We should also bear in mind that to each of them have been applied, in whole or in part, conceptions from the various social sciences which, in turn, have developed individual emphases and technical terms of their own. Finding the one language, or the combination of languages or concepts, that best meets social work's needs for a particular purpose is not a simple matter. We should, however, be wary of drawing all our theoretical assumptions or research strategies from any one source. Moreover, while some of the administrative issues in social work are peculiar to the social work profession, many are not, and there is every reason to draw on knowledge and ideas wherever they can prove useful.

---

[35] Jacobson, E.; Kahn, Robert L.; Man, F. C.; Morse, N. C. "Research in Functioning Organizations," *Journal of Social Issues,* Vol. VII, 1951, No. 3.

[36] March, James G. & Simon, Herbert A., *op.cit.,* p. 5.

AUTHOR'S COMMENTS

In introducing discussion of his paper, Dr. Stein outlined some of the reasons for the dearth of research on administration, some of the problems in undertaking such research in social work, and some of the problems in administration on which social science theory might be helpful.

Administration is not ordinarily thought of as an area of research in social work, for several reasons: (1) It is not regarded as a primary method in social work. (2) Analysis of organizational behavior is conceded as a more legitimate area of inquiry for social science than for social work research. (3) Appropriate methodologies have not been clearly worked out. (4) Administration is accepted as a given, an inevitable fact outside the sphere of responsibility of the researcher. (5) Research on organizational behavior is difficult in any organization, but especially so in a social work organization, where the agency administrator may not only be unwilling to leave the researcher sufficiently free but be prevented from doing so by the nature of agency policy.

While a case can be made for the need for research on social work administration, much preliminary work remains to be done. One problem is the identification and definition of the variables in agency structure that need to be examined. We have not yet worked out a method of classifying agencies in a way that permits analysis of relevant material, with respect to size, degree of autonomy, and so forth. Measurement of effectiveness has proved difficult in clinical terms; determination of effectiveness in organizational terms is even more elusive. (Dr. Stein cited a recent bibliography of 300 items on "Measurement of Organizational Effectiveness" issued by Cornell.) He suggested that the accumulation of some organizational life histories would provide useful data for study.

The following are some of the problems in social work administration on which social science theory might offer leads for research:

1. The prevention of strains arising out of bureaucratization;

2. Understanding such key roles as that of supervisor;

3. The relation of informal to formal structure as it affects administrative behavior—ways in which the executive tries to penetrate the informal structure, ways in which informal structure works for and against agency aims;

4. Division of staff loyalty between agency and other reference groups;

5. The importance of differentiating degrees of bureaucratization.

Dr. Stein concluded by noting that social science gives promise of help in minimizing the strains and maximizing the benefits of bureaucracy.

DISCUSSION

The group found it difficult to differentiate administration research from the broader topic of research related to the concerns of the administrator. Discussion of this point led into consideration of the problem of identifying goals and determining success in implementing goals. It was agreed that there is strong need for experimental research to determine the patterns of organization and deployment of staff conducive to efficiency in goal attainment.

If administration is viewed as goal implementation, as the process of translating objectives into services, then the administrator is interested in evaluation of effectiveness and determination of ways of increasing it. He is therefore concerned with research that will indicate: (1) ways of eliminating dysfunctional strains within the organization; (2) organizational forms conducive to goal achievement; and (3) predictive factors of use to him in such administrative decisions as allocation of personnel. (For example, if it were known that patients with certain characteristics were likely to require rehospitalization regardless of the amount of social service offered to them in the community, the administrator might assign less of his limited staff time to these cases.)

Evaluation presupposes identification of criteria of effectiveness, which may be phrased in terms of effect on client, standards of performance, or community expectations. Thus, a prior research consideration is identification of goals. Although organizations have stated goals, it is difficult to operationalize them. The conflict of professional versus bureaucratic interests cited in the discussion of community organization was suggested as the nexus of administrative problems as well, and as a possible point of attack on the problem of goals. To what extent does the profession dominate in goal-setting? How compatible are the goals of the board and those of staff derived from their professional reference group? One point of view expressed was that goals cannot be examined directly but must be deduced from study of structure, since goals are mediated through organizational structure.

Attention was called to the distinction between the problems of multiplicity and of ambiguity of goals. It is possible to deal with several goals, if they can be operationalized, but the problem of ambiguity of goals is more vexing. One function of the researcher is to help his research client (the organization) to clarify its goals, just as the caseworker assists the individual client in clarifying goals. The customary role of the council researcher exemplifies this function.

Assuming that goals have been identified, it may be useful to delineate a series of steps that represent partial goal attainment or preconditions to goal achievement. For instance, in a group work setting, there might be ten steps in getting the client involved therapeutically—getting him in the door, getting him to play basketball, involving him in discussion of certain problems, and so forth. Knowing how many clients arrive at each step might add something to the picture given by data on the number of clients in whom behavioral change is effected. Further, measurement of change becomes relevant only when the client reaches the point where he can be provided with the service whose effect one wishes to measure. It is important therefore to specify as many as possible of the necessary conditions to effective service.

Administration is concerned not only with quality but with quantity. How can effectiveness be maximized through appropriate distribution of personnel or modification of structure or procedures? The importance of experimentation was stressed. The recent experiments in the nursing field with different patterns of assignment of nursing personnel were cited. Several illustrations were also cited from the social work field, including an experiment in a public assistance agency in which one group of cases was assigned on a categorical basis and a second group on the basis of the family problem presented. Optimism was expressed about the possibility of expanding such experimental research in casework. Agency resistance was seen as a less serious obstacle to such research than uncertainty about the variations in program that should be introduced, since program modifications are very costly in terms of staff time and cannot therefore be recommended by the researcher without strong conviction about their reasonableness.

12. The Study of Organizational Effectiveness

In a paper prepared by the writer for the 1959 institute of the NASW Social Work Research Section, stress was placed on the necessity of considering consequences for administrative practice deriving from bureaucratic theory.[1] Difficulties in the study of organizational effectiveness were cited, and writings of Pfiffner, Cuber, Gouldner, and others were referred to in this connection. The present paper carries further the discussion of organizational effectiveness and presents, in non-research terms, a statement of administrative implications of bureaucratic theory as one area for study within the framework of a systems model of analysis.

There are varied approaches to the analysis of organizations.[2] With respect to organizational effectiveness per se, two general directions have been taken: the goal model and the systems model.[3]

The goal model deals with the extent to which an organization meets its objectives or goals, stated or implicit, public or private. Etzioni's critique of the goal model rests partly on the grounds that the results of such analysis tend to be stereotyped, *i.e.,* they usually show that the organization does not realize goals effectively nor that the organization has different goals than those it claims. He prefers the systems model where the starting point is not

Reprinted with permission from David Farshel, editor, *Research in Social Welfare Administration*, Report of the Institute on Research in Social Work Administration and Community Welfare Organization, sponsored by the National Association of Social Workers Research Section (New York: National Association of Social Workers, 1961).

[1] Herman D. Stein, "Organization Theory—Implications for Administrative Research," in Leonard S. Kogan, ed., *Social Science Theory and Social Work Research* (New York: National Association of Social Workers, 1960), pp. 80-88.

[2] See Alvin W. Gouldner, "Organizational Analysis," in *Ibid.*, pp. 46-62.

[3] Amitai Etzioni, "Two Approaches to Organizational Analysis: A Critique and a Suggestion," *Administrative Science Quarterly*, Vol. 5, No. 2 (September 1960), pp. 257-278.

the goal of the organization, but the working model of a social unit capable of achieving a goal. The basic question becomes then not "how devoted is the organization to its goal," but rather, "under the given conditions how does the organizational allocation of resources approach an optimum distribution."

GOAL MODEL OF ANALYSIS

While it is maintained in this paper that research addressed to analyzing the presence and consequences of bureaucratic strains and their countermeasures should draw on a systems model type of analysis, it would be hazardous to accept the premise that the more traditional goal model has outlived its usefulness. Such a premise is questionable, if only because of the prevailing lack of clarity with respect to social agency goals and the absence of studies in the social work field which attempt to define explicit or implicit goals in a manner that makes it possible to determine whether these goals are being met. Generalized public relations objectives of "serving individuals and families in distress" or "enabling youth to develop wholesome interests and democratic attitudes" hardly permit operational evaluations of goal attainment. Despite shortcomings in evaluations based on the goal model, it is at this stage necessary to encourage the analysis of both stated and implicit goals in social agencies in order to permit and encourage a more realistic and hard-headed examination of agency objectives, and to provide the basis for comparative studies of social welfare organizations in terms of goals.

It is important to define agency goals, whether of voluntary or governmental agencies, in such a way that one can determine whether goals are or are not being achieved, without reducing such definitions to the level of technical procedures. Operational definitions may vary from agency to agency even within the same field, and they may be changed in the course of time with further experience and actual changes in objectives. Nevertheless, the establishment of "hard" objectives, in contrast to the over-generalized "soft" objectives, would put the agency on notice to itself as well as to others about what it is in business for and how it intends to determine whether it is indeed achieving its purposes. The agency could thus be more truly accountable, the process of community planning for agency coordination could be more rational, and the possibilities of innovation of new organizational arrangements to meet newly recognizable goals could be enhanced.

One may suggest for a voluntary family agency, for example, the following types of questions which would have to be answered to make it possible to judge whether the agency is fulfilling its objectives, no matter how its global or ultimate purposes are stated:

1. What segments of the population are to be served, in demographic terms—ethnic, religious, age levels, socioeconomic groupings, geographic boundaries?

To answer this question the agency would require demographic information about the larger community within which the potential client population is located, as well as decisions about how this client population should be defined.

2. What is the range of needs to be met by the agency?

A statement of intake policy is required to provide an answer to this question. The terms should be sufficiently clear so that one may, if only speculatively, tell who among those meeting these needs criteria are not being served.

3. What proportions of those with stated need is the agency designed to serve? (Now? In five years?)

In other words, what proportions of the estimated potential client population, as defined, is the agency actually intending to help?

4. What types of service are to be rendered?

"Types of service" would include, in a family agency, such help as financial assistance, individual casework, family or group counseling, diagnostic service, "family life education" meetings, and so on. A decision on the proportionate agency investment (in professional manpower, for example) in each type of service within the agency range should normally tend to follow the definition of such services in relation to needs to be met.

5. What are the desirable standards of quality of service?

Quality refers to definitions of what constitutes help, and what constitutes "success" and "failure"—in other words, what kinds of help should the agency be giving? Shall the agency be geared for "success" only? What tolerances should it accept for "non-help" or "failure"? That quality levels are difficult to define, let alone measure, goes without saying. It is equally important to recognize that in the absence of some definition of quality objectives, whether or not these are immediately subject to measurement, the assessment of organizational effectiveness in terms of goals can hardly be adequate.

6. What are desirable standards of productivity, e.g., ratios of clientele to professional staff?

Quality can be maximized at the expense of cost. Some relationship between quality expectancies and productivity requires explicit statement, whether the agency is experimental with deliberately low productivity, or provides a mass service restricting quality to certain limits in order to meet needs of the most urgent priority.

None of these questions are simple to answer, yet the effort to provide answers to as many of these questions as possible can put us on the road toward analysis of effectiveness in terms of organizational objectives. The effort may also provide a basis for comparative evaluations between agencies, in addition to evaluations of the same agency over a period of time. These kinds of questions, which may vary with different kinds of agencies, are not ephemeral or unrealistic, no matter how far we may be from a position to state required definitions in clear terms. The well-run corporation asks similar questions in terms of objectives for given time periods—for example, what products shall be manufactured? What share of the market for these products should the corporation aim for? What profit ratio should be achieved? What level of quality maintenance should be achieved? It is in these terms that its progress and purposes are evaluated.

A statement of operational criteria of goal achievement would have to precede any research into organizational effectiveness (and the development of indicators for these criteria) by the goal model. There is utility in such efforts not only for research purposes which can themselves yield new kinds of utility, but because such efforts are important for more planful administration and for greater accountability of agencies to the communities they serve.

We are, perhaps, not *ready* to utilize the goal model in social agency research, and the need is to prepare for such analysis. Whatever shortcomings there are, in Etzioni's terms, should first be experienced before this general direction of examining organizational effectiveness is written off in the social agency field.

SYSTEMS MODEL OF ANALYSIS

The systems model, which does not concern itself with organizational goals as such, and therefore cannot answer questions regarding goal achievement, provides quite a different pathway to the assessment of organizational effectiveness. This model is designed to help answer questions regarding the best utilization of energy and resources. The assessment would, therefore, be in terms of instrumental or middle-range criteria rather than in terms of devotion to, or achievement of, ultimate objectives.

Georgopoulos and Tannenbaum, in their presentation of research into organizational effectiveness, develop three basic criteria subsumed under this concept, all of which may be regarded as intermediate rather than long-range objectives: (1) organizational productivity, (2) organizational flexability—successful adaptation to internal and external changes and, (3) absence of tension.[4]

In social work we have no generally conceded Operational definition of productivity, and the development of standards of productivity related to different types of agencies remains an important requirement for research.

A case in point of the possible use of the "organizational productivity" criterion is a study, now being completed, that is concerned with the relative effectiveness of utilizing different levels of staff competence (senior caseworker, caseworker, case aide, secretary) for different kinds of case situations, or for different purposes in the same case, in a hospital social service department.[5] The objective of the study was not to determine whether the department was achieving its "goals" but rather to see whether a different distribution of staff resources could yield greater economy of service, in terms of productivity in a quantitative sense (e.g., cases per worker, staff time per case, cases closed per month, and so on) without loss of quality (i.e., without decreasing the effectiveness of its service per case), or could attain higher quality without loss of productivity. In this purpose, the study conformed to the systems model approach. Moreover, with respect to gauging both quantitative productivity and quality of service, the instruments developed were designed to gauge changes in the same agency over a period of time, rather than to establish any appraisal in accordance with a set of external, uniform standards.

The second and third criteria noted by Georgopoulos and Tannenbaum, flexibility and absence of intra-organizational strain, may be utilized in the understanding of social work organization, and have particular relevance for the analysis of bureaucratic strains.

[4] B. S. Georgopoulos and A. S. Tannenbaum, "Organizational Effectiveness," *American Sociological Review*, Vol. 22, No. 5 (October 1957), pp. 534-540.

[5] The exploratory project has been conducted at the Albert Einstein Medical center in Philadelphia under the direction of Margaret Heyman, Director of Social Service. The writer has been senior research consultant for the project, *Effective Utilization of Social Workers in a Hospital Setting*, to be published in 1962 by the American Hospital Association.

Two approaches toward such study may be noted as desirable and feasible:

1. The longitudinal study of agency behavior over a period of time, through observation, records, guided interviews, and questionnaires, can provide data showing the presence of such strains, their consequences, how they were resolved, how significant they were, whether this approach to the understanding of the organizational system is fruitful. Subjective elements can easily creep into such an analysis, and the data will be largely descriptive in nature and will depend upon the accuracy and objectivity of the observer. These possible shortcomings, however, should prove no serious barrier to such undertakings and should not mar their usefulness. While organizational research is tending to move away from longitudinal studies, the absence of such studies in the social work field leaves the student of social work organization dependent upon organizational studies in other settings. Valuable as these are, there is something to be said for the stimulation of new hypotheses and insights that derive from a critical appraisal of organizational behavior within one's given field of interest. Social agencies have rarely sat for full-length portraits. Case studies focusing on the kinds of problems bureaucratization induces and their modes of resolution are sorely needed. What would seem to be required, in other words, is a systematic account of a period of agency history, focusing on the organizational problems it encountered and the ways in which they were or were not met, and interpreting such developments in the light of organization theory, which includes taking exception to existing theory.

2. Research methods are gradually being worked out, as the guiding concepts emerge, for non-longitudinal empirical research in organizational effectiveness. The work of Georgopoulos and Tannenbaum, cited above, is an example. Scales were developed for the rating of each of the three criteria by experts, and an empirical basis was provided for testing the utility of these criteria as an over-all index of effectiveness. If one is to appraise the prevalence of bureaucratic strains and judge the effectiveness of counter-measures, instruments would have to be developed for detecting or judging the presence of such strains, once they are defined in operational terms.

The presentation which follows reviews, in non-research terms, certain bureaucratic strains—ritualism, overconformity, inadaptability to change, self-protectiveness, incompatibility between formal and informal systems—and action consequences or administrative implications.

The multiple questions would be raised, in a line of analysis deriving from the systems model: In view of total conditions of pressure on the system from outside and the necessity of mediating different interests from within the system, how far can the organization go in minimizing such strains, what consequences are there for organizational behavior in such alternatives, and in attempting directly to alleviate one or more of such strains?

BUREAUCRATIC STRUCTURE

In the social scientific sense, the term bureaucratic structure has no necessarily invidious connotation. It refers, rather, to a form of rational organization conceived thus far to be indispensable to the mass production of goods and services. The extension of bureaucracy has been a concomitant of technological development in all countries where such development has taken place.[6] Government bureaus, industrial organizations, the armed services, trade unions, schools, and hospitals have all reflected this trend in the United States; and, as has been amply demonstrated, social agencies, whether public or voluntary, have not been strangers to this development.[7]

The key features of bureaucratic structure are relatively large size, departmentalization with specialized offices and functions, a hierarchical form of organization, and written or well understood policies, regulations, and procedures.

Inherent Strengths

Bureaucracy, as a rational form of organization, depends for its most effective functioning upon planned co-ordination of its parts, clarity in its policies, specificity in the roles of all who are part of the organizational system, and impersonality in its discharge of functions. When referring to *inherent strengths* of bureaucratic structure, one is not suggesting that every organization so characterized includes these virtues; rather that the central tendencies of bureaucratic structure, when the most rational principles are applied, are consistent with these attributes. Such "strengths" may be characterized as follows:

---

[6] Peter M. Blau, *Bureaucracy in Modern Society* (New York: Random House, 1956).

[7] Harold L. Wilensky and Charles N. Lebeaux, *Industrialization and Social Welfare* (New York: Russell Sage Foundation, 1958).

Economy and efficiency. These are contributed to by rational division of labor and pooling of expertise.

Stability and permanence. A bureaucracy is not easily shaken by the loss of one person, since it is the office to be filled which tends to be more important than the particular individual who occupies it. Such structures maintain a high investment in stability and permanence.

Role security. Occupational roles tend to be highly specific. What is expected on the job is relatively clear. Job descriptions and formal communication processes tend to be defined.

Relative job security. Bureaucratic structures have an investment in retaining personnel in the interests of stability, and thus tend to promote not only fringe benefits but in-service training programs, retirement programs, and so on.

Impersonality of policies. Bureaucracies tend to minimize subjective elements in determination of policies and to maximize the establishment of objective and impersonal criteria, with the following results:

1. For the consumer of the organization's goods or services, this can have the effect of democratization through uniform applicability of criteria, as long as the consumer meets established criteria. Whether it is having the amount of money to purchase the goods or services, or the requisite financial need to obtain public assistance, the tendency is to minimize discretion based on subjective considerations.

2. For the personnel of the organization impersonality of policies tends to make for relatively objective criteria for evaluation, promotions, sick leave, vacations, and so on. Aside from inducing expectations that can be realized and providing clarity for job conditions, the application of the principle of maximum impersonality tends also to reduce interpersonal competition for advancement within an organization. The competition may be related to the achievement of certain experience or skills deemed necessary for promotion and not, for example, to competition between two or more people for the favor of a superior.

Inherent Strains

While bureaucracy tends to bolster such strengths, its structure also contains *inherent strains.* By strains, in this sense, we refer to tendencies which are likely to arise unless specifically planned for and prevented and which tend to weaken the capacity of the organization to maintain itself and fulfill its objectives. These strains may be viewed in four areas: personnel, the consumer, management, and the community.

Personnel. 1. Ritualism.[8] This is the condition where means become ends. The very fact that roles are defined, that the job tends to be precisely described, provides a congenial situation for the employee who feels constrained only to do his particular job right without reference to its meaning for the total organization, and not to deviate from established routine or to exercise judgment.

2. Mediocrity and overconformity. These are the tendencies which have recently been emphasized on the public rostrum, in the press, and in books, such as *The Organization Man.*[9] "Not getting into trouble" and "playing it safe" tend to be requisites for maintenance of job tenure and among the criteria for eventual promotion when length of service is a prime factor in this regard. The system may both attract conformists and remove the potential for constructive nonconformity by adhering rigidly to prescribed policies and procedures. In the long run the diffusion of mediocrity serves to militate against the most important *raison d'etre* of bureaucracy itself, namely, economy and efficiency. Another aspect of this condition is lack of stimulus for imagination or creativity.

The consumer of the organization's goods or services. The very impersonality of criteria when applied to the consumer can make it difficult for the individual to be properly served and leave the organization incapable of meeting crisis situations or emergencies. When the consumer confronts an organization in this context he has the sense of dealing with a system, not with a person. It is at this point that the epithet "red tape" is most frequently applied.

Management. Lack of adaptability to change can be a consequence of the investment in the organization's stability and permanence. Ritualistic, unimaginative, and overly formalized behavior may become norms of management, as well as of other personnel.

Community. Bureaucracies tend to be self-protective and it is difficult for the outside community, except in cases of violation of law or other crises, to gain access to the organization or affect its structure (more so, of course, in voluntary than in public agencies). While the cohesiveness of the organization can be an asset, it also promotes unwillingness to expose its internal system to public scrutiny because of the danger of upsetting the authority balance within the organization, or to reveal practices deemed necessary

---

[8] Robert Merton, "Bureaucratic Structure and Personality," in Merton, ed., *Reader in Bureaucracy* (Glencoe, Ill.: The Free Press, 1952).

[9] William Whyte, *The Organization Man* (New York: Doubleday & Company, 1957).

for internal stability but not easily reconciled with public or official goals of the organization. This condition of protective shielding from the public can become particularly important in social agencies, which in the final analysis are supported by tax funds.

Administrative Implication[10]

One general principle should govern an approach to preventing, mitigating, or compensating for strains arising from bureaucratic organization, namely, preventive countermeasures should themselves be consistent with bureaucracy. That is, such means should themselves be rational and official, maintain specificity of roles and clear procedures, maximize impartiality, and the like. In other words, a bureaucratic organization would not be consistent if, in attempting to lessen overconformity, it would say to personnel, "Just use your own judgment," but it may more consistently say to a specific department or level of personnel, "In these situations discretion may be exercised up to this point, utilizing the following criteria as guides."

Further, it is obvious that no organization, however ingeniously run, is without its problems while it lives, grows, and changes. It is with the capacity of the organization to strengthen itself, to detect and deal with its problems—not to remove all problems for all time—that any consideration of administrative practice must be concerned.

The prevention of ritualism. Ritualism develops in organizations when personnel are either permitted or encouraged to wear "organizational blinkers" so that they see neither to left nor right but keep their eye on the immediate job for which they have been hired. It can pervade not only personnel who do routine mechanical operations, but professional and managerial personnel as well. Ritual behavior is unconcerned with the larger organizational purposes and can lead to the aggrandizement of one's own job or one's own department at the expense of others, or at the risk of disturbing the organization's rational balance and co-ordination of functions.

The prevention of ritualism is, therefore, in the direction of policies and procedures which make it possible for personnel to be oriented to the central objectives of the organization, to see how their functions relate to those of others, and to be concerned about such interrelationships. Some of the

---

[10] The discussion in this section pertains only to implications for bureaucratically organized agencies. Bureaucratic theory also provides a basis for deriving implications for nonbureaucratic agencies, i.e., those which are small, in which roles are more diffuse, and so on. Such organizations have their corollary strengths and potential strains.

simple techniques in this area are well known, for example, the orientation of new staff by physically taking them around an office or plant, general meetings of the entire staff, annual reports, interdepartmental meetings, and so forth. An appropriate program for a given organization will depend partly on its complexity and partly on the precise character of its organizational cast, as well as its function and objective. As will be noted below in another connection, the supervisory chain of command is crucial to the mitigation of this as well as other strains, if nonritualistic behavior is regarded as a positive criterion of performance and evaluated accordingly through the entire organization.

Programs may vary for different echelons of the organization, and when carried out "nonritualistically" may have the effect of reducing the tendency to encapsulate one's own task as if it were the only important one in the organization, without reference to its meaning for others, and may encourage flexibility and judgment when the need arises.

Provision of opportunities for new ideas. The accent on stability and permanence can have the effect of making "not rocking the boat" a central concern. Where such is the prevailing norm, not only will potential ideas in the service of the organizational purposes not be tapped, but their sources will be dried up. One is familiar with primitive devices such as the suggestion box, or more recent notions such as "brainstorming" in executive idea sessions, as devices for encouraging or stimulating imaginative contributions. Some industrial organizations have attempted to cope with this problem partly by creating "islands of creativity" where scientists and professionals who have achieved superior standing within the organization are permitted a place to work and resources without restriction on what they do, and without having to abide by the normal routines of the organization.

To utilize individual initiative and imagination would seem to require, however, a pervasive, built-in policy through the entire administrative structure which pervades the organization and is effectuated through its entire supervisory apparatus. Thus, every supervisor at whatever level would have as part of his obligation the need to inquire as to suggestions or ideas, to evaluate them, and to utilize what is possible, and would *himself* be evaluated partly on his capacity to fulfill this supervisory requirement. The organization itself can thus better harness its potential from personnel, and for those who are able to contribute ideas, rewards—whether in economic or noneconomic terms—should be forthcoming.

*Prevention of rigidity toward the con*sumer. Bureaucracy requires policies and regulations, but also ways of individualizing and dealing with the exceptional situation or the emergency. It is possible for a bureaucracy to develop ways of dealing with the exceptional case in a manner which is consistent with the needs of such a structure. Essential in any method of dealing with the emergency or exceptional case is for the organization to recognize that such cases may arise, situations which are not anticipated by existing policy. Responsibility for emergencies or special cases should, therefore, be centralized and clarified to avoid that exasperating phenomenon of a representative of an organization who says, in effect, "I'm sorry I can't deal with that and I don't know who does."

Emergencies that are anticipated can be met by policies which set the levels of discretion appropriate to different staff. For example, a family agency might be able to permit its workers to grant emergency financial assistance at their discretion up to a certain amount without further check, increase the amount at the discretion of supervisory personnel, and beyond this limit it may require authorization from the executive. Such policies with regard to limits of discretion are possible when emergencies can be anticipated.

When emergencies or special cases begin to assume recognizable patterns, policies can be developed for such situations and responsibilities allocated for carrying them out, so that these situations no longer assume the character of emergencies or special cases.

Adaptability to change. The processes of change in large organizations are still not too well understood, but change does occur and often stems from imagination and creative planning rather than being simply accidental. To develop the actuality of change toward well-understood goals requires, of course, that the function of planning be dearly located within the organization. Unless planning is a conscious activity it will not tend simply to happen. There will be changes, but they will be uncontrolled and at the mercy of external factors rather than self-directed, or planned to meet the influences of external pressures in the environment of the organization.

The centralization of a planning function does not mean, however, that participation in planning and in policy formulation must be restricted to a specific individual or group of individuals. On the contrary, participation in planning can and should be widespread through an organization. In making this point one is not referring to so-called "democratic administration" where everyone in an organization has an equal voice in planning or where the right, if not the fact, of such "democratic" participation is conceded. In large formal structures "democratic administration" in this sense is a contradiction in terms and virtually impossible. What is possible, however, is tapping the understanding, ideas, and motivations of people in an organization according to their special competence and their special interests, that is, through *relevant participation*. One way of making the bureaucratic structure more adaptable to change is to build into the administrative process modes of participation that would elicit the contribution of all those in the organization who have something to contribute out of their legitimate roles, experience, and organizational interests. This can be true whether one is dealing with planning for budget, for locating unseen problems, or for devising new approaches to meet existing conditions.

The concept of relevant participation does not mean having everyone responsible for everything, and certainly is not the same as trying to have participation for its own sake as a morale-builder. Such specious involvement can only lead to cynicism and is self-defeating. More to the point is the concept of maintaining at all times appropriate channels for the raising of questions related to the work problems of staff at any level in the organization. In effect, the approach would be to seek systematically such evaluation of work tasks, procedures, and relationships by personnel, and to recognize this process administratively as desired behavior, without having the executive branch of the organization abdicate its authority for decisionmaking.

Client or consumer participation. In considering participation in policy formulation and in raising questions at various levels, one must not overlook client, consumer, or patient participation. A longstanding practice in membership organizations, such as in group work agencies, has been to involve clientele in program-planning, although the extent and the modes of participation may often merit re-examination. Now there is increasing attention to the importance of participation among resident populations, such as those in general, rehabilitation, and mental hospitals. Whether and how such participation is possible for nonresident groups, as in casework agencies, remains to be seen.

Participation of clientele does not have to be complicated. One might remind oneself that retail customers "participate" when they are asked to register suggestions on cards in restaurants or in airplanes, and such participation can be quite valuable to an organization if the cards are actually read and followed up. Clients in agencies participate when they are involved in the follow-up study of practice. The utilization of client or consumer participation as a gimmick to demonstrate organizational interest and response to "the voice of the people" can in the long run only be self-defeating, since even the public relations utility of these devices will probably eventually suffer, and the chances of actually utilizing the opinions of consumers will be minimized. What is much more to the point is, first, the right of the consumer to participate at his level of legitimate interest and experience, and second, the contribution he can make by such participation, even if it is elicited by simply asking in a systematic way, what did he think of the service, and does he have any suggestions. Robert Vinter has stated that the client is "lowest on the authority continuum" in social agencies.[11] This is, by and large, true. It hardly means, however, that the client has nothing to contribute in the formulation of policy. It means, rather, that the opportunity to participate has to be structured for the client and that this opportunity should be meaningful.

Accountability. The tendency that can develop in agencies toward self-protection and insularity from outside community pressures can lead to inadequate discharge of the agency's responsibility to be accountable for its activity. This source of strain can to some extent be solved by executive decision. A clear understanding is necessary of the public or publics to whom reporting should be made, as well as the development of appropriate means for such reporting. In the absence of such measures for accountability, accumulated pressures for reporting may press on the agency at a point when it is least prepared to meet the demand. While public relations is an element in accountability, it should not be construed as synonymous with it; rather, the genuine right of groups to know what is appropriate and legitimate for them to know and to react about should be emphasized. Not only external groups such as legislatures or chests and councils are involved in agency accountability, but departments and total staff of the agency as well.

Formal and Informal Organization

Phillip Selznick stated three hypotheses in his article on "An Approach to a Theory of Bureaucracy."[12]

1. Every organization creates an informal structure.
2. In every organization the goals of the organization are modified by the processes within it.

---

[11] Robert Vinter, "The Social Structure of Service," in Alfred J. Kahn, ed., *Issues in American Social Work* (New York: Columbia University Press, 1959).

[12] *American Sociological Review*, Vol. 6, No. 1 (February 1943), pp. 47-54.

3.   The processes in modification are effected through the informal structure.

Informal organization has been given considerable research attention, yet again relatively little has been said about action implications in the relationship of formal to informal structure. It may be noted that in referring to formal structure one is essentially speaking of what can be blueprinted in the organization—staff positions, lines of authority, job functions, procedures and regulations, committees, and so on. The informal structure includes virtually all else—sentiments, loyalties, informal interaction, friendships, animosities, and cliques.

When the goals of the informal organization are the same as the formal, one has the essential precondition of high morale. It is generally conceded that such a situation contributes to efficiency, productivity, and flexibility of an organization. People will do more, work more, think harder, for the organization when its purposes are incorporated not only in the formal tasks but in the sentiments and personal orientations of those in the organization. When the methods and goals of the formal organization are not shared by the informal, more rigid controls become necessary, and the investment in management activity tends to be toward organizational control and overcoming impediments to carrying out the objectives of the organization. This is the situation, for example, in most correctional institutions or in any organization which for longer or shorter periods of time contains disaffected, alienated employees, or resident populations of patients or inmates with sentiments or aspirations in conflict with those of formal authority.

For the executive and management group there is the recurrent dilemma in most noncustodial organizations of having to be sensitive to the informal structure without interfering with it or attempting to manipulate it. Such manipulation is not only ethically questionable, but in the long run destructive to organizational interests. It is important to recognize, at the same time, the danger inherent in permitting formal processes and formal decisions to be usurped by the informal structure. One can accept the hypothesis that processes of modification in the formal organization are constantly being effected through the informal structure. Ideas, sentiments, biases within the informal structure have an effect, sooner or later, on changing conditions within the formal structure. However, for an organization to remain viable and in control of its destiny without being seriously beset by nonrational influences requires that the formal structure be recognized as super-ordinate. It thus becomes the responsibility of all personnel to see that decisions that belong within formal channels are not made within informal groupings, and to make sure that policy questions that should be raised become located in proper administrative channels. If there are no such channels available, staff can seek that they be created. Should informal groupings be able to manipulate the formal structure, the results—with the best intentions in the world—can become corrosive to the organizational fabric.

In summary, therefore, one may note at least two directions for executive and other personnel in an organization to follow, from an understanding of the inherent relationship between formal and informal structure:

1.   The executive should not seek to manipulate the informal structure. He can be sensitive to its climate through the normal processes of administration without seeking to intrude or to develop special channels of communication.

2.   For all staff it is important to locate recommendations and policy questions within appropriate levels and channels of the organization, whether or not they originate within the informal structure, in order to safeguard the long-range interests of organizational purposes, processes, and stability.

SUMMARY

This paper has discussed organizational effectiveness in social agencies and has considered both the goal model and the systems model of analysis. The former was suggested as having considerable merit in the present stage of social work development, despite the disadvantages noted particularly by Etzioni. The systems model, however, was suggested as an appropriate framework within which to analyze the presence of, and consequences inherent in, bureaucratic strains and countermeasures. A summary of certain predominant strains arising from bureaucratic organization has been provided from existing theory. In relation to each, inferences were drawn as to the direction of administrative practice in preventing, mitigating, or compensating for such strains. It is understood that no organization can be stress-free and that the direction of resolution of bureaucratic strains should be consistent with bureaucratic organization. The importance of supervisory evaluation through the entire line organization in mitigating stress, and the concept of relevant participation in policy formation, were emphasized.

13. The Concept of the Human Service Organization: A Critique

The expression "human service organization" is explored in reference to an organization's essential societal functions, the development of HSOs as a growing movement, their special functional attributes or domains, the workplace of particular kinds of personnel, and the federal umbrella organization approach to service planning and delivery. The author discusses the utility of HSO as a concept and speculates as to why social work finds it agreeable; and he comments on the ways in which it remains confusing and illusory when used as an analytic construct rather than as the European equivalent of "the social services."

Each of the words in the expression "human service organization" is so pleasant and straightforward that, placed together, they produce a term that fairly shines with a sense of hearty and effective good will. It was bound to sell. I like the sound of it, too, but I am not sure what it means.

The term has caught on rapidly during the past 10 or 11 years. It has substantially replaced the more traditional categorical names, such as social service agency or health and welfare organization. A review of social work journal articles and books over the past 10 years reveals that HSO is commonly used without definition, as if it were so readily understandable and obvious that no explanatory statement is necessary. Where there have been serious efforts to define the term, the variations, ambiguities, and contradictions among definitions have been considerable.

The interpretations or definitions of HSOs may be grouped in the following categories: (1) Societal Function; (2) Movement; (3) Special Attributes; (4) Workplace of "Human Service Professionals"; (5) Governmental Designation.

Reprinted with permission from *Administration in Social Work*, Vol. 4, No. 2 (Summer, 1980), this article was prepared while the author was a fellow at the Center for Advanced Studies in Behavioral Sciences, with the support of the Lois and Samuel Silberman Fund, for a conference on Organization and Human Services.

SOCIETAL FUNCTION

Sarri (1971) presented an interpretation of the societal function of HSOs which has since been widely used or adapted. She states in a footnote to this early article that "the distinguishing features of human service organizations" were elaborated in an article by Vinter (1963). However, Vinter's incisive analysis of "treatment organizations" in fact does not refer to HSOs at all. Sarri went far beyond his statement, referring to HSOs as "-community agencies for welfare, education, social control, and the preservation of social values (that) are mandated by society to contribute to the fulfillment of essential societal functions." As illustrations, she includes juvenile courts, mental health and correctional agencies, family service and children's agencies, general and special hospitals, and agencies for the physically handicapped, retarded and aged, "as well as a large number of specific health and welfare organizations."

She states further, "The substantive goals of the organization are to process and change people as a means toward social rather than nonsocial ends. Furthermore, the clients who are served both the major input and output of the organization."

Vinter's (1963) article refers to "people-changing organizations" and two major types that compose this category; that is, socialization and treatment agencies. The first include schools and youth-serving agencies preparing individuals for adequate performance of their social roles. By contrast, treatment organizations seek to resolve problems of deviants. Since delinquents and criminals, emotionally disturbed persons, and the chronically unemployed are regarded as possessing defective attributes or as improperly motivated and oriented, they therefore are to be "treated" in such organizations with means an the way from coercive repression to manipulative persuasion. Vinter's essay is principally a critique of the treatment organization thus defined, where professionals assert the principle of autonomy in the exercise of their skills. He argues that treatment organizations therefore tend to become contexts for professional practice rather than goal-directed enterprises. Or, they become agencies overvaluing organizational stability, administrative convenience, and preservation of good order. "Thus, a high degree of doctrinairism is cultivated throughout the entire range of treatment organizations. . . . Deprived of confident knowledge about goal attainment, the treatment organization encounters difficulties in assuring external public that it is both competent and effective. "

In their book of readings on HSOS, Hasenfeld and English (1974) also refer to Vinter as their source, in generalizing about HSOS: "A key derivative of the technological problems encountered by human service organizations is their difficulty in developing reliable and valid measures of effectiveness" (Vinter, 1963).

Hasenfeld and English define HSOs as follows: "We shall denote the set of organizations, whose primary function is to define or alter the person's behavior, attributes and social status in order to maintain or enhance his well being, as human service organizations." They go on to say, first, that their "input of raw material" consists of human beings and their "production output" are persons processed or changed in a predetermined manner; and secondly, that their general mandate is that of "service," that is, to maintain or improve the general well-being or function of people. In giving their illustrations, they include schools, social and recreation centers, universities, youth-serving agencies, police and other agencies, hospitals, prisons, and all social service agencies. A similar context for human service agencies is provided by Brager and Holloway (1978) and other publications.

Their line of interpretation and the expanded scope of organizations included blurs Vinter's distinction between socializing organizations that try to assist in preparing people to move "along normal developmental gradients," and those that try to alter personality or motivation or otherwise control deviance. Vinter at no point refers to hospitals, universities, police departments, etc.

Hasenfeld and English (1974), drawing on a number of resources, present two typologies for human service organizations. One dimension of HSOS, they state, is the nature of the clients they serve, that is, how normal or "malfunctioning" are the clients? A second dimension relates to the services offered by the organization, i.e., whether it is "people-changing" or "people-processing." These two dimensions are combined into one typology of function and domain.

Their second typology of "organization-client relations" combines Etzioni's classification of normative, utilitarian, and coercive compliance systems, with Lefton and Rosengren's dimension of the nature of the organization's interest in the client.

These classifications are not designed to decide when an organization is an HSO, but to denote ways in which they might be analyzed or researched once they are so defined.

Hasenfeld and English conclude their introductory essay by noting the difficulties in applying the "new science of management" to HSOs, such as hospitals, police departments, and schools. They state that the success of "sophisticated management tools," like operations research and management information systems, has been limited to the more routine and peripheral aspects of the organization. However, they conclude, "full cognizance and understanding of the unique parameters that shape the service delivery system of human service organizations may enable the development of a new science of human service management that is applicable to these organizations." The inference to be drawn is that there is sufficient commonality in "these organizations," including, as earlier specified, schools, law enforcement agencies, hospitals, and correctional institutions, as well as all manner of social service agencies, to warrant an applicable "science of human service management."

There are approaches other than that of Hasenfeld and English, taken by those oriented to the status-enhancing, people-processing, or people-changing function of human services. However, more mundane distinctions in the social work literature for purposes of classification are rare, such as whether there is governmental or private sector funding or auspice, whether the organization is for profit or is nonprofit, whether it is custodial or not, whether it is large or small (although HSOs are frequently referred to as complex and bureaucratic and sometimes simply assumed to be governmental). One result is ambiguity about boundaries. While most definitions include education, health, and social work services, by some interpretations, one can include under the HSO umbrella a dentist's office, a law firm, a maximum security prison, a public library, a for-profit marital counseling agency, a state public welfare system, and a barber shop.

AS A MOVEMENT

Schulberg, Baker, and Rowen (1973) interpret the concept of human - services as a reaction from the isolated clinic or other agency to designing "far-flung human service systems which seek to provide comprehensive and coordinated assistance to clients." The emphasis is on new care-giving systems incorporating the following features: comprehensiveness of services, decentralized facilities located in areas of high population density, and integrated program administration that permits continuity of care from one service element to the next with a minimum of wasted time and duplication. Their underlying premise is that the increasing tendency to designate a community's variety of health and social welfare services as human services organizations reflects not only the desire to provide services more efficiently but also a growing societal as well as professional recognition of the common denominator inherent in the various problems presented us by clients.

Thus, traditional child guidance or adult psychiatric clinics, not part of comprehensive systems, would fall outside the human services framework. The "involvement and cooperation of the target community" are essential to this premise.

Demone and Harshbarger (1973) refer to human service organizations as

organizations in the public or voluntary sector that have as their mandate primary, secondary and tertiary prevention of biosocial problems. Moreover, they carry the implicit mandate that their combined efforts should contribute to the social welfare and the development of proadaptive and active rather than passive ecological behaviors among the population.

They state that HSOs are similar to "other" complex organizations by sharing problems of differentiation-integration, resource acquisition, and role strain and role conflict. However, they are supported at a public and voluntary resource level and do not expect to make a profit, the authors thus apparently eliminating the for-profit organization from the concept. At another point, however, they say that "profit making in the human services represents a significant future development" in the health and education industry. "The human services complex is a growth industry of the profit making sector and is moving into this larger arena."

Demone and Schulberg (1975) interpret the concept of human services as a reaction to decades of growth, expansion, and specialization, insufficiently related to comprehensiveness and linkages for client service.

The increasing tendency to designate a community's variety of education, health and social welfare interventions as human services reflects both a discontent with existing practice and a recognition of the common elements underlying the helping actions of diverse professional and nonprofessional care givers.

In a doctoral dissertation reviewing HSOS, Bridenbaugh (1975) interprets the movement features of the human services concept more drastically as an attack on the traditional helping services in health, welfare, and rehabilitation for being over-professionalized, over-bureaucratized, and too distant from those they are intended to serve. However, two additional elements are essential to this interpretation of the human services organization: one, a denial of the "objective, value-free non-political approach to human problems" toward planned organizational and social change (although how the organization is to be changed is left to "future research"), as well as relieving client distress. The second is the preparation of a new cadre of generalist "human service workers," imbued with the necessary skills and values, who can function in any of the existing HSOS. Indeed, such training has been under way in recent years, at both undergraduate and two-year graduate levels, "in conflict with the established professions" (Sunderland, 1975).

The movement interpretation is no doubt accurate in referring to the sense of dissatisfaction, both on th epart of the public and political bodies with expansion, over-specialization, and lack of coherence in both the public and private sectors. It begs the question, however, of whether a given organization becomes an HSO only when it joins other HSOs in coordination and comprehensiveness or, in the more militant approach, when it engages in social change efforts. In general, the boundary or classification concerns are left untouched by this usage and line of interpretation.

A variant of the movement notion is given by Alexander (1978). He explains human services as resulting from the pressure by graduates of expanded programs in "psychology, theology, law, sociology, education and social work," and to the creation of new vocations such as urban and health planning and counseling. The graduates of these programs, according to this view, tried to "rationalize" national, state, and local service efforts and to establish new domains in which they were identified as experts. These attempts, he observes, to move away from the more traditional "social welfare" or "social service" agencies led to the title "human service organizations."

Alexander's contribution to the *Encyclopedia of Social Work* illustrates some of the confusion resulting from cloudy terminology. He states: "Human service organizations are now a major industry in the United States. For example, in 1975, approximately $389.7 billion in public and private funds were spent on social welfare" (p. 844). Note may be taken of the sudden, and in the literature not infrequent, equation of HSO and social welfare." What is much more important is that no reference was made to the precise definition and usage peculiar to the source used by Alexander (Skolnik & Dales, *Social Security Bulletin,* January 1977) of "public and private social welfare expenditures. " In this usage, such expenditures, in addition to health, education, and welfare programs, include life insurance programs, railroad retirement, industrial in-plant health services, and a variety of expenditures of employee benefit plans. Of the $387.7 billion actually noted for total expenditures in 1975, $24.6 billion were expended for "welfare and other services" in both the private and public sector (Table 10, p. 17). This is the sector to which Alexander apparently has reference. $24.6 billion is a large enough total to warrant being referred to as constituting "a major industry," but it is hardly $387.7 billion. When it comes to assuming what is meant by HSO or social welfare in reading, caveat lector!

SPECIAL ATTRIBUTES

A recent statement of HSOs in terms of their essential attributes rather than their societal functions is provided by Sarri and Hasenfeld (1978) in their introduction to *The Management of Human Services.* First, they introduced their now familiar theme that "HSOs work on people by processing and/or changing them individually or collectively. The persons directly handled by these organizations are simultaneously their input, raw material and product." This last phrase, reflecting a factory analogy, developed also in Hasenfeld and English (1974), and apparently drawn from Hasenfeld's previous work, seems to suggest that in a counseling service, for example, what the professional staff does is not input, nor is any other resource applied for service to the clientele; that in a hospital, what the staff does is not input, that research is not a product, but that the hospital "produces" patients. I find their use of input, raw material, and output awkward and confusing.

The accent, however, by Sarri and Hasenfeld now has moved from their previous concentration on the social function of HSOs to observations about their characteristics and the ways in which they work.

Thus, "HSOs must adopt ideological systems to justify their activities, yet always face the risk that these ideologies will be contested by various social groups. " Second, HSOs are characterized by a "precarious domain consensus. . . . They confront multiple expectations and conflicting demand sin a pluralistic society." Third, "human service organizations, particularly in the public sector, acquire very limited autonomy in relation to their task environment. . . . These organizations are highly dependent on resources controlled by other organizations and are often subject to extensive regulation by various legislative and administrative bodies." Fourth, "the lack of determinate and effective technologies. With few exceptions, particularly in the health field, most human service technologies are based on limited and fragmented knowledge bases while having to deal with complex human behavior. . . . Consequently HSOs develop ideological systems in lieu of technologies which guide and justify the behavior of staff."

The editors then make a plea for an organizational theory that accounts for all of these characteristics. "These four mentioned characteristics indicate that, at the very least, organization and management theories must incorporate them into their explanatory models and prescriptive paradigms in order to be of any relevance to HSOS."

WORKPLACE OF "HUMAN SERVICE PROFESSIONALS"

A number of statements in the literature, directly or indirectly, suggest that HSOs are essentially those where "human service professionals" work. Who the human service professionals are may be as unclear as what human service organizations are, by those who attempt to define them. Thus, Turner (1968) uses the term "human service professions" as being broader than social work, and mentions education, health, housing, economics, and the law. Hokenstad (1977) refers to them as including services that promote social and psychological well-being, as well as physical and economic. They include "self-development and self-actualization, hard and soft services, health and social services."

Morris (1974) forthrightly focuses on social workers and states that "the term human services covers several subsystems of the social welfare system that employs social workers in either a dominant or peripheral position. The subsystems include health and medical care, law and justice, education, income security, and reinforcement of personal growth and family cohesiveness (family services, character building, and the like)." He recognizes that in many states, "the human services thus interpreted include as much as 50% of state government employees and account for between 50 and 65% of state, government expenditures."

GOVERNMENTAL DESIGNATION

Most states have by this time adopted the approach of human service umbrella organizations, under various titles such as the Department of

Health and Rehabilitation Services or Department of Human Resources. All of the agencies reporting to the superagency then automatically become identified as human service organizations. In most states these would include public welfare, health, mental health, retardation, youth services, aging, children, medical programs, and vocational rehabilitation. Sometimes corrections agencies are included. Education, however, rarely appears within this comprehensive rubric.

By such designation, not only would the governmental organizations defined in a given state as within the human service orbit be so included, but also those that are within the private, nonprofit sector. Thus, which organizations are within or outside the "human service industry" (Austin, 1977) become administratively defined. Whether grouping these categories of organizations under one overall state administration provides greater comprehensiveness or greater cost saving and ease of administration is still under review. It has, however, been a process further stimulated by the HEW reorganization in 1977, during which the Office of Human Development Services was established, consolidating the former Social and Rehabilitation Services and human development programs.

This is not a conceptual, but a managerial approach. What is and is not an HSO is administratively designated. A program now in, may later be out, or vice versa, in a reorganization, but at any one time what is declared a human service organization for these purposes is clear. This is not, however, how social work literature currently prefers to use the term.

WHY HSO?

"Human service organization" seems to provide for the social work onlooker whatever ideology, attributes, and behavior one prefers to espouse for it, a seductive catchall of a phrase. Richan (1969) called the term "social services. . . a marvel of imprecision." By comparison to human service organization, it is a model of clarity.

But why has this term become so popular with social work?

Educators don't call schools HSOs.

Doctors and nurses don't call hospitals HSOs.

Lawyers don't call their offices HSOs.

Judges don't call courts HSOs.

Even wardens don't call prisons HSOs.

Yet in the social work literature they are all called HSOs, along with the familiar family agencies, mental health clinics, and child care institutions.

One reason may be a perspective within social work which is sensitive to the commonalities of working with people. An awareness of the interconnections of different fields of service is intrinsic to the very activities of social workers and social agencies. HSO may have these connotations, when no precision is required for usage.

Another reason for the affinity to the expression is perhaps similar to social work's fondness for "the helping professions, " a term alien to the older, more prestigious professions. That is, it may in some measure be a need to be associated with institutions and professions more solidly rooted, and to find social work located more securely within a broader social context.

There can be no great objection to the use of global generic terms that are loose and comfortable, particularly where there is sufficient understanding of their sense for general communication. "Social services" is one of these terms. It defies consensus, but will not cause more confusion unless used for serious analysis without further definition. "Human services" likewise poses no serious problem. However overflowing and ambiguous its boundaries are, it signifies direct services to people, in usage implicitly, if not necessarily, of a nonprofit variety. "Human service professions," by suggesting that there are commonly understood identifiable professions thus subsumed, is even more risky, and "human service organizations" begins to fade into a haze barely to be rescued by the caveat, "for present purposes the term will be used to mean."

No serious problem yet arises until this voracious shark of a term, swallowing diverse organizations like so many schools of fish, becomes reified, treated as if it were a recognizable entity. The employment of the term for analysis of organizational structure, function, and processes causes mischief by suggesting that HSO is part of an authentic taxonomy of organizations, and this, I argue, is an illusion. The contrast is striking between Vinter's careful analysis of the treatment agency, which is definable, and the way in which his precise formulation has been inflated and transmuted into the current diffuseness of the HSO-blanketing courts, public welfare agencies, schools, hospitals, libraries, and occasionally any et ceteras that seem at hand.

There can be little objection to the use of the term as connoting a movement, if that is the way some wish to use it. Whether one agrees or not that there is or should be such a movement is immaterial. The sense of the term in this context is at least clear, and requires no precision as to boundaries or internal arrangements of organizations, for these are virtually irrelevant to the ideological message.

Neither is its use for administrative or regulatory purposes trouble-some. As an omnibus term to specify services within the scope of Title XX, for examples or falling under a state coordinating umbrella of "human re-sources agency" or "Human Service Development Office," it poses no con-ceptual dilemma.

The very special usage of defining the human service organization as an agency wherever social workers practice, is awkward, and possibly un-necessary, but at least is not misleading. It is its employment as a generic kind of organization with generalizable functions and attributes that is troublesome.

The typologies of HSOs presented by Hasenfeld and English provide useful perspectives for understanding and researching certain aspects of organizations. However, they reflect conceptual and analytic concerns of interest to particular researchers. They do not derive from a general scheme of organizational classification, nor do they attempt to identify the vari-ables necessary to define boundaries within which organizations can be located, either structurally or functionally, for theory development, aggre-gation, comparative analysis, or simply for systematic description. No one system of classification can satisfy all interests, but it would help advance organizational research and theory, particularly with respect to nonprofit, so-called "human service" organizations.

Blau and Scott (1962) made a major effort at classification, utilizing their *cui bono* criterion. There they distinguished among mutual benefit as-sociations, business concerns, service organizations, and commonweal or-ganizations. However insightful and forward-looking their analysis, at the time, it no longer serves as a sufficient basis for classification, for it concen-trates on one dimension of societal function.

An interesting and valuable effort was made by Harshbarger (1974) to outline "dimensions for a taxonomy of complex organizations, " by attempt-ing to incorporate Blau and Scott's approach with that of Etzioni (1961) and Katz and Kahn (1966). Harshbarger's own' use of it, to contrast production and service organizations, is insightful and provocative but replete with questionable assumptions. Although he narrows the field by generalizing only for "public sector human service organizations," it is still too heteroge-neous a catchall. His position on the need to develop a taxonomy of organi-zations for purposes of theory and research is, however, unexceptionable.

Developing a comprehensive taxonomy of organizations is far from simple, particularly if it is to achieve consensus. It is, however, a necessary context within which the growing nonprofit sector in the economy can be better understood.

Efforts are being made to understand this sector better, both globally and with respect to specific fields such as hospitals, schools, or employment services (the last, it may be noted, does not yet seem to figure within the et ceteras noted in social work literature as falling within HSOS). One of the most promising directions is the study of the economics of the private nonprofit sector as a whole, a field which Weisbrod (1978) describes as being in its infancy. "Researchers are far from a consensus on organizational goals or on trade-offs among the probably multiple goals, and there has been scarcely any empirical testing."

CONCLUSION

The interpretations underlying the use of the term "human service organization" vary as among societal function, movement, special attributes, workplace for certain kinds of professionals, and by governmental designations. All of these interpretations can live side by side, as long as their particular meaning is made clear in specific usage. Moreover, the term can be used generically to blanket-in organizations commonly grouped in Europe as "the social services." However, the use of the term to connote a defined type of organization with specific behavioral, functional, and management characteristics, is confusing, because it does not reflect reality but gives that illusion. In current usage, it usually lumps together service agencies which differ markedly in function, auspice, relationship to the marketplace, size and structure, and other critical variables, and therefore does little, when used as an analytic concept, to help in understanding organizational behavior, management, or implications for service delivery. There is a need for a general taxonomy, within which the variety of organizations can be appropriately identified so that analysis and research, and understanding of management implications, can progress.

REFERENCES

Alexander, C. Management of human service organizations. *Encyclopedia of Social Work*, 1978, 17, 844-849.

Austin, M. J. Defining the nature of human service work for personnel system management. *Administration in Social Work*, 1977, 1, 31-41.

Blau, P. M., & Scott, W. R. *Formal organization: A comparative approach*. Chandler Publishing Co., 1962.

Brager, G., & Holloway, S. *Changing human service organizations politics and practice.* New York: Free Press, 1979.

Bridenbaugh, W. D. *A descriptive study of the development, organization, and implications of human services: An interdisciplinary analysis.* Unpublished doctoral dissertation, St. Louis University, 1975.

Demone, H. W., & Harshbarger, D. A. The planning and administration of human services. In H. C. Schulberg, et al. (Eds.), *Developments in human services* (Vol. 1). New York: Behavioral Publications, 1973.

Demone, H. W., & Schulberg, H. C. Human services trends in the mid-1970's. *Social Casework,* 1975,56,268-279.

Etzioni, A. (Ed.). *Complex organizations: A sociological reader.* New York: Holt, Rinehart, & Winston, 1961.

Hasenfeld, Y., & English, R. A. (Eds.). *Human service organizations: A book of readings.* Ann Arbor: University of Michigan Press, 1974.

Hokenstad, M. C. Higher education and the human service professions: What role for social work? *Journal of Education for Social Work,* 1977, 13, 52-59.

Katz, D., & Kahn, R. L. *The social psychology of organizations.* New York: Wiley, 1966.

Morris, R. The place of social work in the human services. *Social Work,* 1974, 5, 519-53 1.

Patti, R. J. Organizational resistance and change: The view from below. *Social Service Review,* 1974, 48, 367-382.

Richan, W. The two kinds of social service in public welfare. *Public Welfare,* 1969,27, 307-3 10.

Sarri, R. C. Administration in social welfare. *Encyclopedia of Social Work,* 1971, 16, 42-5 1.

Sarri, R. C., & Hasenfeld, Y. (Eds.). *The Management of human services.* New York: Columbia University Press, 1978.

Schulberg, H. C., Baker, F., & Rowen, S. R. (Eds.). *Developments in human services (Vol.* 1). New York: Behavioral Publications, 1973.

Skoinik, A. M., & Dales, S. R. Social welfare expenditures, fiscal year 1976. *Social Security Bulletin,* January 1977.

Stretch, J. Increasing accountability for human service administrators. *Social Casework,* 1978, 56, 323-329.

Sunderland, S. C. Creating the new profession: The human services. *Education and Urban Society,* 1975, 7(2).

Turner, J. B. On response to change: Social work at the crossroads. *Social Work*, 1968, *13*, 7-15.

Vinter, R. The analysis of treatment organizations. *Social Work*, 1963, *8*, 3-15.

Weisbrod, B. The forgotten economic sector: Private but nonprofit. *Challenge*, September-October 1978.

Weissman, H. *Overcoming mismanagement in the human service professions.* San Francisco: Jossey-Bass, 1973.

14. Administrative Implications of Bureaucratic Theory

The general development of bureaucratic theory, stemming from Max Weber's original formulations, has received impetus in the past decade, and the understanding of organizational behavior has been greatly enhanced as a result. The inferences to be drawn by administrators and others in a position to influence organizational development have, by comparison, received little attention. This discussion is, therefore, related to specifying a tentative series of such inferences rather than to an attempt to examine or extend the area of theory. Two themes of existing theory are considered for these purposes: strengths and strains related to structural attributes of bureaucracy, and the relationship between formal and informal organization.

STRENGTHS OF BUREAUCRATIC STRUCTURE

In the social scientific sense, the term "bureaucratic structure" has no necessarily invidious connotation. It refers, rather, to a form of rational organization conceived thus far to be indispensable to the mass production of goods and services. The extension of bureaucracy has been a concomitant of technological development in all countries where such development has taken place.[1] Government bureaus, industrial organizations, the armed services, trade unions, schools, and hospitals have all reflected this trend in the United States; and, as has been amply demonstrated, social agencies, whether public or voluntary, are not strangers to this development.[2]

Reprinted with permission from *Social Work*, Vol. 6, No. 3 (July 1961), this article is an adaptation of part of a presentation given at a conference on research in administration and community planning sponsored by the NASW Research Section, Chicago, November 1960.

[1] Peter M. Blau, *Bureaucracy in Modern Society* (New York: Random House, 1956).

[2] Harold L. Wilensky and Charles N. Lebeaux, *Industrialization and Social Welfare* (New York: Russell Sage Foundation, 1955).

Bureaucracy, as a rational form of organization, depends for its most effective functioning upon planned co-ordination of its parts, clarity in its policies, specificity in the roles of all who are part of the organizational system, and impersonality in its discharge of functions. When referring to *inherent strengths* of bureaucratic structure, one is not suggesting that every organization so characterized includes these virtues; rather that the central tendencies of bureaucratic structure, when the most rational principles are applied, are consistent with these attributes. Such "strengths" may be characterized as follows:

Economy and efficiency. Contributed to by rational division of labor and pooling of expertise.

Stability and permanence. A bureaucracy is not easily shaken by the loss of one person, since the office to be filled tends to be more important than the particular individual who occupies it. Such structures maintain a high investment in stability and permanence.[3]

Role security. Occupational roles tend to be highly specific. What is expected on the job is relatively clear. Job descriptions and formal communication processes tend to be defined.

Relative job security. Bureaucratic structures have an investment in retaining personnel in the interests of stability, and thus tend to promote not only fringe benefits but in-service training programs, retirement programs, and so on.

Impersonality of policies. Bureaucracies tend to minimize subjective elements in determination of policies and to maximize the establishment of objective and impersonal criteria, with the following results:

1. For the consumer of the organization's goods or services, this can have the effect of democratization through uniform applicability of criteria, as long as the consumer meets established criteria. Whether it is having the amount of money to purchase the goods or services, or the requisite financial need to obtain public assistance, the tendency is to minimize discretion based on subjective considerations. (The owner of a small neighborhood grocery store may provide credit to his customers based on his personal knowledge and opinion of them. In a large urban supermarket there would either be "no credit" for anyone, or it would be established on the basis of uniform procedures.)

---

[3] A maxim in administrative circles is that "the easiest way to start a permanent organization is to start a temporary one."

2. For the personnel of the organization impersonality of policies tends to make for relatively objective criteria for evaluation, promotions, sick leave, vacations, and so on. Aside from inducing expectations that can be realized and providing clarity for job conditions, the application of the principle of maximum impersonality tends also to reduce inter-personal competition for advancement within an organization. The competition may be related to examinations or to the achievement of certain experience or skills deemed necessary for promotion and not, for example, to competition between two or more people for the favor of a superior.

INHERENT STRAINS

While bureaucracy tends to bolster such strengths, its structure also contains inherent strains. By strains, in this sense, are meant tendencies likely to arise unless specifically planned for and prevented. These strains may be viewed in four areas: personnel, the consumer, management, and the community.

Personnel. 1. Ritualism.[4] This is the condition where means become ends. The very fact that roles are defined, that the job tends to be precisely described, provides a congenial situation for the employee who feels con-strained only to do his particular job "right" without reference to its mean-ing for the total organization, and not to exercise judgment or deviate from established routine. A "ritualist" in a mail-order house whose job it is to seal up envelopes on the assembly may continue to do so even if the enve-lopes she is sealing happen not to have anything in them. A "ritualist" in a hospital will wake a patient soundly asleep in order to give him a sleeping pill because that is the routine practice for that precise hour.

2. Mediocrity and overconformity. These are the tendencies which have recently been emphasized on the public rostrum, in the press, and in books such as *The Organization Man.*[5] "Not getting into trouble" and "playing it safe" tend to be requisites for maintenance of job tenure and among the criteria for eventual promotion when length of service is a prime factor in this regard. The system may both attract conformists and remove the po-tential for constructive nonconformity by adhering rigidly to prescribed

---

[4] Robert Merton, "Bureaucratic Structure and Personality," in Merton, ed., *Reader in Bureaucracy* (Glencoe, Ill.: The Free Press, 1952).

[5] William Whyte, *The Organization Man* (New York: Doubleday & Co., 1957).

policies and procedures. In the long run the diffusion of mediocrity serves to militate against the most important *raison d'etre* of bureaucracy itself, namely, economy and efficiency. Another aspect of this condition is lack of stimulus for imagination or creativity. The absence of a demand for one's thinking and evaluation and the adherence, rather, to making sure that the defined job is done can have the effect of stifling potential imaginative contributions which could add to the effectiveness of the organization.

The consumer of goods or services. The very impersonality of criteria when applied to the consumer can make it difficult for the individual to be properly served and leave the organization incapable of meeting crisis situations or emergencies. When the consumer confronts an organization in this context he has the sense of dealing with a system, not with a person. It is at this point that the reproach of "red tape" is most frequently applied. A customer who is making a fast purchase when a store is closing and is told that he cannot complete the purchase because the store closed at that very moment is bound to be frustrated. The employee in such a situation is not concerned with the customer but with conforming to the prescription of his job, and when the bell sounds slams the register shut. The parent in distress after his child's accident is depressed by the impersonality of eligibility criteria when he is compelled to see that the proper forms are filled out at the hospital to assure his financial condition before he can return to his child.

Management. Lack of adaptability to change can be a consequence of the investment in the organization's stability and permanence. Ritualistic, unimaginative, and overly formalized behavior may become norms of management, as well as of other personnel.

Community. Bureaucracies tend to be self-protective, and it is difficult for the outside community, except in cases of violation of law or other crises, to gain access to the organization or affect its structure (more so, of course, in voluntary than in public agencies). While the cohesiveness of the organization can be an asset, it also promotes unwillingness to expose its internal system to public scrutiny because of the danger of upsetting the authority balance within the organization, or to reveal practices deemed necessary for internal stability but not easily reconciled with public or official goals of the organization. This condition of protective shielding from the public can become particularly important in social agencies, which in the last analysis are accountable to the public, whether or not the agencies are supported by tax funds.

ADMINISTRATIVE IMPLICATIONS

One general principle should govern an approach to preventing, miti-gating, or compensating for strains arising from bureaucratic organiza-tion: that preventive countermeasures should themselves be consistent with bureaucracy. That is, such means should themselves be rational and offi-cial, maintain specificity of roles and clear procedures, maximize impar-tiality, and the like. In other words, a bureaucratic organization would not be consistent if, in attempting to lessen overconformity, it should say to personnel, "Just use your own judgment," but may more consistently say to a specific department or level of personnel, "In these and these situa-tions discretion may be exercised up to this point, utilizing the following criteria as guides."

Further, it is obvious that no organization, however ingeniously run, is without its problems while it lives, grows, and changes. It is with the capacity of an organization to strengthen itself, to detect and deal with its problems-not to remove all problems for all time—that any consideration of administrative practice must be concerned.

Following are observations bearing on the reduction or prevention of organizational strains. While they are grouped in relation to implications for personnel, consumer (of service), management, and community, it should be clear that measures taken in relation to any one of these poten-tial strains may affect more than one of these components of the agency network.

PERSONNEL

Prevention of ritualism. Ritualism develops when personnel are either permitted or encouraged to wear "organizational blinkers" so that they see neither to left nor right but keep their eye on the immediate job for which they have been hired. It can pervade not only personnel who do routine mechanical operations, but professional and managerial person-nel as well. Ritual behavior is unconcerned with the larger organizational purposes, and can lead to the aggrandizement of one's own job or one's own department at the expense of others or at the risk of disturbing the organization's rational balance and coordination of functions.

The prevention of ritualism is, therefore, in the direction of policies and procedures that make it possible for personnel to be oriented to the central objectives of the organization, to see how their functions relate to those of others, and to be concerned about such interrelationships. Some of the simple techniques in this area are well known, for example, the orientation of new staff by actually taking them around an office or plant, general meetings of the entire staff, annual reports, interdepartmental meetings, and so forth. An appropriate program for a given organization will depend partly on its complexity and partly on the precise character of its organizational cast, as well as its function and objective. As will be noted below in another connection, the supervisory chain of command is crucial to the mitigation of this as well as other strains, if nonritualistic behavior is regarded as a positive criterion of performance and evaluated accordingly through the entire organization.

Programs may vary for different echelons of the organization, and when carried out "nonritualistically" may have the effect of reducing the tendency to encapsulate one's own task as if it were the only important one in the organization without reference to its meaning for others, and may encourage flexibility and judgment when the need arises.

Provision of opportunities for new ideas. The accent on stability and permanence can have the effect of making "not rocking the boat" a central concern. Where this is the prevailing norm, not only will potential ideas in the service of the organizational purposes not be tapped, but their sources will dry up. One is familiar with primitive devices such as the suggestion box, or more recent notions such as "brainstorming" in executive idea sessions, as means for encouraging or stimulating imaginative contributions. Some industrial organizations have attempted to cope with this problem partly by creating "islands of creativity" where scientists and professionals who have achieved superior standing within the organization are permitted a place to work and resources without restriction on what they do, and without having to abide by the normal routines of the organization.

To utilize individual initiative and imagination would seem to require, however, a pervasive, built-in policy through the entire administrative structure, pervading the organization and effectuated through its entire supervisory apparatus. Thus, every supervisor at whatever level would have as part of his obligation the need to inquire as to suggestions or ideas, to evaluate them, and to utilize what is possible, and would himself be evaluated partly on his capacity to fulfill this supervisory requirement. The organization itself can thus better harness its potential from personnel, and for those who are able to contribute ideas rewards, whether in economic or other terms, should be forthcoming.

CONSUMER

Prevention of rigidity toward the consumer. Bureaucracy requires policies and regulations, but also ways of individualizing and dealing with the exceptional situation or the emergency. It is possible for a bureaucracy to develop ways of dealing with the exceptional case in a manner which is consistent with the needs of such a structure. Essential in any method of dealing with the emergency or exceptional case is for the organization to recognize that such cases may arise—situations not anticipated by existing policy. Responsibility for emergencies or special cases should, therefore, be centralized and clarified to avoid the exasperating phenomenon of an organization representative who says, in effect, "I'm sorry I can't deal with that and I don't know who does."

Anticipated emergencies can be met by policies that set the levels of discretion appropriate to different staff. For example, a family agency might be able to permit its workers to grant emergency financial assistance at their discretion up to a certain amount without further check, increase the amount at the discretion of supervisory personnel, and beyond this limit require authorization from the executive. Such policies with regard to limits of discretion are possible when emergencies can be foreseen.

When emergencies or special cases begin to assume recognizable patterns, policies can be developed for such situations and responsibilities allocated for carrying them out, so that the situations themselves no longer assume a special or emergency character.

MANAGEMENT

Adaptability to change. The processes of change in large organizations are still not too well understood, but change does occur and often reveals imagination and creative planning rather than being simply accidental. To develop the actuality of change toward well-understood goals requires, of course, that the function of planning be clearly located within the organization. Unless planning is a conscious activity it will not tend simply to happen. There will be changes, but they will be uncontrolled and at the mercy of external factors rather than self-directed, or planned to meet the influences of external pressures in the environment of the organization.

The centralization of a planning function does not mean, however, that participation in planning and in policy formulation must be restricted to a specific individual or group of individuals. On the contrary, participation in planning can and should be widespread through an organization. In making this point one is not referring to so-called "democratic administration" where everyone in an organization has an equal voice in planning—or where the right, if not the fact, of such "democratic" participation is conceded. In large formal structures democratic administration in this sense is a contradiction in terms and virtually impossible. What is possible, however, is tapping the understanding, ideas, and motivations of people in an organization according to their special competence and interests—that is, through *relevant participation*. One way of making the bureaucratic structure more adaptable to change is to build into the administrative process modes of participation that would elicit the contribution of all those in the organization who have something to contribute out of their legitimate roles, experience, and organizational interests. This can be true whether one is dealing with planning for budget, for locating unseen problems, or for devising new approaches to meet existing conditions.

The concept of relevant participation does not mean having everyone responsible for everything, and certainly is not the same as trying to have participation for its own sake as a morale-builder. Such specious involvement is self-defeating and can only lead to cynicism. More to the point is the concept of maintaining appropriate channels at all times for the raising of questions related to the work problems of staff at any level in the organization. In effect, the approach would be to seek systematically such evaluation of work tasks, procedures, and relationships by personnel and to recognize this process administratively as desired behavior, without having the executive branch of the organization abdicate its authority for decision-making.

Client or consumer participation. In considering participation in policy formulation and in raising questions at various levels, one must not overlook client, consumer, or patient participation. A long-standing practice in membership organizations such as group service agencies has been to involve clientele in program-planning, although the extent and modes of participation may often merit re-examination. Now there is increasing attention to the importance of participation among resident populations, such as those of general, rehabilitation, and mental hospitals. Whether and how such participation is possible for nonresident groups, as in casework agencies, remains to be seen.

Participation of clientele does not have to be complicated. One might remind oneself that retail customers "participate" when they are asked to register suggestions on cards, in restaurants, or in airplanes, and such participation can be quite valuable to an organization if the cards are actually read and followed up. Clients in agencies participate when they are involved in the follow-up study of practice. The use of client or consumer participation as a gimmick to demonstrate organizational interest and response to the "voice of the people" can in the long run only be self-defeating, since even the public relations value of these devices will eventually suffer, and the chances of actually utilizing the opinions of consumers will be minimized. What is much more to the point is, first, the right of the consumer to participate at his level of legitimate interest and experience; and second, the contribution he can make by such participation, even if it is elicited by simply asking in a systematic way what he thinks of the service and whether he has any suggestions. Robert Vinter has stated that the client is "lowest on the authority continuum" in social agencies.[6] This is true, by and large. It hardly means, however, that the client has nothing to contribute in the formulation of policy. It means, rather, that the opportunity to participate has to be structured for the client, and that this opportunity should be meaningful.

COMMUNITY

Accountability. The tendency that can develop in agencies toward self-protectiveness and insularity from outside community pressures can lead to inadequate discharge of the agency's responsibility to be accountable for its activities. This source of strain can to some extent be solved by executive decision. A clear understanding is necessary of the public or publics to whom reporting should be made, as well as the development of appropriate means for such reporting. In the absence of such measures for accountability, accumulated pressures for reporting may press on the agency at a point when it is least prepared to meet the demand. While public relations is an element in accountability, it should not be construed as synonymous with it; rather, the genuine right of groups to know what is appropriate and legitimate for them to know and react about should be emphasized. Not only external groups such as legislatures or chests and councils are involved in agency accountability, but departments and total staff of the agency as well.

---

[6] Robert Vinter, "The Social Structure of Service," in Alfred J. Kahn, ed., *Issues in American Social Work* (New York: Columbia University Press, 1959).

FORMAL AND INFORMAL ORGANIZATION

Philip Selznick has stated three hypotheses in his article on "An Approach to a Theory of Bureaucracy."[7]

1. Every organization creates an informal structure.

2. In every organization the goals of the organization are modified by the processes within it.

3. The processes in modification are effected through the informal structure.

Informal organization has been given considerable research attention, yet again relatively little has been said about action implications in the relationship of formal to informal structure. It may be noted that in referring to formal structure one is essentially speaking of what can be blueprinted in the organization: staff positions, lines of authority, job functions, procedures and regulations, committees, and so on. The informal structure includes virtually all else: sentiments, loyalties, informal interaction, friendships, animosities, and cliques.

When the goals of the informal organization are the same as for the formal, one has the essential precondition of high morale. It is generally conceded that such a situation contributes to the efficiency, productivity, and flexibility of an organization. People will do more, work more, think harder, for the organization when its purposes are incorporated not only in the formal tasks but in the sentiments and personal orientations of those in the organization. When the methods and goals of the formal organization are not shared by the informal, more rigid controls become necessary, and the investment in management activity tends to be toward organizational control and overcoming impediments to carrying out the organizational objectives. This is the situation, for example, in most correctional institutions or in any organization which for longer or shorter periods of time contains disaffected, alienated employees, or resident populations of patients or inmates with sentiments or aspirations in conflict with those of formal authority.

For the executive and management group there is the recurrent dilemma in most non-custodial organizations of having to be sensitive to the informal structure without interfering with it or attempting to ma-

---

[7] *American Sociological Review*, Vol. 8, No. I (February 1943), pp. 47-54.

nipulate it. Such manipulation is not only ethically questionable, but in the long run destructive to organizational interests. It is important to recognize, at the same time, the danger inherent in permitting formal processes and decisions to be usurped by the informal structure. One can accept the hypothesis that processes of modification in the formal organization are constantly being effected through the informal structure. Ideas, sentiments, and biases within the informal structure have an effect, sooner or later, on changing conditions within the formal structure. However, for an organization to remain viable and in control of its destiny without being seriously beset by nonrational influences requires that the formal structure be recognized as superordinate. It thus becomes the responsibility of all personnel to see that decisions that belong within formal channels are not made within informal groupings, and to make sure that policy questions that should be raised become located in proper administrative channels. If there are no such channels available, staff can seek to have them created. Should informal groupings be able to manipulate the formal structure, the results—with the best intentions in the world—can become corrosive to the organizational fabric.

One may note, therefore, at least two directions for executive and other personnel in an organization to follow, from an understanding of the inherent relationship between formal and informal structure:

1. The executive should not seek to manipulate the informal structure. He can be sensitive to its climate through the normal processes of administration without seeking to intrude or to develop special channels of communication.

2. For all staff it is important to locate recommendations and policy questions within appropriate levels and channels of the organization, whether or not they originate within the informal structure, in order to safeguard the long-range interests of organizational purposes, processes, and stability.

CONCLUDING OBSERVATIONS

This paper has summarized from existing theory certain predominant strains arising from bureaucratic organization. In relation to each, inferences were drawn as to the direction of administrative practice in preventing, mitigating, or compensating for such strains. It is understood that no organization can be stress-free, and the direction of resolution of bureaucratic strains should be consistent with bureaucratic organization. The importance of supervisory evaluation through the entire line organization in mitigating stress and the concept of relevant participation in policy formation were emphasized.

While the focus of this paper has been the bureaucratically organized agency, the theory has implications as well for the nonbureaucratic agency, characterized by relatively small size, less defined roles, and more informality in relationships. The inherent strengths of such organizations at their best lie in their high potentiality for flexibility, responsiveness to change, and the use of imagination and creativity. The inherent potentialities for weakness lie in the dangers of instability, role confusion, stress on the maintenance of affable personal relationships, and ambiguity of norms for both personnel and consumers or clientele. The virtues of informality are also its dangers if relationships are strained or systematic procedures neglected. The potential organizational assets and liabilities of the nonbureaucratic agency are thus the reverse of those in the bureaucratic agency. The direction of administrative implications would be to maintain enough structure to minimize role confusion, personnel insecurity, and policy ambiguity without sacrificing the essential values of adaptability and informality. Although concepts related to the nonbureaucratic agency cannot be elaborated in this paper, they should not be overlooked in our attention to bureaucratization, and merit development in their own right.

Part Five
**INTERNATIONAL SOCIAL WORK:
TOWARD A WORLD VIEW**

15. International Responsibilities of U.S. Social Work Education

We are here to consider the contribution of social work in helping to fulfill two responsibilities: first and foremost, the responsibility which our government has assumed in aiding other countries, particularly its concern with enabling the poorer countries of the world to develop more rapidly, their own way; second, our responsibility to exchange experience and knowledge with other countries in order to enhance the worldwide progress of our profession and our capacity for service.

Social work education in the United States is in a unique position. It is seen in most parts of the world as being in the forefront of this profession, and social workers in the United States are turned to for expert guidance more than are those in any other country.

Moreover, there is a great reservoir of interest and talent to be drawn upon for staffing the international field. Many factors have contributed. Social workers from the U.S. have served overseas with the Red Cross, UNRRA, IRO, and with many voluntary agencies with foreign programs. We have received more international social work students than any other country, and they have helped quicken the interest of schools and of the general social work community in the international dimension of our field. The International Conferences of Social Work are always well attended by U.S. social workers and American schools of social work have been actively represented in the International Congress of Schools of Social Work from its beginning. There have been committees on international social welfare in many of the chapters of the National Association of Social Workers.

Reprinted with permission from *The Time Is Now*, Proceedings of the Conference on International Social Welfare Manpower, December 13–15, 1964, Washington, DC (Washington, DC, and New York: U.S. Department of Health, Education, and Welfare, Welfare Administration; U.S. Department of State, Agency for International Development; and Council on Social Work Education, 1965).

Can we use the interest and experience that has been developed more rationally than we have to date, in order to help other countries in the development of their manpower resources in social welfare and also to benefit ourselves through experience and exchange?

It is the conviction of many of us that social work education in the U.S. is seriously lagging behind other fields in fulfilling its international responsibilities. It is regrettable, for example, that in the Great Lakes Consortium[1] there are apparently as yet no schools of social work involved.

We do not deny the fact that the contribution thus far made has been considerable—but it has been relatively formless and haphazard. The time is more than ripe for an intensive and concerted move to enlarge this contribution along several dimensions and to make it more rational and more purposive.

We say several dimensions, because they are interdependent and mutually reinforcing. If one of these is not pursued, it will adversely affect the progress of the other three, creating bulges and gaps. I believe economists refer to this as the principle of complementarity. These dimensions are:

1.   The *development of faculty* towards greater competence in international service and greater knowledge of social welfare on the international scene.

2.   A greatly improved process of *selection and preparation*, through the use of university resources, for social welfare advisors and training consultants for overseas service.

3.   *Strengthening the curriculum* of professional education with particular reference to the selection and needs of international students and other social work participants from abroad, as well as for domestic students.

4.   Projecting *research in the international field*.

We are interested, as the proposal for the Conference states, in an integrated, long-range plan for optimal use of our social work educational resources. To consider these areas for purposes of a long-range view will also mean to examine and possibly to expand the relationship of schools of social work in the U.S. to governmental, non-governmental and international bodies, with respect to contractual arrangements in the field of social work education and training.

---

[1] The State universities involved are: Wisconsin, Michigan State, Illinois, and Indiana. The program for the development of the universities' international consortium is supported by the Ford Foundation.

FACULTY DEVELOPMENT

All American universities should improve the competence of their graduate and professional schools to teach and conduct research on international aspects of their disciplines and professions.[2]

The faculty member who has taught abroad is likely to be a better teacher for having gained a broader view of his subject. Because he has faced new kinds of teaching problems, his ability to impart this knowledge to students will be improved. New courses, and new ways of teaching old courses may result from the insights he acquires. Both inside and outside the classroom, the teacher with experience abroad can have a significant impact on the world outlook of students. His courses lose some of their cultural bias; he gives his students perspective on their own society and culture. He becomes more effective in preparing students for study abroad and in teaching foreign students, since he understands some of the problems they face. And, finally, whether or not he was engaged in research, new ideas for research projects often develop.[3]

With these sentiments I think we can heartily concur.

Any program based on the contribution of social work education must rely heavily on the competence of faculty members in the schools to teach international content, to be knowledgeable about comparative developments in their own specialties and to have overseas experience of a responsible nature in consultative, teaching or research positions.

At the present time, there is no organized and substantial way in which faculty members in schools of social work who want this experience and this knowledge can get it, with the exception of the Fulbright programs. While individual faculty members here and there have been able to secure specialized experience, and have studied their fields from an international point of view, this has been a matter of happenstance. It has been too much the result of individual interest and initiative against obstacles, and too little influenced by encouragement from university and school adminis-

---

[2] *The University and World Affairs*, Ford Foundation, 1960, p. 4.

[3] *The College and World Affairs*, Report of the Committee on College and World Affairs. New York: Ford Foundation, 1964, pp. 15-16.

trations. Moreover, there has not often been the opportunity, the incentive, or perhaps the capacity to translate this specialized experience and knowledge into course teaching, counseling with international students, or other educational use.

Faculty members are frequently the first kind of group to be looked at when openings occur for advisers, consultants and trainers overseas. If there has not been prior overseas experience on which one can rely (and one cannot always rely on the fact that overseas experience has been a genuinely constructive experience), the selection of a faculty member for such assignments simply because he is on a faculty, is a most unreliable criterion. It would be important to consider what elements other than individual interests should go into selection of faculty members to be given special encouragement and resources to pursue overseas experience, or special training to enable them to be more competent in the international field.

There are two principal directions that may be considered. One is a program that would enable faculty members to acquire greater expertise in international social welfare so that they can teach and do research in this area, give leadership to programs for international students and bring an international perspective to the curriculum. The second direction concerns the utilization of faculty in advisory and training posts abroad.

With respect to the first, there are of course programs that permit foreign study by social workers and social work faculty. These have been utilized and they are helpful, but they are not enough. For one, they depend largely on who is available for sabbatical leaves. For another, they have been concentrated in countries in Western Europe. And finally, although there is no research I am aware of to back up this impression, relatively little of this experience has been transmuted into teaching, research or curriculum development.

We should be considering whether and how specialists can be developed, not in every school, necessarily, but in sufficient numbers and in enough schools across the country so that an impact on teaching can be felt and an international perspective can gradually be seen as imperative by all schools. A commitment by a number of social work faculty members to the area of international social welfare would imply not only keeping up with the literature but contributing to new knowledge and giving service. Arrangements should be thought of whereby selected interested and qualified faculty members could devote themselves to special language study and area study related to their special interests or to comparative international study on particular social work programs in which they have special authority, whether it is in child welfare or community development or any other field. All facilities now existing that would make such concentrated study possible outside of the accident of sabbatical leave should be made known and be assessed, and we should be able to indicate whether these opportunities are sufficient for the scope of development we have in mind. Undoubtedly an additional investment is going to be called for to permit the release of faculty time for such intensive study, whether in this country or abroad.

With respect to the second direction, namely, the availability of faculty in our schools to serve in advisory or training capacities overseas, we are fortunate in having the responses, for at least 14 schools, to the questionnaire on the subject sent out in the spring of 1964 by the Welfare Administration. The deans responding to the question about impediments to release of faculty indicated, among other obstacles, the following: difficulty in meeting their own immediate needs for staff to man the basic curriculum; the fact that when faculty are on leave there are no funds available for replacement, and the problem, when there are such funds, that engaging part-time faculty tends to weaken continuity and the educational experience for the students; the lack of language facility among faculty; university regulations which often make a leave of more than one year difficult; the inordinate amount of time between the initial inquiry and statement of interest on the part of the employing agency and the firm commitment on appointment, which makes planning by the school extremely difficult. One may note in this connection that in the Ford Foundation-sponsored consortium of the Great Lakes Universities, provisions have been made to take care of most of these difficulties.

One of the directions we should be considering very seriously, is the matter of exchange programs with schools of social work in other countries. At the present time, contracts for assisting other schools of social work have been granted only to the Council on Social Work Education and one School of Social Work (St. Louis University). I believe the Council is not only prepared, but would encourage the development of exchange relationships by individual schools with counterparts in other countries, particularly in the developing countries of the world.

This kind of possibility, however, immediately brings into focus at least one of the points raised by John Gardner in his report,[4] namely, his emphasis on the relationship not between departments or schools of two universities, but between the two universities themselves. We would have to examine the extent to which this is, for the immediate future, both realistic and advisable, granting the general merit of the principle. In several overseas universities where exchange programs in social work would be advisable, other American universities are already in the picture, in teaching, mining, agriculture or other fields. Shall the arrangement be confined to schools of social work in universities already having contracts, or can one graft on additional university relationships?

What are the various kinds of experience overseas, which might be made available to faculty members, assuming that the schools have the wherewithal to replace the faculty member while he is away? Several have been suggested, such as:

- A tour of duty as a social welfare adviser overseas through the UN, AID, Organization of American States, a voluntary agency or some other arrangement.

- Fulbright lectureship or study.

- Intensive studies of a region or a country including study of language, politics, the economics of the area.

- Participation in country and regional seminars.

- Participation in international conferences.

- Specialized experience in programming the training of international students.

- Arranging for faculty to study comparative education and other international courses.

- Arranging for faculty to participate in seminars of the Foreign Service Institute.

Or, we might take a look at the statement in *The College and World Affairs*:

---

[4] Gardner, John. *AID and the Universities*, Agency for International Development, Washington, D.C., 1964.

The faculty can enlarge their competence in their own disciplines in a number of ways. Some ways that have already proved effective are the on-campus faculty seminar; the summer faculty seminar, organized either by discipline or foreign area, at a major university center in the U.S. or at a comparable institution in the foreign area to be studied; an academic year of study at a major university center, supplemented in some cases by a teaching internship, and followed ideally by several months of study and travel in a foreign area; and lastly, an academic year of study abroad.[5]

RECRUITMENT, SELECTION AND ORIENTATION

The problem of personnel selection for international service is acute, especially in the recruitment for professional, scientific and administrative posts. As the volume edited by Dr. Torre on *The Selection of Personnel for International Service*[6] indicates, it costs between ten and twenty thousand dollars to get a senior overseas employee to his first day of work abroad with his family. In addition to the initial and subsequent financial investments which are at stake, the success or failure of an overseas assignment can have far-reaching consequences. There are career and personal considerations for the recruit himself, and the fact that the course of a significant program in the country may be affected—but we should also note that the assignment can affect relationships with a particular international or national agency and, in some measure, even the reputation of the sending country.

It has been a tacit assumption among agencies in the intergovernmental and voluntary fields who send personnel overseas, that it is most difficult to know beforehand who is going to work out, and that successful domestic experience is hardly a sure-fire criterion for effective work in other cultures and in other administrative and political contexts. One does the best one can through direct impressions, references, and knowledge of previous work experience.

---

[5] *The College and World Affairs*, Report of the Committee on College and World Affairs. New York: Ford Foundation, 1964, pp. 15-16.

[6] Torre, Mottram, ed. *The Selection of Personnel for International Service.* World Federation for Mental Health, U.S. Committee, 1963.

There is now a growing body of information on selection techniques developed to a substantial extent in relation to our own Peace Corps, but systematic evaluation based on predictive factors of who will succeed in overseas service has not been undertaken in any comprehensive way. It is probable that subjective impression, hopefully increasingly expert in nature, will remain a large factor in the selection process.

The difficulty for many international agencies of engaging in a systematic combination of selection and orientation is very great. For the most part, international agencies, and U.S. agencies hiring in the international field, cannot engage in a selection-orientation program for potential oversea personnel without first hiring them. The realities of such commitments on both sides, that of the hiring agencies and the particular potential recruit, are hard to overcome. The Peace Corps program is an exception. There the training program is deliberately set up as part of the selection process and there are no grave risks taken by the potential recruit if he is dropped or decides to drop out in the course of this process. The same considerations do not obtain when senior personnel engaged by international agencies have to sever connections with their current employment or take official leave with all that signifies for their personal as well as professional lives.

By the time someone is hired, it is too late. (Think of all the farewell parties!) Everyone involved is too committed, and it may be just as well not to find out that someone whom one has hired may really be a very questionable candidate for the job. There are careers at stake, leaves arranged, clearances endured, host countries informed. In this respect, the United Nations, AID, and other international and national organizations are in a quite different position from the Peace Corps.

There is no problem about eliminating those who are clearly unqualified on grounds of inexperience, incompetence in domestic performance, or who are, on the other hand, clearly desirable because of truly verified successful prior experience overseas. But the vast majority of potential recruits to international service in the social work profession lie in between.

How does one locate the large pool of potential interest and quality, and the smaller pool of desirable recruits? The first answer may be provided by the roster developed by the Welfare Administration. For the second question we now have no answer.

There is a need, it seems to me, for a new approach with an organizational device which will have the following characteristics: It should be independent administratively of operating agencies, but sensitive to their requirements. It should provide orientation for overseas services without requiring a commitment from a potential recruit or from the orienting program. It should have the responsibility, quite clear to all concerned, of evaluating the capacity of the trainee. It should provide counseling for trainees. And it should provide usable, objective, candid references for prospective employing agencies.

If an organizational approach of this kind is accepted as desirable, it can take several forms. It might be exclusively concerned with the recruitment, orientation and selection of social workers for international service. Or it might—both for economical use of resources and to break down overspecialization—deal with a group of related professions concerned with interpersonal communication, social policy and direct service to people. For example, social welfare might be tied in with public administration and public health. Education would be a natural allied field, but the numbers in education may be too large, realistically, to be part of such a program.

Such a program need provide no training in technical fields. On the contrary, technical qualifications would be among the essential criteria for admission to the program. One can visualize a program of four to six weeks duration in residence during the summer, to be attended by both academic and nonacademic people from the practice fields. The content of such a program could be principally to provide orientation to given roles in overseas service (i.e., the expert advisers consultant, trainer) and orientation to overseas opportunities in their fields and requirements for U.S. nationals. Observations, tests, individual interviews and consultation would be undertaken by the staff. For those who pass muster, follow-up programs at universities in their own geographical areas could be initiated so that those selected can take specific training to bolster their capacity to function in overseas service; for example, area courses, international studies, or language training.

Such a program should be university-based, but it is not necessary that it be lodged in a given university. This could be a cooperative interuniversity arrangement. As a matter of fact, we should be, it seems to me, more and more thinking in terms of inter-university cooperation.

There is now no career route for people interested in overseas work. We can tell someone who asks to register in a roster about the possibilities, but how should he prepare himself? The plan I have outlined is one device. There may be others. We should be thinking of internships, of use of graduate students in international programs directly. The evaluation of the experience of overseas personnel is also haphazard and archaic, and this matter should receive our attention. There is a responsibility for schools to select and orient social workers from practice for assignments abroad. How do we best go about it? We have a large amorphous interest, we are losing good people. What can we do about it?

CURRICULUM AND INTERNATIONAL STUDENTS[7]

> It is no longer possible for universities to regard their foreign students (and particularly those from outside North America and Western Europe) as no different from American students. Curricular offerings must often be redesigned to meet the distinctive needs of foreign students and the nations from which they come. At the same time, special efforts have to be made not to isolate the foreign students either in their course work or their extra-curricular life.[8]

In the long view, the subject of North American professional training for nationals of other countries should be placed in the perspective of international professional manpower requirements. In the case of social work, it would require concern not only with what our domestic training programs and policies should be for students from abroad, but what more and what else we can realistically do for the development of social work resources and training patterns indigenous to the needs and capacities of the countries themselves—for example, in sending faculty and graduate students abroad, and having overseas faculty come here. This is why these dimensions interlock.

Professional social work education in North America should not be regarded, by and large, as the basic preparation for social work practice for students from overseas. It is time we faced up to this. While the profession of social work is international and common elements are increasingly in evidence, it is not a technology or a science requiring only minor adap-

---

[7] For this section, the writer has adapted liberally from his essay on "Issues in the Professional Education of International Students in Social Work in North American Schools", pp. 151-186 of *The Professional Education of Students from Other Lands*, ed. by Irwin Sanders, Council on Social Work Education, 1961.

[8] *The University and World Affairs*. Report of the Committee on the University and World Affairs, New York: Ford Foundation, 1961, pp. 29-30.

tations to be universally applicable wherever taught. Rather, it is still shaped in its methods, its structure, and to a considerable extent in its ideology, by the underlying social, economic, and cultural elements in each particular society in which it develops. In these respects education in social work poses, at least in degree, a different situation from that faced by the overseas student in other professions, such as engineering or medicine.

Ideally, therefore, the basic preparation for practice should be provided in the student's own country, with education abroad seen as adding new perspectives and deepening his knowledge and skill, as well as providing the cultural enrichment traditionally sought in travel abroad for educational pursuits. This pattern has not been followed consistently. Many candidates have been accepted for graduate study without prior training in their own country, even when such training was available.

We are very well equipped to meet the educational needs of appropriately selected students from European and other Westernized countries who have previous experience and established position in their own countries and who are heading for positions in government or community agencies back home similar to social work positions here. Indeed, the one systematic study of returnees has found that such students were overwhelmingly "satisfied" with their training in North America, after they had returned to their own countries and were working, and that they had experienced fewer difficulties in transition to their own jobs than students from other countries.

What, however, is the situation with students from the poorer countries in Asia, Latin America, the Middle East, or the newly independent nations of Africa? Are we equipped to offer them what they need, in addition to a degree, for their responsibilities and local conditions? Livingstone[9] answers this in the negative, not on the grounds that we have nothing useful to teach, but that we (that is, Western social work education, including the United Kingdom) tend to have an undesirable influence by shaping welfare systems elsewhere in our image, rather than encouraging an indigenous development that may head in quite different directions. "However inevitable it may have been, there is cause for alarm at the extent to which social welfare training in Asia and Africa has been dominated by Western concepts of social welfare goals and social welfare organization." He deprecates the contribution of individualism, Freud, and

---

[9] Professor of Overseas Studies in University of Manchester.

Western social welfare policy as having any marked relevance for the conditions of large portions of our globe.

I have shared the concern Livingstone expresses over some aspects of the influence we have had in helping to shape social work organization elsewhere. The implication, inherent in some of our earlier and more naive exportation of North American social work, of our being at the apex of professional development and other countries moving at various stages up to our august position, has been painful to witness. I also share Livingstone's caution that we cannot train international students for practice in their countries by historical analogy, whether in North America or the United Kingdom. Yet, I do not share his sense of alarm. For one thing, the countries of Asia and Africa and Latin America, as is true of most countries, are finding their own emphases in social welfare training and programs, with certain core trends that serve to give a common base to social work education internationally. If our contribution in education is transmitted to mature, experienced people from such countries, we minimize the risk of making them unfit for their own country and maximize the prospect of their utilizing what we have to offer on their own terms or, if they question what we have to offer, of their knowing with what they are taking issue.

The fact is, we do have much to offer that is of underlying value, that does not stem from provincial or ethnocentric attitudes or a particular restricted cultural system. The capacity for self-discipline and self-awareness the significance of objectivity not only in professional roles but in personnel practice, the understanding of resistance to change on the part of groups as well as individuals, the possibilities or relationship between voluntary and governmental programs, an increasingly scientific approach to prevention and treatment of social and individual problems, an increasingly broad international perspective on social programs and need priorities, and a concern with social research are among the transferable assets. Moreover, since our schools of social work are located in universities, we can provide academic work, as needed, in diverse subjects of direct bearing on the students' national problems, such as public health, rural sociology, economic trends, and so on.

We cannot provide a specific social strategy for a particular country through our teaching here at home, but we can provide a basis for evaluating and comparing social needs and programs and offer a wider base for the selection of alternatives. This is no mean contribution. Provided we raise no false expectations and do not pretend to have the best answers to every social work situation, social work education in this country has a good deal to offer the student from an economically developing country who is prepared to cope with our special requirements and pressures.

Social work education is undergoing important changes. There is now more content on analysis and skills in formulation of social policy, more integration of social science with practice, more emphasis on broad social welfare objectives and social action, greater concern, in field instruction, with a wider base of teaching beyond primary methods, greater attention to underlying principles, the development of administrative sophistication, and a growing emphasis on an international perspective in viewing the place of social work in society. These directions are apparent in many quarters. They will make education more relevant to the needs of our foreign students; indeed, experience with such students has helped stimulate us in some of these directions. These changes are being pursued because they make for better education for all and are organic to our social work development. They will provide the context for better education of our international students, but far more flexibility is needed: flexibility in field work arrangements, wider use of electives, not confining students necessarily to two years of study in one method, more work taken in other departments of the university, good counseling. None of these will work, however, if the student is not properly selected.

There is also the need for much more curricular attention devoted specifically to international content.

This concern was examined by a committee of the Council on Social Work Education in 1957. At that time we thought it was quite important for schools to develop a world perspective on the part of their students. We inquired of schools interested in this area about their curricular objectives, and these may be grouped as follows:[10]

1. To provide information on programs and conditions in countries in various parts of the world at various stages of technological development.

2. To sensitize students to trends and methods in other countries that may be applied to their own.

3. To develop greater awareness of the ways in which economic, political, cultural and religious influences shape social welfare needs and programs.

---

[10] Stein, Herman D. *An International Perspective in the Social Work Curriculum*, Workshop Paper presented at the Annual Meeting of the Council on Social Work Education, January 23-26, 1957, Los Angeles, California.

At that time we recommended building an international perspective into the basic curriculum, with content on the following:

1. Knowledge of social work developments in various parts of the world.

2. Understanding of the effect of economic, political, demographic, religious and cultural influences in shaping social welfare needs and resources.

3. Understanding the problems in application of social work method principles under these differing conditions.

4. Knowledge of the work of the international agencies.

5. Awareness of the common as well as the different interests of social workers in various parts of the world.

6. Awareness of the potential contribution of developments abroad to social welfare in the U.S. as well as vice versa.

In addition, we felt it was important for some social work centers to develop specialized courses in comparative social welfare and related subjects.

These were statements of hope. They had agreement. They moved in the path of many other noble hopes and agreements. Little happened, except on the part of those few schools already committed. This conference is an opportunity to develop a program of implementation, if these are still among our hopes.

RESEARCH

As we have been informed, there has been a very active program administered by the Welfare Administration in cooperative research in the fields of social welfare and maternal and child health under the special foreign currency program begun in 1962, with 33 projects having been approved, 21 of them in welfare.

This is an excellent beginning and I think we would agree it is a very salutary way of using these funds. In addition, there are the research programs in the international field, of the Bureau of Educational and Cultural Affairs in the Department of State, considerable AID-supported research in the field of education, and research programs in the Division of International Education of the Office of Education.

It is time that we try to pull together the research that has meaning for the social welfare field, to see what we can learn from it that we can usefully apply now, or that suggests future research directions of high potential yield. Why make the same mistakes here that have been made elsewhere in losing track of previous research and repeating steps?

One obvious area for research is in the field of comparative social work education, itself. We have relatively little that is systematic in this field, except for the material periodically supplied by the United Nations Bureau of Social Affairs, and, as we have been informed, even this is rather general and not always documented in sufficient detail.

We also have a special need in this country for the evaluation of our educational programs for our overseas students. Thus far we have had several narrative reports based on informal observations and replies to questionnaires, and one systematic questionnaire follow-up survey. All of these suggest that there may be merit in more intensive analysis of such issues as the re-entry problem for students of different backgrounds and levels of responsibility, and the issues involved in the integration and use of learning in the social work field in the U.S., as applied to the context of other countries. Basically, we need evaluation of the entire range of our present and future investment in social work education for international use.

We face a question of priorities in research, however, to the extent that we can control its direction. Once the world is opened as our arena for research in social work, there is a world of choice, both by the countries requesting research help, and from U.S. educators and researchers who wish to do research in the international areas. What kinds of priorities shall we set? Shall we give priorities to background studies of welfare programs in other countries? Shall we give priority to the assessment of manpower needs or to the development of longitudinal evaluation studies of returned international students? Or shall we engage in basic theoretical research on evaluations, motivations, social factors related to development, and the like?

How can we tie in the research that is most relevant to the social work field to that going on in other disciplines related to the utilization of training in this country? How can we make the best use of the research already done? How can we aid countries in the development of their own research capacity?

Clearly there is a need for the promotion of research in the social field and for better ways of helping countries to develop their own priorities in social welfare, and particularly in the development of appropriate manpower resources.

Professor Harbison suggests a rule of thumb in requirements for high level manpower: "The rate of net accumulation of high level manpower for expansion of activities is calculated at 1.5 times the increase in G.N.P. Thus, if G.N.P. increases by 4% per year, high level manpower for expansion should increase by about 6% per year." For intermediate categories, he suggests that in most cases the number should increase twice as fast as G.N.P. [11]

Do such estimates apply in the case of social welfare manpower? Whom do we call "high-level" social welfare manpower? We have a considerable need for better methodology in manpower assessment in the social welfare area, and any contribution here will be useful domestically as well as internationally.

There is a general push towards research in development planning, a growing recognition among economists that this is not exclusively an economic problem, and that the social and economic aspects of development are intertwined. There are questions of developing incentive for change, and dealing with the consequences of the breaking up of traditional values and traditional family organization, as well as with preventive steps. There is the issue of community development as an instrument of social change. What do we in the U.S. have to offer now in relation to such questions, and what must we know and study and test so we can be more useful for the future in this field?

CONCLUDING COMMENTS

There are questions which cut across all of the areas discussed. There are issues raised by the Gardner report, for example, other than those already cited, with which we should be concerned:

- The need for greater autonomy on the part of the university.

- The caution on the part of the university against aggressive "tactics" in obtaining contracts.

- The capacity of the university to "deliver" on its contract.[12]

There is the issue of publication referred to in the Bulletin on International Education.[13] Sometimes publishing *all* the findings growing out of the overseas experience can do harm to international relations. The prob-

---

[11] Harbison, Frederic, from his paper delivered at the conference on "Education and the Modernizing of Nations" at Detroit, Michigan, September 1964.

[12] Note suggested criteria in *Bulletin on International Education*, Vol. 2, No. 4, May, 1964.

[13] *Bulletin on International Education*, Vol. 2, No. 6, July-August, 1964, pp. 5-6.

lem here, it has been suggested, is not one of security but of discretion: the need for a balance to be struck between the freedom to publish as a scholar and the public consideration one assumes as a public servant.

There should be a way of regularizing the relationships of American schools with those in other countries so that we have a rational and balanced distribution of our resources. There are now 220 schools of social work in some 40 countries which are members of the International Association of Schools of Social Work, excluding schools in the United States and Canada. Many of these schools are in developing countries which are struggling both to define and to meet minimal manpower requirements in social work. We should be thinking of ways of extending ourselves in some orderly manner.

We have seen, not only in the field of social work education, but in all professions and disciplines, despite the most sincere statements of aspirations, that it is not quite possible for all schools and departments to excel, or to become specialized in everything. Are we dealing in the international field with an area of responsibility which represents a specialty rather than one which can be discharged with at least a minimal level of competence by all schools across the country? Can we develop priorities for the selection and encouragement of schools who would be participating in this field as centers of specialized strength? What should the relevant roles be of the Welfare Administration, the Council on Social Work Education, and other bodies close to the schools? How can we develop a balance between the necessary autonomy and the indigenous interest and capacity of the schools on the one hand, and the need for some control in quality and over-all sense of direction in the use of our own scarce resources, on the other?

What should our relationship be, if any, to undergraduate training in social work and to in-service training in other countries? These, for a number of countries, provide the major sources of social work manpower. Are we equipped to aid at these levels, or shall we restrict ourselves to graduate programs?

There is also the question of geographical priorities. To what extent shall our resources be distributed among the more and the less economically developed countries? If we go by Fulbright requests, we should note that about half of all of our Fulbright lecturers and research-posts are filled in the United Kingdom and Italy. Very few have been in the developing countries.

The field of social work education has many pressures on it—to do something about manpower for social welfare in our own country, to contribute more substantially to the poverty program, to develop mental health services and programs for the aging, and do more about corrections, and alcoholism, and a whole slew of other problems which press for priority concerns all legitimate. The graduate professional curriculum consists of only two academic years. Every segment of the field wants "in". What is the point of adding training for international social welfare as another special cause to plead? There are three major reasons:

The first is that we are already involved. Hundreds of social workers are going overseas. There is demand from international and U.S. agencies, government and voluntary, and there is great interest among schools and practitioners.

Second, we have to do more about the international field in order to fulfill our responsibilities. We neglect our responsibilities in social work education when we do not provide a worldview to our students, and we neglect our responsibility to our profession and our government when we do not contribute to international service.

Third, this is the time to act. Ten years ago we were not equipped to launch a systematic program. Ten years from now it will probably be too late to have an impact, particularly on the developing countries. We would have a great deal more to give in social work education if there were a plan and the wherewithal to execute it. We have learned much, mainly through a hit and miss approach. Now we should be systematic. There is now much greater maturity in our international activities, much less assumption of superiority, much more willingness to listen and learn, much more "feel" for this field of work than ever before. The time is ripe.

This can be a landmark conference. We should develop consensus on points of principle and policy and get these out of the way quickly. We should also identify areas of difference, but mostly develop a plan of action for implementation of what we can readily agree to. There is no need to go over the material amply discussed in other conferences and reports.[14] The point for us to address is how we get our convictions, principles and policies into some program of practical action, That is the focus of our conference, and our charge.

---

[14] For example, the two publications edited by Irwin Sanders on *The Professional Education of Students from Other Lands*, and *Interprofessional Training Goals for Technical Assistance Personnel Abroad*, both published by the Council on Social Work Education.

16.   Realities Facing Social Work Education

Each congress has its own personality and character and one never knows beforehand what form this will take. I could characterize this Congress as clearheaded and sobering, the latter not in the sense of being solemn or depressing but in its realism and absence of polemics and platitudes. It has been a time of sometimes painful appraisals from its opening to its present closing session.

In part, this was due to the theme itself—"Social Realities and the Response of Social Work Education." The litany of realities is so overwhelming and the capacity of social work and social work education so small, sometimes so pitifully small! What has happened here, I believe, is an effort to gain perspective on troubling concerns. Is our work at all worthwhile? Does it make any difference? The needs are so great, the causative factors so complex and deeprooted. How can social work make a constructive impression of the world? How can social work education help social work make a dent?

There was an effort during this Congress to try to come to grips with the possible and obtainable as well as with the ideal, but there was also an increasing recognition of the difference between them. The written presentations for regions and national associations, and the vivid sectional presentations with audio-visual aids were impressive. They provided us with a formidable array of information in precise and thoroughly unvarnished forms.

The contrasts between the regions of the world—those with backgrounds of colonization, exploitation, and subjugation and those

Reprinted with permission from *Social Realities and the Social Work Response: The Role of Schools of Social Work*, Proceedings of the 19th International Congress of Schools of Social Work (International Association of Schools of Social Work, 1976), this chapter consists of summary observations from the Congress. It has been edited slightly for this volume.

harbouring the rich industrialized countries—have come through strik-
ingly. For the developing countries, the extent of poverty, illiteracy, and
disease, the ravages of urbanization without adequate availability of employment or education, the strain between population growth and resources, and the inequities within as well as among countries have been
graphically presented. The more industrialized countries have also delineated their problems in relation to poverty, inequity, migration, urban
sprawl, alcoholism, delinquency, and so forth.

There is some overlap in the nature of the problems of the richer and
poorer countries, but there is no mistaking the fact that the scale and depth
of the problems make them different in kind as well as degree, in their
complexity and in their overwhelming and massive impact in the poorer
countries of the world. Although it has been repeatedly observed here that
the richer countries as well as the poor countries have social problems, the
richer countries have problems that come with affluence. They are problems that the richer countries can afford better than can the poorer, and
the richer countries have the means if not always the will, to address them.

Progress in the realities of social and economic development have been
noted in many reports. Many of the areas of the world have seen genuine
progress, but I hardly need tell you that the picture is not rosy and it has
not been presented as such at this Congress. The response of social work
and of social work education to these realities is less than impressive by
the testimony given here. Over and over again the inadequacies of resources
and capacity, of status and power in social work, have been noted in various parts of the world, and the inadequacies seem much greater in the
light of the staggering problems that have been identified.

We must bear in mind a theme touched on in Professor Pusic's paper,
that social problems cannot be dealt with by any one profession. These
problems are too huge; they all require extraordinary combinations of resources and skills. The most important of them lie beyond professions and
disciplines; they, are deeply embedded in the political structure of their
societies. There are problems that have been discussed here about which
social workers can clearly do very little in their roles as social workers.
What can social work or social work educators contribute to slowing the
armament race, to industrial and agricultural production, or, for that matter, to the interregional distribution of wealth and resources? Moreover, if
we are not responsible for either the cause or the remedy of any one social
problem, and if there are factors which lie beyond anything we can touch

in our work, why is it necessary to confront these realities in social work education? Such were our sobering and innermost questions.

I believe there was an underlying response which emerged in many of the meetings of this Congress. We have found that, for ourselves as well as for our students, we have a fundamental need, sometimes a desperate need, to locate ourselves, to know where we are, and to know what the pressures are that affect those for whom the profession of social work is presumably organized—that is, the poor and most vulnerable in our several societies. In short, we have an imperative need to comprehend the social, economic, and political environment in which we are located, so that we call understand ourselves a little better and have a clearer sense of self-direction. That is why, again and again, there has been reference to "the raising of our Consciousness" or to the "stimulation of awareness." Whether one call do something about a problem or not, one should at least know what and where it is, how it affects one's self, students, and the society, and perhaps what ought to be done about it. If any one theme emerged from this Congress, it has been this insistence that we bring home to whatever extent possible, to both students and ourselves the broad context of the political, economic, and social realities of our respective societies. Whether it can or should be done through a curriculum in social work education or whether such awareness should derive from other kinds of education or participant activities, it is an awareness which must be achieved for successful social work.

There was a time when the word "politics" was not used in schools of social work. That time has gone now. The discussions in the Congress have helped us to develop and understand a central concept of the professional— that social work is undeniably related to the realities of the distribution of power and resources and, therefore, to the political economy of the nations in which social work is practiced and taught. Even when the concentration is solely on direct service activities, it is important that such activities are seen within the context of the societal structure and processes as well as from the perspectives of the problem-ridden families and the individuals themselves.

It is this relationship of perspective and contest that creates the essential link between policy and planning in social work on the one hand and services on the other. When these two emphases are separated and considered as mutually exclusive in social work education, we have a situation that is destructive to the profession as well as to social work education.

Another underlying theme that has been re-emphasized in this Congress has been "indigenization." However clumsy the word, which we indirectly coined at the XVIth International Congress in The Hague, the idea is of great importance. It refers to the process by which societies develop their own way of defining their needs and their own ways of teaching about social work, and by which they develop teaching materials related to the needs of their own cultures and national situations. It means an end to reliance on the domination of western materials and the breaking up of the "cookie-cutter" type of curricula that have existed not only within but also among countries. We need not expand on it now, but what we have seen and heard at this Congress is evidence of the very rapid progress in the development of indigenous materials and frames of reference.

Popular participation in the development of social programmes was another theme frequently alluded to as important for social work education. In this connection there is one element that I found of particular interest because it has not been self-evident. Not only has it not been "universal," but in some places it has not even been "particular." I am referring to the learning process whereby the students themselves have some way of participating in the decisions that affect them as students in their schools, as building social workers, and as people who can discuss issues directly not only with their teachers but also with all those with whom they work. Popular participation starts at home. If one wishes to have social workers engaged in stimulating and leading popular participation, the must have the experience of participation in the course of their own preparation for the work they are being trained to do.

Let me now refer to some of the realities of social work which have been voiced loudly, clearly, and repeatedly during the sessions of this Congress. I will simply note the phrases and all can draw the context most vividly, for there is no need to elaborate on these items: low budgets, low priorities for social work and social programmes, government controls that provide constraints, absence of manpower planning in social welfare, inadequacies of research efforts, archaic curricula and outmoded reaching that still persist, separation between research and action, and separation of theory and practice.

I note this litany of shortcomings because this has been a Congress which did not pour syrup on realities, and which identified these difficulties and inadequacies wherever they emerged. At the same time, however, there has been a good deal of illustration of positive directions, of a struggle for forward movement. There has been experimentation in field training for developmental roles in social work and increasing research related to the identification of social problems and directions for action. We have heard of the participation and, in some cases, of the leadership given by schools in public policy decisions. We have already referred to the development by schools and by national and regional associations of their own teaching materials related to indigenous needs. We have seen evidence of the spread of social work education beyond the confines of a professional group to encompass a broader scope and to reach all those who can use this training effectively at levels below as well as above those that are traditional. We have also seen evidence of research-oriented training, including, for example, that advocated in the presentation from the European region.

Many dilemmas emerged during the course of the diverse discussions. These were dilemmas of both principle and practice. They have evolved as a result of the active involvement of social work and not because of its passivity, and they are therefore a sign of vitality. I refer to the dilemma for example, of advocacy and what it means, and of the relationship between political and professional roles and whether it is possible to put them together. Indeed, there are risks in taking advocate positions. In one country an aggressive statement with respect to public policy might only cause raised eyebrows among colleagues. The same kind of statement about or attack on existing public policy in another country might result in the speaker losing his job or even being imprisoned. One can no longer generalize about how militant social workers should be in their advocacy.

The issue has been raised as to whether it is possible to have equivalence of training within a given region. This question came out particularly in reference to Latin America. The chronic search for underlying values and the presentation of universal and particular elements in social work set off still another chain of consideration, as to whether it is possible to have universal values that can include both tile individual and as well as the collective values.

We have been apprised again of the dilemma as whether to try to change conditions through reform approaches as against those that fall under the term "reconceptualization." How do we respond to the demand of many social work students to be allowed to participate in instituting social change when they are told that they should be "change agents"? Some question how much of this "change agentry" is real and how much is rhetoric. Is the social work "change agent" a clear and realistic concept, or is social change happening so fast that the question more often may be not how to become a change agent but how to cope with those changes that are already upon us and to help other people make sense of such changes so that they might also be able to cope with them.

There has been a strong recurrent refrain on the significance of the developmental role for social work, and considerable thought was given to this theme. However, it is not always crystal clear as to just what this means in a given society. The underlying agreement is that it does not mean confining one's self to remedial patch-up activities. More positively, there is increasing consensus that it means helping large sectors of the population to improve their living conditions, whether through government policy, community action, or both.

We have learned of the growth of continuing education, which is increasingly being considered as essential and not simply as a cosmetic addition in the preparation of social workers. Courses in a school of social work simply cannot provide the entire basis for what one needs to know in the future, and there is a limit to what one call learn on one's own.

The question has also been raised of how prepared social work educators themselves are for their work when they may not have had enough experience or enough expertise. Times change and there is need for continuing education, not only for the graduates of social work schools but also for the educators themselves in order to keep current their ties to practice.

The answers to these dilemmas and questions were not explicitly forthcoming from the Congress as such. A congress of social work educators is not designed to provide definite answers in the form of resolutions; however, the search for answers, the identification of the questions, the delineation of the dilemmas form part of the solutions. Direct questions have been asked and many useful answers have been given. The exchange of experiences among social work educators from so many countries has not been as diffuse as in former years. The exchange has tended to crystallize on these very questions and dilemmas. One of the greatest values of a Congress is such interchange, and it is all the more valuable when the issues are common, however differently they are brought to light in the realities of the different countries.

At this Congress we have tried to see the relationship of social work education to the world of which it is a part. We have not gotten mired down in a solipsism, where social work and social work education constitute the centre of the universe of discourse, and everything else is seen only in relation to how, it affects our work. When professional meetings do this, everything is examined so myopically that inadequate attention is paid to the waves of change and the momentous forces surrounding us, and to the very shape of the world to which we are related.

It has been the other way around in this Congress. It was almost as if we were inundated by the elements of our economic and political environment. We have been trying hard to gain perspective and to see what foothold we have. Strangely enough, and painful as it must frequently have been to be made cognizant once again of the weakness of our position in the face of all we have to confront, the process has been reassuring. We have become increasingly aware of the true limitations, not the fancied ones, not the mythical dragons, but the authentic forces and constraints, and the forward movements as well, within which we are located and to which we can accommodate or oppose or be neutral. We have a better grip on what our contribution can be. We have given ourselves an opportunity for reaffirmation of underlying premises about ourselves and about the people we serve, reaffirmations about the direction of our work toward equality and justice, of what we stand for as a one-field and one-profession microcosm in the macrocosm of all occupations and fields of work.

The panelists have given evidence that I believe illustrate the general observations I have made. My function has been principally to provide closure to the Congress and not to extend its already formidable contents. I therefore now say adieu both as President of the IASSW and as summarizer for this Congress.

17. Learning and Doing in International Social Development

I am deeply moved and honoured to receive the René Sand award. The vision of this founder of the International Council on Social Welfare and the International Association of Schools of Social Work, and indirectly the International Federation of Social Workers, extended beyond narrow professional confines. He transcended his own field of social medicine, in which he was also a pioneer, to a broader concern with human well-being, cutting across vocational and national boundaries. With his colleagues in Europe he planted the seedlings not only of these important organizations, but of a network that we can see today extending to almost all the world, and ever growing. It is a network for social justice, for recognition of our global interdependence, for collective support in understanding and coping with the issues we face.

Those of us who entered the international field, and became part of this expanding network begun by the founders, became involved through different pathways. For me, it was a combination of the university and work with international agencies, with the opportunity of alternating between them.

I was fortunate to be invited to a faculty post at Columbia University at a rather young age. I left this position two years later, in 1947, at my first opportunity to work in war-devastated Europe. I was told by a kind and very distinguished professor that I was making a serious mistake to leave, and might ruin a promising career. After some three and a half years overseas, I returned to the same school which indeed became my home base, and a happy one, for many years. I was permitted to rejoin the faculty, but

Reprinted with permission from H. Philip Hepworth, ed., *Social Welfare in a World in Crisis* (International Council on Social Welfare, 1984), this chapter is the address given by Dr. Stein on the occasion of the René Sand Award from the International Council on Social Welfare and International Association of Schools of Social Work.

was told I would have to return to the salary I had started with years back, for after all, I was reminded, I had "lost" all those intervening years.

I thought of the European communities starting to rebuild from the carnage and destruction of the war, of the Displaced Persons camps, the movement of refugees, the soul-scarred survivors of concentration camps trying to rise from the depths of human despair and degradation. I thought of my missions in North Africa, where I experienced for the first time what infant mortality rates of 150 to 200 per 1000 really means close up, how trachoma could blind thousands of children, and how oppressive colonialism could be. I thought of what I had learned of mass emergencies, of how some organizations could respond with speed, effectiveness, and compassion, and others get caught up in protocol, hierarchy and clumsy bureaucracy. And I thought of the diverse values and behaviours in the cultures I had seen, beneath which lay deep the fears and hopes of a common humanity.

These years were hardly "lost," whatever I might be doing in the future. I had rather found a part of myself to which I would be committed for the rest of my life. I speak, I believe, for many among us, who found the same commitment, whether from that era or others, whether from origins north or south, east or west, who whatever our other kinship, community and national identities and loyalties, could never again separate ourselves from a worldview. We became committed to try to avoid ethnocentrism, and the pretensions of universal relevance, let alone superiority, of how things were done in one's own country. Most of all, as Eugen Pusic wrote in an essay called "Toward World Welfare" in the ICSW 50th Anniversary Publication: "It becomes less and less possible to conceive of anybody's welfare on this earth separate from, and independently of everybody else's" (ICSW, 1978, p. 144).

To make a difference in our world, we must learn and put what we learn to practical use. We learn from experience, from research, from each other, and most of all from the people themselves, in their own communities and we must also learn to unlearn, not only to avoid past errors but to be able to think and act creatively, breaking with outworn patterns.

We have learned the pit-falls and frustrations of the first, second, and third development decades. The wealthy countries, with few exceptions, have not provided their projected share in international aid. Trade concessions have not been made. Expectations of quick and massive results from community development programs were unrealistic. In Africa the desert continues to expand, and hunger spreads. Of the 122 million children born during the International Year of the Child, one in ten was dead within two years, almost all in conditions of preventable disease and poverty, dying in urban slums and favelas, in shanty-towns and rural villages, and refugee camps. The goals had been set, but the list of short-comings is long.

There have been achievements, however. The World Bank recognized the importance of investments in social sectors for economic as well as social development, and a few years ago began to make such investments. Many of us know how often this issue has been debated. In the excellent and fruitful seminar on "Social Welfare in a Developing Economy" held in New Delhi in September 1963, I recall the patient argument of the economists that social expenditures must be seen as consumption expenditures and might be justified as good in themselves, with which we agreed, but not as contributing to national productivity, with which we did not agree (Government of India, 1963). The debate goes on, and social expenditures usually continue to get hit first, and most, on the basis that they are the most expendable, despite the evidence that economic development, as well as a rise in health indicators, is buttressed by strong social supports, ensuring literacy, better health, lower infant and child mortality and lower population growth rates (United Nations Children's Fund, 1984).

Primary health care, with its do-it-yourself components, has been taking hold successfully in many countries, with the strong backing of many agencies, and it has been working. For communities to become prepared to deliver much of their own health services, as well as introduce public health measures, in the absence of any doctor or trained nurse, was a powerful idea. Like many important new ideas, it met with resistance. This is to be expected, for if there is any truism with respect to social change, it is that if there is no resistance, the chances are the change is not significant.

Recognition is finally being given to the importance of development movements rooted in the culture of the people, operating without state control and with little or no external funding. Movements such as Sarvodaya Srimadana in Sri Lanka and Project NAAM in Upper Volta, different as they are in their organizational and cultural framework, have in common a strong premise of self-reliance, and a deep commitment to improving both the material and non-material quality of their lives through common effort. Gone is the over-emphasis on the external change agent, which used to dominate development thinking.

We have learned the importance of women in development, how ignored they had been, for example, in agricultural training, especially in Africa, even though they are responsible for much, if not most of agricultural production. Research and experience have shown that investment in the education of girls in primary grades reaps extraordinary dividends, not alone for the enrichment of their lives, but in the protection and advancement of their families, and that infant mortality bears an inverse relation to female literacy.

We have sometimes embodied what we have learned in conferences and documents, such as that of the historic 1968 United Nations Meeting of Ministers Responsible for Social Welfare, in which 89 country delegations participated, along with many United Nations agencies and nongovernmental organizations. It took place when the United Nations Bureau of Social Affairs was alive and well in New York, and I well remember the extraordinary job of Aida Gindy, Jean Iliovici and their colleagues in mounting this Conference. This meeting placed before the nations of the world the functions of social welfare, giving emphasis and clarity to the developmental function. Permit me to quote one of the paragraphs of the report:

> 17. The Conference gave emphasis to the principle that the objectives of national development everywhere were designed to enhance the well-being of people by raising their level of living, by ensuring social justice and a more equitable distribution of the national wealth, and by enhancing the opportunity of people to develop their highest capacities as healthy, educated, participating and contributing citizens. Social welfare, whatever the precise meaning given to its programmes in different States, was an essential component force to such development objectives. Its contributions were manifold. They could be characterized as developmental, preventive and remedial. They might also be supportive to other services. Those functions, however, were not disparate. They reinforced one another, and at any one time a given programme might embody several of those characteristics, but the emphasis given to those functions would vary within countries and in the same country at different times. To achieve an appropriate balance, social welfare policy needed to be consciously

wrought, within the framework of total national planning (United Nations, 1968).

This paragraph still holds up, a cornerstone for building further.

The immediate aftermath of the conference was not a surge in developmental social welfare. However, a new bench-mark was set for the international social welfare agenda, and initiatives were taken among many countries through bilateral and international action, and universities in both poor and rich countries gradually picked up the developmental challenge.

Organizations in the international field also can learn and change, and thereby become increasingly effective. Since it is through my back-and-forth involvement with UNICEF at Headquarters and in the field over twenty years, that I have gained most of my international experience, permit me to refer to it. There is, parenthetically, an interesting connection between Dr. René Sand and UNICEF. In 1952 Dr. Sand spoke at the Madras meeting of the International Council on Social Welfare on "Health Standards of Living" (ICSW, 1953). His paper was so forward-looking in relating health to different sectors, that the UNICEF Regional Office in Asia reprinted his message in the UNICEF Staff News for all to study (UNICEF, 1953).

After its first stage in the last 1940s, to help meet the post-war needs of children, mainly in Europe, UNICEF shifted to helping children in developing countries, always on the premise that it was not engaged in UNICEF projects, but in cooperating with countries on their plans and with the resource commitments of the national and local bodies responsible for implementation. It later moved, in another major change, to emphasize the combined delivery of water, health, literacy, nutrition and educational services through a basic services approach emphasizing the involvement of people at the community level. UNICEF then entered the planning arena, since it became clear that the public sectors must be seen in their interaction—that it was largely futile, for example, for a health ministry to mount a nutrition program for children with kwashiorkor in a region where the agricultural ministry was substituting cash crops for food crops.

UNICEF learned to advocate—such as the campaign for breastfeeding instead of infant formula substitutes—and recognized that it could be most effective only when it joined with other international and bilateral agencies, and especially the whole range of non-governmental agencies concerned with common objectives, and which were often the spearheads for change, as in this case. The need for such close association with non-governmental organizations came most vividly to light during the International Year of the Child.

Recently UNICEF helped mount a major effort to reduce infant and child mortality in the developing work through the use of inexpensive but effective methods of oral rehydration, growth monitoring, breastfeeding and mass immunization, known widely as the child survival revolution. Again, it is not UNICEF trying to do this job itself, but working with the countries themselves, with the cooperation of the World Health Organization and other international agencies, with non-governmental organizations, bilateral agencies and by the mounting of a worldwide campaign of public understanding and support. If infant and child mortality are to be drastically cut in the third world within this decade, which is a powerful idea because it is possible, international cooperation is essential.

UNICEF continues to learn, and to evaluate its role and performance. I dwell on this agency not because it is a perfect organization, because it is not, or that it has no problems, because I am sure it has. I emphasize it rather to identify some principal sources of the capacity of an agency to be learning, changing and responsive, for much of what we accomplish in social development is through organizational means. One source for UNICEF is the pattern of participation of its staff in sharing knowledge, experience, problems, shortcomings and new ideas, from both field and headquarters. Another is the progress made in decentralizing decision-making authority, so that its representatives in the various countries can act swiftly and decisively within broad guidelines. A third is its readiness to join other organizations in cooperative effort towards common objectives.

We in international social welfare are not alone in trying to learn and change and to act. We need to connect with other groups, other networks moving in the direction of a safer and more humane planet. Early this year 75 leaders of science, government, industry and citizens groups from some 20 countries met to consider the central question "Can the world reverse fundamental resource and environmental deterioration while at the same time promoting a better quality of life for all and achieving a marked improvement in the living standards of the world's disadvantaged?" (World Resources Institute, 1984).

While the conference was focussed on natural resources, they recognized that nuclear warfare was the greatest potential disaster of all. Meanwhile, there are threats to the global environment in which no one country and no one region is either the sole cause or can control the damage. They refer to the build-up, for example, of carbon dioxide other gases in the atmosphere which may change the world's climate in ways we can not anticipate or control, and to deserts expanding and forests retreating, to entire species disappearing. Among the participants in this conference were people familiar to most of us such as Soedjatmoko, Maurice Strong, and Ariyaratne. Their summary report entitled "The Global Possible" answers the central question affirmatively. It is possible, they say, to reverse the rapid deterioration of global resources and the global environment if there will be international cooperation within and between the developing and industrialized countries. In technical papers they specify action steps which must be taken, not only in areas of science and technology, but also in the social field, because they are all connected—in the reduction of poverty, the stabilization of the world's population, the improvement of the position and employment of women, and the reduction of mortality and fertility rates.

There are also peace networks, with which we can connect. One such, according to a recent analysis,

Has gone a long way towards formulating a distinctively third world perspective and project. It is "peace and global transformation," now the framework of the peace programs of the United Nations University. Their central message is that, for third world people peace is not simply a matter of survival; the cause of peace and disarmament is in no way a status quo cause. As they see it, it is inextricably linked with the radical transformation of global society and the uprooting of many of the currently accepted patterns of privilege between countries as well as within them (Feith, 1984).

CONCLUSION

It is timely that we here take stock, mindful of the huge threats that hang over our world, of the potential for obliteration of one more species, this time our own, but mindful too of where we can make a difference in our concern with the eradication of poverty and disease, injustice and indignity. We can draw on what we have learned, especially the enormous promise that exists when the means become available for people to participate in making decisions affecting their own lives and their own communities, in solving their own problems. It is timely also that we entertain and debate new approaches.

A distinguished historian suggested that, in the broad sweep, the twentieth century will be chiefly remembered in future centuries not as an age of political conflict or technical innovations, but as an age in which human society dared to think of the welfare of the whole human race as a practicable objective. This is a new and inspiring concept, worthy of our energy and commitment.

We in social welfare are among those who have contributed to this vision, and we have to find new ways of keeping it alive and moving toward realization, no matter what the frustration and resistance.

We do this by educating ourselves and each other to the nature of the issues and the possibilities for action. We do it by how we behave in our own lives, our own communities, our own countries, and how we reach out beyond them to join in support across national boundaries, across ethnic and religious lines, and across lines of class and caste.

We contribute by bringing into our work perspectives from other disciplines, other professions, other occupations so that we avoid a professional myopia. Some of us make our contribution as well by studying and writing and teaching and advocating. As a world-wide social welfare network, all of us contribute by learning together, by involving and joining other groups in coalitions and movements towards common interests, and to further common values that would lift the burden of abject poverty from almost one fourth of the human race, and give our children and our children's children a chance for a better and more hopeful life, so that they will not have to attend a conference on how to deal with a world in crisis.

May I, in conclusion, pay my respects to the International Council on Social Welfare. It has throughout the years promoted a broad view, permitted the widest diversity, raised our consciousness about critical issues and ways to address them, and provided through its international and regional programs the means and the environment for learning and action. To receive the René Sand award from this great body makes me profoundly privileged and grateful.

REFERENCES

Feith, Herbert, "The Emergence of Peace Politics in the Third World," International Peace Research Newsletter, Vol. XXII, No. 1, 1984.

Government of India, Planning Commission, Report of the Seminar on Social Welfare in a Developing Economy, 22-26 September, 1963, New Delhi.

International Council on Social Welfare, Proceedings, 1953.

International Council on Social Welfare, Human Well-Being: The Challenge of Continuity and Change, 50th Anniversary Publication, Paris 1928— Jerusalem 1978, New York, 1978.

UNICEF STAFF NEWS, 2 July, 1953.

United Nations, Proceedings of the International Conference of Ministers Responsible for Social Welfare, 3-12 September 1968, New York, 1968.

United Nations Children's Fund, The State of the World's Children, 1984. New York: Oxford University Press, 1984.

World Resources Institute, The Global Possible: Resources, Development and the New Century, The Statement and Action Agenda on an International Conference Sponsored by the World Resources Institute, Washington, D.C., 1984.

18. Epilogue
Goldilocks (An Integrated Generic Version)
June 4, 1958

Goldilocks, a hyperkinetic child of five, suffering from absence of peer group relationships due to inadequate community planning, and at the peak of her oedipal conflict, indulges in a pattern of the old American culture influenced by the frontier tradition, and strides through the forest, which she does not see for the trees, in pursuit of a butterfly, symbolizing the escapist fantasies of the beat generation.

She there encounters a typical suburban ranch-type residence, naturally housing three bears. Unaware of this fact because of the anonymity of modern life, she boldly enters, violating a legal statute for which she could have been classified as a juvenile delinquent were she apprehended, indicating the unreliability of criminal statistics.

Meanwhile, back on the ranch—that is, ranch-type house—this overactive child dashes about among the various articles of furniture, revealing unusual sensitivity for strength and texture—an important factor to be kept in mind for later occupational therapy should this be needed—but at the same time displaying a neurotic, self-destructive streak in destroying those articles she loves the best. Goldilocks, who requires more than the normal caloric intake for a five-year-old because of her overactive thyroid and her fear of losing her mother's love, consumes an appreciable quantity of carbohydrates which she discovers in the form of a cereal suspected of being advertised by subliminal techniques and, exhausted, her chin smeared with cereal, she falls asleep, enabling her bodily tissues to regenerate. Note, if you will, the sequence of activities in which Goldilocks engages—eating, sitting, and going to bed, corresponding to three well known phases of psychosexual development—but there is no significance to this. We have considerable evidence that many children eat, sit and go to bed without having any phases at all.

Now, the three bears who inhabit this residence consist of mother, father, and child—a typical middle-class nuclear bear family, but with strong traces of a patriarchal kinship pattern in their background, as evidenced by the fact that the father has the last word. Noting the destruction and expropriation of their belongings, and concerned principally with the abuse of property, thus exhibiting a materialistic bias which is destroying American influence among the uncommitted nations of Asia, they face this child with her offenses as seen in legal-property terms, and ignore the underlying moral and psychological problems. Without the feeling of acceptance and support, and without even a referral, Goldilocks is panic-stricken and flees, guilt-ridden and still smeared with cereal.

Only a positive program of reaching out, reaching under, and reaching in, of public sponsorship, of adequately staffed services, of $5,200 a year for beginning workers, greater support for professional education, and full participation in the political life of the community and nation can prevent such cases of personal and family breakdown as represented by Goldilocks!